Thirteenth

Robyn at Raine Island, 1987.

"You can't cross the sea merely by standing and staring at the water."

—**Rabindrath Tagore**

Thirteenth Beach

◆

Diving Adventures Around the World

Wade Hughes

iUniverse, Inc.
New York Lincoln Shanghai

Thirteenth Beach
Diving Adventures Around the World

Copyright © 2004, 2007 by Wade and Robyn Hughes

All rights reserved. No part of this book may be used or reproduced by any means, graphic, electronic, or mechanical, including photocopying, recording, taping or by any information storage retrieval system without the written permission of the publisher except in the case of brief quotations embodied in critical articles and reviews.

iUniverse books may be ordered through booksellers or by contacting:

iUniverse
2021 Pine Lake Road, Suite 100
Lincoln, NE 68512
www.iuniverse.com
1-800-Authors (1-800-288-4677)

ISBN-13: 978-0-595-31098-2 (pbk)
ISBN-13: 978-0-595-76070-1 (cloth)
ISBN-13: 978-0-595-75928-6 (ebk)
ISBN-10: 0-595-31098-2 (pbk)
ISBN-10: 0-595-76070-8 (cloth)
ISBN-10: 0-595-75928-9 (ebk)

Printed in the United States of America

SOME WORDS OF THANKS ...

For Robyn, my wife. You are my safe harbor, Robbie.

For the mateship of Neil Wehlack, Wayne Osborn, John Butler, Herb Ilic, Dave Strawn, Steve Sutton, Graham Stevens, Gretar Gretarsson, Michael Costa, Frank Wirth, and, longest standing of all, Ron Moon; kindred spirits all.

We all need role models, and Professor Hans Hass, with his books and films, was my first. It was Les Leaney who made it possible for me to finally meet Hass in Vienna. Brian Rodger and Rodney Fox shared their skills, showed me their courage and determination, and helped knock some sense into those formative teenage years.

And there's this kid I met at Thirteenth Beach. He'd just qualified as a scuba diver, he was filled with a sense of wonder for the sea, and he's the one who prompted me to sit and write this book. Ostensibly, I've written this for him, although I haven't got a clue who he is. Thirteenth Beach is the only address I have for him; hence the title of the book! I hope he gets to read it.

I've had the invaluable editorial support of Kelly O'Toole, with her fine eye for detail and her insightful critique. Any errors in the text are mine, not hers. Rebecca Osborn added her unique artistic touch, too; that's her handiwork on the cover, along with some of her dad's and my own photographs. To you too, thanks!! Let the adventure continue!

Wade Hughes
New York, October, 2006

Sea Sweeper: Two joined broom handles, spiked with sharpened wire, propelled by a strip of tire inner tube posed little threat to local fish. The rugby jersey did little to retain body heat. Yet every swim was a new adventure. The author, at Christie's Beach, South Australia, early 1960s.

Photo: Ron Moon

Contents

1960s

CHAPTER 1	Diving to Adventure	3
CHAPTER 2	First Breath	7
CHAPTER 3	With Ron and Barb	9
CHAPTER 4	Flash of Silver	21
CHAPTER 5	Off the Leeuwin	26
CHAPTER 6	When Predator becomes Prey	31
CHAPTER 7	Nerve of A Bandit	40
CHAPTER 8	Gung-ho!	49
CHAPTER 9	Down the Sinks	52

1970s

CHAPTER 10	In the Dam Black	59
CHAPTER 11	Skeleton in the West	64
CHAPTER 12	Images on the Wall	66
CHAPTER 13	Tail of the Typhoon	68
CHAPTER 14	One Last Dance	77

1980s

CHAPTER 15	Cathedral Deep	81

Chapter 16	Coconut Logs	86
Chapter 17	Raine Island Moon	94
Chapter 18	Diving in the Desert	99
Chapter 19	Torn Along the Dotted Line	108
Chapter 20	Similan Nights	117
Chapter 21	After Ataturk	121

1990s

Chapter 22	Two Men in A Leaky Boat	131
Chapter 23	Cossack Kid	136
Chapter 24	Hass, Armstrong, and A Very Big Tarpon	141
Chapter 25	Polynesian Blue	146
Chapter 26	Wounds of Truk Lagoon	151
Chapter 27	The Fish that Roared	157
Chapter 28	From Xarifa to the Danube	161

2000s

Chapter 29	Southwind over Erie	167
Chapter 30	Xel-há	173
Chapter 31	Wolf in the Sun	182
Chapter 32	From the Irish Shore	190
Chapter 33	Iceberg in A Glass	193
Chapter 34	Cloudbreak on the Abrolhos	208
Chapter 35	Last Ascent	219

Scientific Names of Species Mentioned in the Text............227
Selected Bibliography 231
Notes on Thirteenth Beach..................................235
About the Author 239

1960s

1

Diving to Adventure

We rubbed spittle into our face masks to prevent them from fogging, rinsed them in the sea, snugged them down over our eyes, and with our home made fish-spears extended out in front of us, flopped face down into the water. We shuddered and gasped as the chill quickly soaked through layers of woolen sweaters and, when the shock of the plunge had worn off a little, we kicked away from the shore, towards deeper water to begin the hunt. A few silvery juvenile whiting, almost invisible against the pallid bottom, ghosted nervously away as our wrinkled shadows undulated across the ripples of sand towards them.

Behind us, beyond the shore and the low red ochre cliffs, the small village of Christie's Beach lay lethargic and stifling in the unrelenting heat of the South Australian summer. Forty kilometers south of the State capital, Adelaide, Christies Beach was little more than a few new State Housing Commission homes, perched incongruously atop a bare vacant paddock, and a weather-scuffed collection of beach houses, clustered closer to the shore of St Vincent's Gulf. It offered bored and impecunious teenagers few distractions from the mundane realities of rural life. Time droned on monotonously and predictably.

Ahead of us though, hidden by the chilly veil of hazy visibility, the mystery and adventure of the offshore reefs beckoned irresistibly. Every swim—every newly discovered gutter and ledge—heightened the sense of adventure and strengthened the bond forged between us by common, exciting experience.

Ron Moon and I met on the first day of High School and, in January 1962, with the skittish curiosity of two kittens approaching their first mouse, we were amongst the first divers to probe those reefs.

Just offshore, rippled sand extended out for 30 meters or so. Gradually, sand gave way to patches of low, tufted seaweed, studded with rocks, and then the sloping shoulder of a kelp covered reef loomed into view. This flat-topped reef juts out from the point of Witton Bluff. West and north-west of that reef, the seabed shelves gently into deeper water where, gutters, pebble beds, sand patches, sea-grass meadows, and low limestone ledges tasseled with short kelp, offered rich habitat for fish species.

Boarfish, flathead, mullet, whiting, wrasse, dusky and blue morwong, magpie perch, leatherjackets, zebra-fish, sweep, and snook could all be seen here within a few hundred meters of the shore. Further out, lays the submerged extension of the Port Noarlunga Reef and, to the north of that, the Horseshoe Reef. Beyond that, to the north, lay the reefs off the receding stubby headland separating Christie's Beach from Hallet's Cove. Out to sea from here, the sea bed continues its gradual descent into 20 meters or so of water, and the reefs break up into isolated patches of rock and weed, scattered across a plain of sand and shell-grit.

This far north in the gulf, there is little swell. Onshore wind whips up choppy water but, for much of the year, there's easy entry into the water from the beach and the rocks. Visibility fluctuates considerably. Winter gales turn the water into impenetrable gray-green but, during winter calms, with moderate off-shore winds, visibility can extend out to 20 meters or more. In summer, five to fifteen meters is typical.

It was Hans Hass who first drew me towards diving. His were among the few diving books available when I was in my sub-teens. Guy Gilpatric's *The Compleat Goggler* and Jacques Cousteau's *The Silent World* were there, too. Both are legendary. But the volume that I read most was Hass' *Diving to Adventure*.

Hass had been one of the pioneers of skin diving in Europe. As a teenager, he encountered the tragic adventurer Guy Gilpatric[1] spearfishing off Cap d'Antibes, on the French Riviera, and became entranced with the idea of underwater hunting. Within a few years, he'd become proficient with a harpoon, and sales of speared fish helped fund solitary expeditions to the Mediterranean and the Adriatic. It was the beginning of a love affair. One summer evening, Hass slipped into the water at Juan-les-Pins and proclaimed the emotions and the ambition they were fuelling, "The night was dark, the water warm and soft, my heart pounded. "I love you, I whispered into the ear of the ocean. Ever since I've known you I've loved you. I must see all your marvels, know all your beauty ... and the ocean listened, and snuggled still closer to me."

Rudimentary waterproof camera housings enabled divers to capture the romance and adventure that lay beneath the waves, and Hass turned his agile and creative mind to underwater photography. Photography, he was sure, could deliver the financial means to support his passion. There was a ready market in

---

1. Gilpatric, a passionate adventurer, committed suicide after shooting his terminally ill wife.

cultured, constrained Europe for tales of adventure and derring-do in far-off places. During the mid-1930s, in the cloistered geographical section two storeys above the main reading room in the National Library of Vienna, he had submerged himself in the charts of the world's coasts and reefs. Gradually, his dreams had materialized on a single destination; the Red Sea.

Despite his best efforts, though, the Austrian bureaucracy, paralyzed with pre-war tensions, defeated him. Destructive politics made the Red Sea just too difficult. Hass was urged at every turn to return to his university studies and to ready himself for military service. He refused to succumb. True to his credo—"A life spent in constant anxiety over losing it would be no life at all. It would not be worth a single day really lived. We must be thankful to fate for every single moment, but must not turn one step aside from the path we have entered on."—he shifted his gaze from one tropical sea, to another.

German ships plied freely across the Atlantic, carrying trade between Europe and the Americas. In the West Indies lay unexplored coral reefs. And so, as the evil clouds of Adolf Hitler's *Anschluss* darkened the Austrian summer of 1938, Hass made his way across the Atlantic toward Curaçao and Bonaire in the Dutch Antilles. Accompanying him were fellow Viennese students, Joerg Bohler and Alfred van Wurzian. Their expedition yielded the material Hass needed for his book, *Diving to Adventure*.

In this book, Hass was reachable. His were low-tech adventures. In contrast, Cousteau was high tech. We watched him, on television and in his books, leading teams of advanced, silver-suited aquanauts equipped with three-cylinder scuba sets, traveling the seas aboard their first research vessel, the *Elie Monnier*. It was like watching pictures beamed to Earth by the crew of the space shuttle. We could marvel, and imagine what it might be like to participate—but we could never go there.

Hass and his mates, on the other hand, initially went into the sea with little more than a sharp stick and a primitive camera. They clambered over rocks to reach the water, swam out from the shore, and faced their adventures, naked and naïve. This was something that we could do too.

At night and in winter, when the house shook as gales swept in over the coast, I swam with Hass over those distant reefs, through the pages of *Diving to Adventure*, and read over and over again his accounts of approaching—trembling in every limb—sharks "so beautiful and elegant" and his first glimpses of "landscapes whose alien magic had never been profaned by man." I had no doubt that, whatever it took, I was going out to make those same trembling encounters, and to swim those same magical landscapes. The unpaved limestone road, blindingly white in the southern sunlight, leading from the front door of my parent's house to the shore at Christie's Beach, became the first dusty pathway to those adventures.

2

First Breath

Errol Chinner emerged from his scuba dive on Port Noarlunga reef, clad in a glossy black and yellow wetsuit and strode, streaming water, like an alien aquanaut across the exposed reef-top towards us. When this pioneering South Australian diver noticed us, two enthralled kids, shivering from hours of snorkeling, semi-naked, in the water inside the reef, he asked us if we'd like to try out his aqualung. We couldn't believe our good fortune!

Rough, thick canvas harness straps chafed my bare shoulders, and the heavy steel air cylinder hung low enough on my back to almost reach the rocky reef top. Errol decided that my skinny legs probably couldn't withstand the added strain of a weight belt.

Trained only by his advice, "Don't hold your breath and come up slowly," I splashed forward into five meters of water. With the twin yellow corrugated rubber hoses of the air regulator bobbling up around my face like tentacles of an octopus, I sank to the sandy bottom alongside the brown kelp-covered rocks.

Breathing underwater for the first time was a revelation. Mammals don't do that instinctively. The same reflex that automatically snaps shut the blowhole of a whale or dolphin as they submerge exists in humans, too. It has to be consciously overcome. I'd held my breath as I sank and, without thinking, held it as long as I could on the bottom, too. There was some apprehension as the need to exhale and refill my lungs became irresistible.

Finally, I could hold on no longer and, like an overdue confession, expired air gushed out of my chest and was replaced immediately, easily, with cool, slightly wet and salty fresh air, as I gulped life from the cylinder on my back.

I was breathing underwater. Staring upward, at the underside of the gently undulating surface, confirmed that. Water so clear. So calm.

Almost as soon as my knees had bumped into the sand, leatherjackets, sea sweep, and demoiselles had purposefully swarmed out from the haven of the reef to satisfy their curiosity. Startled by the bubbles from my exhalations, they'd flit back toward the reef, only to return as soon as I began to inhale and temporarily interrupted the stream of drubbing bubbling pouring from the regulator.

After a few minutes, I surfaced and passed the aqualung to Ron, and watched as he sank quickly. Through the transparent water, I could see him immediately surrounded by the same groups of fish that had greeted me.

Ron's wide-eyed delight when he surfaced reflected my own excitement. It would be a long time before we could ever afford to buy scuba gear, but buy it we would! In the dwindling air supply from Errol Chinner's tank, we had tasted new adventure, and we could talk of nothing else for days.

3

With Ron and Barb

Unconscionable for me today, hunting, killing fish, was an early and powerful motivating force on me, as it had been on Hass. In the late 1930s, he and his mates, Joerg and Alfred, relied upon hand harpoons to capture fish in the Caribbean. Enormous grouper, jacks, even tarpon and sharks, fell prey to their lethal thrusts.

Our initial thrusts were not quite so damaging. We did our best to prove Darwinian theory correct by prodding energetically but inelegantly at those few fish that had inexplicably remained unaware of our approach, despite the graceless flailing and splashing generated by our crude technique. But all we could achieve, for quite some time, with our wooden broom handles tipped with cheap and malleable trident heads were three or four loose scales.

Heading off to the sea, and returning home again, was exciting in itself. My parents had forbidden me to skin dive. So, the journey to the sea was broken up into two distinct stages. The first saw me leaving home carrying a fishing rod and a handful of ground meat "for bait." At Ron's house, the fishing rod was swapped for a fish spear, mask, and fins. The first dog we encountered got the meat, and we were off to the sea.

Returning home, we reversed the routine. This didn't cause much of a problem before we managed to start spearing some fish; the salt-caked hair could be explained as the result of a cooling swim. More difficult to explain were the spear holes in the first fish we started to bag.

"We had to use Ron's gaff to drag it ashore" was probably difficult for my parents to swallow when the fish only weighed a kilogram or so. But, eventually, the secret was out and, after some tense exchanges, my parents' anger subsided and was replaced with mute disapproval. When the few fish that we were able to spear started to ease the family budget by supplementing our diet, they were cooked by my mother and consumed at our table without comment.

Then Ben Cropp published his *Handbook for Skindivers* and revealed to us the secrets for constructing a surgical-rubber powered spear gun. All we needed was the money to buy the parts—particularly the prefabricated trigger mechanism. We could raise the money by selling fish ... but we couldn't spear enough fish to sell. Two weekends of brutal work pruning grapevines near McLaren Vale broke the impasse.

High school woodwork lessons provided the tools and time, and we were soon manufacturing our own guns. Two were particularly notable for their innovation, if not their effectiveness.

The RoTa (derived from Ron and Taffy, my nickname) featured short spear shafts—more like crossbow bolts. Each was attached to five or six meters of Venetian blind cord, which was attached to, and stuffed into, short lengths of garden hose. A cork plugged one end of the hose and created buoyancy. The spear shaft was clicked into the trigger mechanism. A clip under the barrel of the gun held the length of hose. When the gun was fired, the spear shaft would pull the Venetian blind cord out of the hose, impale the fish, and then dislodge the hose from its clip under the barrel.

The hose would float to the surface, marking the spot where the impaled fish could be found. The underwater hunter could rapidly reload with a spare spears and hoses, and pursue other fish in the school without pause. Bobbing floats, with their reward of fresh fish could then be harvested at leisure once the combat had ended.

This would revolutionize spearfishing, and would lead ultimately to the belt-fed spear machinegun, which would be ideal for encounters with schools of tuna and kingfish. This was the hypothesis, and we manufactured about a dozen spears and hoses.

If we'd tested the RoTa with the first spear and hose we made, we would have learned then that the alarmingly erratic and unpredictable behavior of the short spear, immediately after the trigger was released, placed us in greater jeopardy than it did the fish. We might then have moved more quickly to the second generation of underwater weaponry to emerge from our garden shed laboratory—the Whopper-Stopper.

It was a simple extrapolation of Cropp's blueprint. It showed that two-centimeter diameter surgical rubber, stretched to a ratio of four to one, provided sufficient killing power to secure small fish at ranges up to about two meters. We couldn't get within five meters most of the time. Disappointing enough when we were pursuing small reef fish, but, clearly, this would prove disastrous when we encountered something really big. We needed a weapon that would be versatile enough to pick off the smaller targets at long range and be able to stop the whoppers when we encountered them.

In the early hours of one rainy, wind-swept morning, while the human residents of Christie's Beach slept, and the fish sheltered from the turbulence surging across the Horseshoe Reef, unaware of the firepower that would soon be unleashed against them, we applied the finishing touches to the Whopper-Stopper. Double rubbers, each five centimeters in diameter and stretched to a ratio of five to one, provided the propulsive force.

After entering the water for the first time with the Whopper-Stopper unloaded, we had to return to shore. It was impossible for one person to pull the super-rubbers back far enough to reach the loading notch in the spear shaft. The only way to load this brute was to jam the butt into the sand on the beach, take one side of the rubbers each, and, on the count of three, heave them down the stock in unison.

Reinforced though the stock was, it creaked worryingly as Ron shuffled his finned feet backward through the gentle surf, reached waist deep water, turned, and began the swim to the silent battleground. The strain exerted on the trigger mechanism was enormous. Ron's knuckles whitened as he squeezed the trigger in an attempt to release the spear in the direction of a decent sized dusky morwong that was loafing, foolishly, about six meters ahead of us. Eventually, it took both hands. By that time, the barrel of the heavy gun had drooped somewhat. Whopper-Stopper bucked mightily, and the steel shaft accelerated more quickly than the human eye could follow.

Our dusky morwong, a fish not renowned for its acute sensitivity to danger, deigned to briefly raise its dorsal spines in curiosity as the marginally subsonic shaft buried into the seabed with a very satisfying *thwack!* about a meter short of the fish. Needle-sharp and highly chromed, the brand new and expensive *Mako* spearhead enabled the shaft to plunge deeply into the compressed ochre clay. When we tried to pull it out, the Mako's hinged floppers, designed to prevent the spear from falling out of an impaled fish, proved their effectiveness. We couldn't budge it. Unconcerned by all the activity, the dusky morwong meandered away, past the permanently embedded spear shaft and into the hazy blue distance.

Undaunted, we were reluctant to abandon the seductive power of the Whopper-Stopper. Snapper fishermen, returning from their expeditions over the scuttled barges beyond the ten-fathom mark off Christie's Beach, were regularly reporting disquieting encounters with a large great white shark. We believed that the Whopper-Stopper offered a prospective solution to this problem.

Power-heads were then readily available. Essentially, these explosive accessories were miniature shotguns and rifles. They consisted of a short barrel, slightly longer than the cartridge they were designed to take—either 12-gauge shotgun or .303 ex-military rounds. Simple in principle, they were attached to the end of a spear shaft and would detonate on impact with a target as the inertia of the spear shaft compressed a stout spring and allowed the firing pin to strike the cartridge. Death came instantly to any target struck in the head, as the rapidly expanding gas created by the cartridge detonation created a massive pressure wave and vaporized the prey's brain and spinal chord. Whopper-Stopper, tipped with a power-head, was clearly capable of taking a big slice out of the "great" in great white.

Unfortunately, when we tried to test the idea against a smaller shark, the acceleration provided by the super-rubbers overcame the resistance of the spring restraining the firing pin. The power head exploded virtually as soon as the spear punched from the gun. The resultant *KABLATT!!* and cloud of gassy bubbles convinced the shark that it should be somewhere else as quickly as possible. It convinced us that the Whopper-Stopper should stay home after that.

Eventually, we settled on a simple, elegant, design and learned to hunt with exuberant and deadly ferocity. Our catches of fish went up dramatically.

As we gained confidence—and our own motor vehicles—our eyes turned west, to the spectacular coasts at the southern ends of South Australia's Yorke and Eyre peninsulas. It is here that the southern coast faces the Southern Ocean. Long fished by commercial lobster, shark, and line fishermen, much of this area was virgin territory to divers. A few hours' overnight drive from Adelaide would see us standing atop an 80-meter limestone cliff at Reef Heads staring down at the sea; jubilant if the water was calm and clear, disappointed if it wasn't.

We could have checked the sea conditions and weather forecast before we left Adelaide—but we seldom did so. Anticipation, planning, packing, and the journey were all part of the adventure. We'd rather spend a weekend bush-bashing our cars through dense coastal scrub and down scarcely negotiable limestone tracks in a fruitless search for suitable conditions, than stay home on the basis of a discouraging weather report.

Night-time camp fires, set in the cliff-top sand, far from any sign of human habitation and sending showers of sparks leaping up to join the millions of stars visible over our heads, were followed by sleep cocooned in snug sleeping bags. Only the timeless sounds of the wind. swishing through the clumps of stunted tea tree, and the sea, fretting at the base of the cliffs, disturbed the silence.

Hans Hass had teased our imagination with his tales of adventure in the Caribbean, an ocean away from his home in pre-war Europe. If only for a weekend at a time, we tasted the same sense of expedition and isolation, separated from our homes by the waters of St. Vincent and Spencer gulfs.

Beetle on the rocks: Lack of tracks leading to some of the most spectacular sections of the South Australian coast punished our street-going cars. Ron and I load fish into the trunk near Memory Cove, 1967

Photo: Dave Bennett

On those mornings when we woke to find the sea lying like liquid sapphire, ruffled and streaked by gentle coastal breezes, we'd scramble down goat tracks leading from cliff top to sea level. We'd load our guns, and, never admitting to each other that our enthusiasm to hunt in this wild and harshly beautiful territory was tinged by a little fear, push off into water that was usually deeper, bluer, clearer, and stocked with more abundant varieties of fish—bigger fish—than any location nearer Adelaide. This was as close to wilderness as we could get.

On one such Saturday morning, Ron and I labored precariously down the vertical cliff at Reef Heads and, for the first time, decided to swim to the left, rather than follow our usual track round to the right and then out to a string of offshore reefs and bomboras—bommies as they're called in Australian shorthand. A wide, wave-cut platform of harder rock rims the base of the cliffs here. Tufted with kelp, and tougher than the softer limestone sediments stacked on top of it, the platform erodes more slowly than the cliffs and offers easy access directly into quite deep water.

As we stepped off the platform on this calm morning, we surprised a school of meter-long yellowtail kingfish hurrying along the cliff front. Sleek and powerful, they bustled past, startled by the swirling bubbles caused by our sudden, plunging, entry. We were surprised, too, so the entire school escaped unharmed. We followed them in the hope that we'd encounter them again. Beneath us, reef fish milled about in their early morning search for food. Swarms of sea sweep, trevally, and drummer darted around nearer the surface.

Ron moved ahead for a while but was soon calling me on. "Come and have a look at this!" He'd found the gaping entrance to a submerged sea cave. We both dived and swam a short distance into the gloomy entrance. It went farther than either of us was willing to swim holding our breath.

We both owned scuba tanks by this stage, but we never took them on spearfishing excursions, and we'd certainly never considered hauling them down and up the cliffs on Yorke Peninsula. This tantalizing sea cave caused us to reconsider all that. Within an hour, we were back at our car, bathed in sweat from the exertion of climbing the cliff in our wetsuits, thigh and buttock muscles burning from the effort of climbing with heavy weight belts buckled around our waists and pressing down on our hips. Late on Saturday afternoon, we were back home in Christie's Beach loading our scuba gear into the car and, with scant explanation to our bemused families, turning around to drive immediately back to Reef Heads.

Climbing down that cliff the next morning with additional weight on our belts and the weight of the scuba cylinders on our backs was hard going and surrendering that weight to the cool buoyancy of the sea brought blessed relief. We swam on the surface toward the cave mouth, breathing through our snorkels to conserve our air supply.

In the pearly half-light inside the cave entrance lay a sandy-floored vestibule, ribbed in serpentine patterns by the constant motion of the sea. Beyond the vestibule, two distinct passageways opened up. On the floor of one, comfortably curved around an angular block of fallen limestone, lay a large wobbegong shark, first covered, then exposed, and then covered again by a carpet of dead and detached kelp moving back and forth in the gentle surge.

Wobbegongs, strikingly camouflaged with cream and brown mottling, spend most of their lives lying in wait for meals to come to them. If they are left alone, they will seldom, if ever, attempt to attack a diver. Behind the wobbegong was its gourmet larder. Lobsters, weighing three or four kilograms each, were jammed nervously under the ledges roughly scoured out of the walls of the passageway. Their only way out, to their feeding grounds among the reefs, lay across the sandy floor of the cave—right past the discerning eye of the waiting wobbegong.

We floated in above the shark, made a mental note to collect a couple of lobsters on the way out, and pushed deeper into the cave. The first passage we chose soon ran into a narrow dead end. Only a fist-wide jagged crack reached down farther into the mass of the cliff. When we tested the second passage, though, we could travel farther. Initially, the buff-brown walls of the cave were encrusted with sponges and gorgonia corals. Drab olive colored in the gloom, they revealed their hidden tones of deep red, yellow, salmon pink, and even white in the beams of our flashlights.

In the darker recesses, the walls were bare limestone, pocked and sharply chipped by the turbulence that no doubt tumbled through the cave whenever winter gales hurled their mountainous swells against the cliff. At the end of the second passage lay a bell-shaped chamber. After scraping through the passage horizontally and in single file, we had room to hover vertically, face each other and, in the dimness sliced by our flashlight beams, silently but elatedly celebrate our discovery. We were confident that we had swum where no one else had yet ventured.

As we emerged from the passage and paused in the rear recesses of the sandy vestibule, we looked out into the intense blue of the open water. Framed by the black, ragged edge of the cave mouth, the water appeared like a wide, bright blue screen on which were projected the images of countless schooling fish. Irresistibly, the brightness drew us forward, across the sandy entrance and out into the blue where, for the lobsters and wobbegong still inside the cave, we, too, became part of the image. We surfaced and chattered excitedly in the choppy water, with the mass of the cream-colored cliff rearing high above our heads, spellbound by our first experience in a large sea cave.

In time, of course, this cave will collapse. Eventually, the ceaselessly probing swirls of the sea will exploit every crack, every weakness, and sufficiently undermine the cliff to bring it crashing down to create new contours on the seabed. With new cliff face exposed, the undermining will start again and the land will continue its retreat.

In the meantime, though, with empty tanks, we were confronted with the upward slog toward our car. First up the low white sand dune humped up against the foot of the cliff, and then, thoroughly warmed up by the exertion of conquering that, up the 80 meters or so of near-vertical scrabbly limestone of the cliff. Under a brassy yellow sun, in thick wetsuits with tanks on our backs and weight belts round our waists, this was a desperately exhausting climb.

At the top, we just collapsed onto our protesting knees, dumped our belts and tanks, and lay on our backs with an arm thrown across our face to shade our eyes from the glare. It was several minutes before our heaving chests settled sufficiently to enable us to speak. "The lobsters," Ron puffed. "We forgot the lobsters."

No matter, this dive rated as a highlight and spurred our enthusiasm for exploration of the west coast.

It was about this time that two more role models appeared—Brian Rodger and Rodney Fox. Both had been South Australian State Champion spearfishermen, both were famous because they were survivors of almost fatal attacks by great white sharks, and both were willing to coach and guide young divers.

Brian buzzed up to me in his Brooker aluminum dinghy one day when I was heading out to sea behind the Horseshoe Reef at Christie's Beach. He'd thought that I was a girl. In those days, long red hair swirled freely around my unhooded head. He grinned in surprise when he realized the unwitting deception. Denied any prospect of a date, he simply asked, "Any fish around?" before he waved me farewell, opened the throttle, and powered away.

I swam on, puzzled by a face I vaguely recognized, wondering where I might have seen it before. Some hours later back on shore, we met again, in Fielding's milk bar, on the Esplanade at Christie's Beach. He shook my hand and introduced himself, and I finally realized who he was. That night, I penned a breathless note to Ron, who by now was in the army. I'd met one of our local heroes!

In one of those serendipitous moments that change the direction of life, I was crossing the beach at Aldinga, heading for the water a couple of weekends later when Brian drove along the sand in his tan Dodge Phoenix. He was towing his boat, recognized me, and offered me a ride out to the Aldinga drop-off, about a kilometer offshore. Sitting in the boat with a celebrity, zipping out to sea at high speed, heading for fishing grounds I had only dreamed about, was an extraordinary twist of good fortune, and I sat watching the approaching dark blue line of the drop-off with a great deal of smugness.

It was in the vicinity of the Aldinga drop-off that great whites had attacked both Brian and Rodney Fox. Going back to spear fish out there, as they both did regularly, was testimony to the quiet courage these two men possessed.

On that first day, Brian's ability to dive holding his breath stunned me. He was superbly fit, but that alone couldn't explain his seemingly interminable capacity to remain submerged. At Aldinga, the limestone seabed drops sharply from a depth of about 14 meters to close to 25 meters. This low underwater cliff face is deeply gouged by ledges and small caves and, in those days, was abundantly stocked with fish. I followed Brian down on one dive and watched as he sank, almost casually, conserving energy and scanning the open water for signs of pelagic fish on the way down to the ledges of the drop-off.

I couldn't go deeper than the first few ledges. Brian went all the way to the bottom and lay among the weed and rock, waiting for a school of trevally to move into range. With a metallic *snick!*, his spear suddenly streaked forward and impaled one of the larger fish. I was out of breath and heading up by the time Brian had reeled in his catch. I waited on the surface, recuperating from what, for me, had been a strenuous effort, expecting to see Brian swimming up toward me with his fish. There was no sign of him. A couple of hurried breaths filled my lungs as I rolled over into a duck dive and headed down again. I made it to the uppermost ledges again, just in time to see Brian reeling in his second fish and beginning his lazy ascent, loading his spear gun again as he went.

On the surface, he cleared the dead trevally from his spear line, dropped them over the gunwale into the boat, swam a few meters up-current, and rolled over into another deep dive without seeming to make any preparation at all. This went on all day, and by the time we were zooming back toward the beach, with the late afternoon sun warming our backs, he'd filled a hessian bag with high-quality fish, such as blue morwong, boarfish, flathead, and trevally.

We parted with a promise that he'd call me the next time he was heading out and, true to his word, he did just that. When Ron came home on leave from the army, Brian extended the same, almost paternal, interest in him and opened our horizons in a way that we could never have done alone. Over time, he taught us how to control our diaphragm to ensure the most efficient expansion of our lungs while we were on the surface.

Most snorkel divers intuitively practice hyperventilation—a series of rapid, deep breaths immediately before a breath-holding dive. This has the effect of postponing the involuntary desire to breathe because it flushes carbon dioxide from the lungs. Under natural conditions, carbon dioxide levels increase to the point that they stimulate the breathing reflex before we have consumed all the oxygen in our lungs. Hyperventilation is, therefore, extremely dangerous because it is possible for breath-hold divers to exhaust the supply of oxygen in their lungs before sufficient carbon dioxide has built up to signal the need for fresh air.

We cannot retain consciousness if our brains are deprived of oxygen. This inescapable fact usually strikes as a breath-holding diver ascends, and is close to the surface. As the water pressure eases and the lungs are able to expand, it creates an imbalance between the pressure of oxygen in the lungs and the pressure of oxygen in the blood. This is because the consumption of oxygen during the dive reduces the percentage of oxygen in the air in the lungs. In essence, there's a partial vacuum of oxygen in the lungs. Simple physics demands that vacuum be filled, and oxygen is sucked from the blood—and the brain—to equalize the pressure. A blackout—instantaneous and without warning—followed inevitably by drowning, is often the result among divers who really push this style of breath-holding technique to the limit.

Brian's disciplined use of his diaphragm stretched the deeper recesses of his lungs, and ensured that he took in the maximum volume of air possible before each dive. On the surface, his measured, rhythmic breathing ensured that his body was always fully oxygenated without depleting the safe residual levels of carbon dioxide in his lungs. And he was superbly fit. With all these factors coming to bear when a fish, or an inviting ledge, came into view, he could roll forward into a duck dive and slip beneath the surface with only a momentary pause to completely fill his lungs.

But there was more than sheer physical conditioning at work. Mental discipline also played a role. Under Brian's coaching, we came to understand that we could reach respectable depths if we were fit enough, and if we believed we could reach them. Swimming down, to just touch the seabed in 25 or more meters of water, seemed an impossible challenge at first. Actually, being able to stay there long enough to achieve the capture of a fish—well, that was clearly beyond us! Fear, doubt, and physical discomfort, all conspired to create reasons for believing that it couldn't be done.

Gradually, though, by exercising to maximize our chest expansion, consciously working to conserve energy on every dive, we started to believe that we could reach 70 feet; 20 meters or so in today's measure. We worked as hard as we could to master the rhythmic breathing techniques given to us by Brian. We learned that we could comfortably hold our breath longer on practice dives, or for that matter sitting in a chair at home, if we ignored the second hand sweeping round our watches, and focused on some other task to take our minds off the time. One weekend, in the unbelievably clear water of the Picaninnie Ponds, Ron, Neil Wehlack, Herb Ilic, and I took turns swimming down to a weight suspended on a shot-line 30 meters below the surface. We'd reached our ultimate goal—100 feet.

With Ron and Barb 19

Photo by Ron Moon

Different times, different values: Autumn breezes scarcely ruffled the sea around South Australia's Althorpe Islands one glorious weekend in March 1967. We went out looking for big fish, and I encountered this giant wrasse in deep clear water. Locally, these fish are known as blue groper, but groper is a misnomer.

It was a male. All wrasse begin life as females and then, guided by signals that science does not yet fully understand, transform into males as they age and grow. With the death of a large dominant male, the largest female in the vicinity will, in a relatively short period, become a male. At 36 kilograms, this wrasse was probably more than 50 years old. After several hours in an open boat, losing weight as its skin dried, it weighed in just half a kilogram lighter than the South Australian State record. At that time, it was probably the heaviest scale-fish ever speared in South Australia. Then, such a trophy was cause for celebration. Today, rightly, these giant reef dwelling wrasse are protected from underwater hunters. There's lots of debate about the merits of spearfishing. Enthusiasts point to it being the most selective and discerning form of fishing. That's true. Provided an undersea hunter has the skills or good fortune to get within range of a fish, the fate of that fish rests with the judgment and integrity of the hunter. Immature, small, rare, endangered, or inedible fish can all be allowed to swim away unscathed.

Opponents counter that spearfishing has devastated populations of unsuspecting reef fish. That's also true. Many species of fish are easy to spear. In remote areas, where they have had little or no contact with divers, they often become curious suicidal targets, shuddering into oblivion as a steel shaft plunges through their muscle and shatters their spinal chord. That might, or might not be an improvement on suffocating to death after being jerked out of the water on a hook and line, or in a net or, on being eaten alive by bigger fish.

One of the major differences between spearfishing and other forms of recreational fishing, of course, is that hunting fish with a spear gun requires the hunter to enter the fish's environment. This exposes the hunter to a degree pf physical risk, absent from other forms of recreational fishing; the odds are a little more balanced. Because of this, there's no doubting that hunting large, wary fish in this way in open water, without the assistance of scuba, brings with it an element of danger that can be both taxing and thrilling.

4

Flash of Silver

My first big fish was a mulloway. I found it, resting amongst boulders, in a gutter off Broughton Island, on Australia's east coast.

Broughton Island, deeply indented and treeless, faces the open Pacific. It was the venue for the 1966 Australian spearfishing championships. Competing as juniors, Ron and I entered the water together from a small sandy cove cramped between rocky headlands, and began our six-hour swim.

Ahead of us, and to right and left, lay tantalizing bommies and reefs; patches and ragged lines of rich brown wreathed in cream and turquoise as gentle swells curled and broke over them. Yellow and orange fish floats dotted the blue water, bobbing along in the wake of the dozens of competitors who were slowly dispersing out into the five-square-kilometer fishing zone. It was a perfect day in an endless summer.

Within half an hour, Ron and I became separated as we each worked our way out of the cove and out to sea. When I was joined, on a small isolated clump of reef, by a few other competitors, I decided that my best chances lay in breaking away from the crowd, and heading to open water off a prominent undercut bluff at the eastern extremity of the fishing zone, about one-and-a-half kilometers away. It was a long swim, interrupted by occasional dives to check for worthwhile fish hiding between boulders and under ledges. A little more than halfway there, I encountered a curtain of hazy, slightly greener water.

Heavy rain had fallen on the mainland over the past few days, so this was probably silted run-off water, carried out to sea by an off-shore current. Being brackish, it floated over the denser, saltier, clear blue water of the open sea, and reduced visibility from around 30 meters to less than ten.

The bottom, 20 meters below me, was now invisible, so it became impossible to spot worthwhile fishing territory from the surface. Hoping that there'd be clearer water off the headland, I pushed on. Green water stayed with me all the way.

At the headland, though, I dived once and discovered that the hazy visibility only extended five or six meters below the surface. Below this depth laid startlingly clear water, dimmed by the dull layer above, but richly populated with fish. Jumbles of pale, rounded rocks, scantly tufted with weed, and gouged by deep gutters shelving steeply into deeper water, lay below me.

Comfortingly, 500 meters or so out to sea from me, Australian senior champion John Black sat manning an anchored aluminum dinghy—the safety boat marking the extremity of the fishing zone. No other competitors had reached this area yet, but knowing that the safety boat was out there eased the edgy loneliness that was creeping into the back of my mind.

Two hours later, with a few good fish hanging from my float, and still no other competitors to contend with, I dived through the green layer again and found myself directly above one of the gutters. As I glided downward, a fish stirred—the biggest fish I'd ever seen up to that time. It was a mulloway, nearly as long as I was. Beautifully proportioned. Powerful. Silvery green.

It had seen me. It was starting to move down the gutter. Slowly at first, just fanning the water gently with its pectoral fins, but with increasing apprehension, it was moving away from me and into the safety of deeper water. I stopped kicking with my fins and allowed myself to sink motionless; spear gun in my outstretched right hand, left arm extended for balance. Heart pounding. With every nerve focused on that fish, the need to breathe was completely and involuntarily blocked out of my consciousness.

There are no sights on spear guns. Aim is achieved by pointing the gun like an extended index finger. Both eyes remain wide open, locked on the precise point where the spear shaft is intended to land. Mysteriously, if the hunter is truly concentrating on the target, the gun automatically follows the gaze.

The mulloway hesitated. That momentary hesitation, we'd learned, signals imminent speedy flight. Some sense, somewhere, squeezed my trigger.

In a flash of silver, that noble fish was smacked over on its side. My spearhead had been driven fatally into the intersection of spine and skull. I kicked hard to get to my prey and jammed my gloved hands into the gaping gills to prevent any chance of recovery and escape, but there was no need. It was stone dead.

I wrenched the mulloway toward me and began the long haul to the surface, staring disbelievingly at its massive face and orange throat centimeters in front of my own. Thin plumes of blood, greened by the depth, snaked out from under the fish's gill plates as my tightly clamped fingers squeezed its gill rakers.

On the surface, I discovered a disconcerting characteristic of mulloway gill rakers. They're not designed to be handled. Needle-sharp spines bit deeply through my cotton glove as I tried to withdraw my right hand. Trying to wave for help with both hands securely snagged inside the gills of a one-and-a-half-meter-long fish proved difficult but, with a combination of splashing and yelling, I managed to attract John Black's attention. He motored across to me to see what all the fuss was about.

I didn't want to trust my fish float to carry this prize to the beach. Competitors were not allowed to touch the safety boats or receive any assistance from them without being disqualified from the event, but the boats were allowed to take fish in an effort to reduce the amount of dead and bleeding shark-bait being trailed through the water.

Eventually, after a series of maneuvers similar to those Harry Houdini used to free himself from straitjackets, I was able to get both hands free with only third-degree lacerations to my fingers. Black was then able to haul my mulloway over the gunwale.

Black then also helped calm my almost uncontrollable elation. He pointed to his watch with his finger, "You're a mile from the beach, and there's only an hour and half to go."

When I hit the beach with only minutes to spare, my exhausted legs could hardly let me stand, and I couldn't speak intelligibly. When Ron came down the beach to meet me, I could only point at Black's boat, "In there!" The mulloway weighed in at 21 kilograms.

That night, back on the mainland, Ron and I carried the mulloway into the kitchen of the Shoal Bay Hotel and bartered it for three-course evening meals for each of us. We had to eat the meals behind a temporary screen to hide us from other diners; the hotel dining room insisted on jacket and tie. Wetsuit jackets, the only ones we had, didn't qualify. So, we sat there dining privately behind the screen in our cleanest dirty tracksuits, scoffing steak and fries and washing them down with a few beers. We were thinking how much better the products of the hotel kitchen were from the diet of canned foods that sustained us on trips like this.

A couple of hours later, I was *in* the hotel kitchen, probing through the revolting scraps drum looking for the head of my mulloway.

This was because, after dinner, we'd headed for the beer garden outside, where we wouldn't have any problem meeting the dress standard and, for the first time, met Ron Taylor. He was then the world champion spearfisherman, having earned that title in New Caledonia, and Australia's preeminent underwater filmmaker. He'd been having a drink with Brian and, when he'd realized that it was me who'd shot the mulloway, he'd asked if I'd taken its ottoliths out before I'd bartered it. Ottoliths are literally the ear-stones of fish. They sit suspended in a gel-filled cavity deep in the skull and provide the fish with its sense of balance.

"They make great cuff-links," Ron Taylor had said. I didn't actually own any shirts that required cufflinks, but the thought of wearing the ottoliths from my first big fish—like the head of a hunting trophy pinned to my shirtsleeve—was enough to make me want to buy one.

Ron Taylor came with me into the kitchen. Once I'd retrieved the head, now smeared with congealed cold gravy and clogged with sprout leaves, diced carrots, and peas, he pointed out the bulge at the end of the spine that housed the ottoliths. A couple of determined swipes with a meat cleaver split the skull—and sent gravy and fish-bone shrapnel spattering across the kitchen—and the ottoliths were mine. With its destruction and humiliation now complete, the once streamlined head plopped back into the scraps drum. We were off for another beer.

At the championship's closing ceremony, Wally Gibbons, the grandfather of Australian spearfishing, presented me with a silver tray for landing the heaviest fish during the weeklong event.

Ron Moon and I also secured another trophy of our trip to Shoal Bay. On the closing day of the championships—New Year's Eve—in broad daylight, we borrowed a ladder and took down the large official sign hanging over the camping ground's community hall. It had been painted onto a three-meter-wide sheet of hardboard and had been destined as a memento for the clubrooms of the host club, the St. George Sea Dragons. The club had intended to post a sentry to watch over the sign during the celebrations that night, to prevent it being taken as a souvenir … so Ron and I decided on a daylight raid, in full view of the passing crowds. Without anyone challenging us, we took the sign down, and drove it away to be hidden in the bush.

There was furor when the illegal acquisition was discovered, but no one could accurately describe the two 'maintenance workers' they'd seen taking the sign down. It traveled back to Adelaide with us in Brian's boat. My parents were not particularly thrilled when they discovered it bolted to my bedroom wall but I'd go to sleep staring at it, and the silver tray that Wally Gibbons had presented to me for the mulloway, living over and over again my first real taste of the exhilaration that comes from underwater big-game hunting. Magnificent fish. Deep water. A hint of fear. A thrilling combination. But they don't always go together!

Flash of Silver 25

Overlanding: Until the early 1970s almost a third of the 2400 kilometer route between Adelaide and Perth lay on rough unpaved surface. Corrugations and deep potholes filled with talcum-fine bull-dust hammered tyres, steering, and suspension. Midsummer temperatures exceeding 50 degress Celsius attacked both engine and passengers. Despite all this, Ron's 1952 FJ Holden (an Australian Chevvy) got us there and back. Nullabor Station, near the head of the Great Australian Bight; 1967

5

Off the Leeuwin

Realization that something was amiss gradually soaked through our feverish enthusiasm to start building our score.

A year after our trip to Broughton Island, Ron and I were competing in the December 1967 Australian spear fishing championships. It was the pair's event, and the venue was Cape Leeuwin on the extreme southwest tip of the Australian continent.

This is exciting territory. Warm Indian Ocean currents wash down the Western Australian coast, bringing tropical fish with them. Here, off the granite and limestone cape, they blend with the cooler waters of the Southern Ocean. Africa lies due west from the cape. Due south lies Antarctica. There's nothing in between.

"There are big fish in the west, but you have to put in long swims to accumulate them," we'd been advised by our Western Australian friends. With that in mind, we'd been puzzled at the start of this competition. All the locals and most of the other interstate competitors had hurried off to right and left, close to the rocky shore. We were too polite to suggest that the best fishing was most likely to be found farther out, in deeper water. Instead, smugly confident that we clearly had some intellectual advantage here, we put our heads down and finned hard out over the limestone seabed, looking for submerged reef in open water.

For the first half hour, we swam over uninteresting, relatively flat bottom, overlaid with the drab brown short kelp that occurs extensively off the southern Australian coast. Few fish appeared to halt our rapid seaward progress. Farther out, a few low ledges offered promise of better fishing grounds ahead. But even though we were now in 20 meters of water, there was no sign of the spectacular fractured and fissured outcroppings of reef that attract and shelter fish in abundance.

Then we realized that there was something curious happening. The bottom, from which we seldom shifted our intent gaze as we searched for the telltale movement of a fish, would be dimly visible through the hazy blue beneath us one moment, then disappear from view, then reappear again a few moments later. Clearly, the seabed couldn't be rising and falling ... so ... by careful deduction ... it must be us!

I put my head up to be confronted by a steep glassy blue wall of water. Oceanic swells sweeping in from the open wastes of the Indian Ocean—or maybe it was the Southern Ocean—were raising and lowering us five or six meters as they rolled under us.

We were in the open sea, well clear of the cape and the string of rounded granite islets lying south of it. We could see the upper section of the 39-meter ironstone Cape Leeuwin lighthouse and the sandy hills rising beyond it, but the shore was hidden, even from the elevated view from the crests of the swells.

We'd been picked up by one of the slowly swirling eddies of the south-setting current and, unless we swam out of it, we'd be making a transoceanic passage!

Swimming back was somewhat more difficult than it had been getting out there. Headway directly against the current was impossible, so we abandoned that idea and set out on a long looping slog across the current. We were hoping that of the three possible landfalls—Australia, Africa, and Antarctica—we'd reach Australia first.

In our lonely blue, hilly void, we were on an invisible treadmill. Each kick of our fins, in the endless succession of kicks, seemed to do little or nothing to move us closer to shore. We swam up and across the face of the swells, breached the surface a little as we tipped over the crest, and dipped down into the following trough.

After a couple of hours, boredom set in and I found myself swimming with my eyes closed for long periods, concentrating on maintaining a regular rhythmic kick, blocking out the tightening pain in my legs, and opening my eyes only when I raised my head to correct course for the shore.

We'd come on this trip carrying a sense of profound sadness. Bob Bartle, one of the Western Australian spear fishermen we had come to know the previous year at Broughton Island, and with whom we'd maintained contact, had been killed in the following August, bitten in half by a great white shark off Jurien Bay. His partner in the water on that day had summoned assistance from a lobster fisherman and, when Bob's floating torso was recovered, his partner had photographed it. I'd seen the photographs when they were offered for sale, without success, to the media in Adelaide. In those photographs Bob lay on his back on the deck of the lobster boat, his peacefully reposed face offering unfathomable contradiction to the evidence of the savagery of his death.

Many times since then I'd lain awake at night, disturbed by those recurring images as they crept like thieves into my consciousness, eager to rob me of my confidence. Now here, vulnerable and with nothing to distract me from them, I found them reaching out for me again. It took some effort to force them back into the shadows.

There's no doubting the comfort afforded by the presence of a dependable comrade-in-arms when things don't quite go according to plan. Off to my left, Ron was pounding away, deep in his own thoughts, arms trailing loosely at his side, spear gun unloaded and clipped to his float line. If he was concerned by our predicament, true adventurer that he is, he didn't show it.

The few fish we saw on the way back, we ignored. To stop swimming was to give up hard-won progress toward the shore.

Eventually, we broke clear of the current but, to achieve that, we'd had to swim far to the east. We were now deep in a wide bay that arcs back from the cape. Strengthening sea breezes scuffed and chipped the surface of the water, but we'd left the swells behind. Deep blue water had faded into shallower sandy yellow-green. Gathering clouds darkened the sky. The cape, although now closer, seemed to huddle down and fade a little into the cold misty haze created by breaking surf on the shore. There was still a long way to go.

Six-and-a-half hours after we'd entered the water, we beached ourselves just inside the cape and squelched off around the rocks to get back to the sign-off desk. It was nearly an hour after the competition had finished and the emergency search and rescue teams had been ready to come out looking for us. One team was dispatched to pick up another South Australian who'd suffered the same ignominy and was limply waving, exhausted, from a little offshore islet. We were exhausted, too. Then we saw the mountain of fish the other competitors had hauled in!

Helpful as ever, one of our Western Australian friends offered more advice. "No, mate, you don't want to swim out deep at the Leeuwin. No fish out there. Just a big booming current. You can get real good fishing in close to the shore. Didn't we tell you that?"

There were other lessons to learn about spearfishing, too. As the attacks on Brian Rodger, Rodney Fox, and the death of Bob Bartle illustrated all too clearly, if you're prepared to go into the sea to hunt fish, you have to be prepared to accept that a fish might come hunting you.

Long swims often resulted in good catches. After several hours patrolling offshore reefs on a gloomy windy day, Barry Paxman (left), Ron Moon (center), and I regrouped on the rocks. Sold over the bar in the local hotel, the fish taken by Ron and me paid for our fuel back to South Australia. Redgate, Western Australia, 1967.

Out in the blue: Swimming alone, and hunting fish a long way out from shore, is one way of really getting to know yourself and developing some appreciation of the natural rhythms of life and death in the sea. Looking back now, though, it sometimes seems a little hair-raising. This was a five kilogram blue morwong taken from a sand-bottomed ledge in about 20 meters of water off West End, Rottnest Island, Western Australia, 1967.

Photo by John Butler

6

When Predator becomes Prey

Sharks don't roar or growl. Eerie, soundless hunters, they issue no audible sign of their intentions. Languid and liquid in their movements one moment; instantly taut, aggressive, and arrow-swift the next.

Late afternoon sun slanted across the brown stubble-paddocks and picked out the bright paint of the first ten Housing Commission homes to be built at Christie's Beach. From my position, in the water nearly one-and-a-half kilometers out to sea, the beach was invisible but, with the sun at my back, it was possible to discern our own house among the ten. White roof. Just south of the hilltop intersection of Gulfview and Dyson Roads. Tantalizingly close. Impossibly distant.

The great white shark had been with me for some time. It had coasted silently into view while I lay among the reef-top kelp, ten meters beneath the surface, trying to lure a blue morwong into the range of my spear-gun.

There had been no warning of its approach. Facemasks blank out peripheral vision. A diver's view is limited to what lies directly in front. With typical underwater visibility in South Australian gulf waters ranging from five to 15 meters, the diver has the equivalent of tunnel vision in dense fog.

Occasionally, large solitary fish such as sharks are detected at the very edge of visibility and, as they approach through the fog, gradually take on form and detail. More often, though, they have already entered the range of visibility before they enter the diver's line of sight.

If a large shark were bent on attack, it would not make any difference anyway. Even if the diver happened to be looking in the very direction of the attack, at moderate attack speed of around 45 kilometers-per-hour, there would be only about one second between the shark entering the range of human visibility and the jaws closing on flesh and bone.

This shark had approached more leisurely. After my initial fright, I had boyishly toyed with the idea of spearing it and took a bead on, of all things, its gill slits. Twitchy and uncertain, it curved away before my trigger finger could commit folly. But, when I could not hold my breath any longer and I pushed up toward the glass-calm surface, the shark turned immediately and swam agitatedly back and forth over the patch of kelp I had just vacated.

Polished great white shark would be a more appropriate description. A shark's skin is covered in tiny denticles—miniature modifications of the nerveless teeth that serrate their jaws. Translucent and densely packed, the denticles flashed refracted light and, like nylon stockings on a shapely female leg, added sensual luster to the hide of the lithe, flexing shark beneath my feet.

Instinct prodded me to lift my face above the surface. A brief glance shoreward—there was our house—and then to left and right. No boats within a kilometer. I lay alone on the surface of the sea, at the interface of two worlds. One modern and modified by humans. The other timeless, natural. Almost indistinguishable ancestors of this shark had been patrolling sunken reefs for about 190 million years. To encounter such a creature in its own element is to swim through the shrouds of time and into prehistory.

Gentle sloshing around my head and shoulders reinforced the hold this prehistoric watery world had on me. Time to reflect briefly on the wisdom of spearfishing alone. Ron was back in his army barracks in Victoria, so it was a matter of hunt alone or don't hunt at all. On days like this, when St. Vincent Gulf lay like a molten crystal mirror beneath a plain blue sky, it was no contest.

But this, the first lone encounter with a shark big enough to inflict serious damage, was also the first test of commitment to the essential difference between spearfishing and other blood sports. This is hunting in its purest form. The hunter is exposed to the same natural laws as the hunted. Predator can become prey in an instant. Bravado and primitive equipment are not much help in a confrontation with a fish bristling with the bulk, power, and will to attack first.

One hint of panic—the reflex urge to flee momentarily overcame my shaky resolve to stay and see this magnificent creature off. I felt like an intruder suddenly unmasked part way through my trespass, and I wanted to run. But flight was not only implausible if I wanted to avoid the risk of stimulating a predatory rush; it was also impossible. Great whites have been estimated to top 50 kilometers-per-hour in short sprints.

Comfort came from needless housekeeping. I flicked the spear-cord retaining clip on the side of the gun and carefully re-looped the cord so that it would be certain to fall free if I did pull the trigger. Tangled cord can halt a spear within centimeters. I checked that the stainless steel bridle, attached to the ends of the propulsive rubber bands, was lodged in the most rearward of two notches filed into the spear shaft. The second notch ensures that as much power as possible could be squeezed from the 20-millimeter-thick surgical rubber tubing. Then, awfully, dreadfully, I came back to reality.

Many sharks have eyes that outwardly resemble those of a domestic cat. In the marvelous biological engineering that we call eyes, rods capture light and shade. Cones yield sharp detail and color. Sharks' eyes are stacked with rods. Eyes designed like star-scopes on a sniper's rifle to capture the feeblest rays of light. A silvery membrane behind the retina collects and reflects stray light and turns it back onto the rods to generate even more light sensitivity. Yet there are only few cones. Sharks apparently don't see color or sharp detail very well—but they can pick out likely prey from their background in very dim light.

Daylight close to the surface expands the retina until only the thinnest slits remain. Impish slits that convey a simple and primitive inquisitiveness. Eyes that somehow belittle the creature's fearsome reputation; like a world heavyweight boxing champion with a squeaky voice. Great white sharks' eyes don't seem to be governed by the same laws of physics.

One arcing circuit brought the shark up from the bottom and within about three meters of the point where I was slowly revolving to keep it in sight. Eye contact triggered more fear in me than I have ever known. No cat-like slit. The retina was flared wide open into a terrifyingly vacant, black hole. A dispassionate data gatherer feeding signals to a programmed predator. Whatever signals had been sent so far had eliminated the twitchiness. The shark was now swimming more purposefully, perhaps even slightly more quickly, than before.

It never quite left my range of visibility. Just as its form disappeared into the haze, and all that could be detected with human vision were the creamy blotches that seemed to have been carelessly slopped up its sides from its pale underbelly, the shark would turn and return. I strained to keep those blotches in sight. A degree of calmness came from knowing with certainty where the shark was.

When it swam seaward of me and merged into the dazzling scattered light of the lowering sun, the suspense and fear in me increased until such panic bubbled just below my skin that it seemed impossible to constrain.

Meanwhile, bobbing sluggishly on the surface 30 meters away from me lay my fish float; a plastic ball beneath which was strung a sharpened steel rod on a length of 12-strand copper wire. A tiny grapnel, attached to 20 meters of nylon rope, anchored the float to the bottom.

Earlier versions of this type of float had been tied to spearfishermen's weight belts. Extra freedom to investigate ledges and holes happened when the idea of detaching the float from belts and anchoring it came along. Some divers attached a shiny, hookless fishing lure just above the anchor and dabbed it up and down in holes and ledges to see if it attracted any attention before committing themselves to an energy-sapping breath-holding dive.

There's always some risk in retaining speared fish in the water. Skewered fish, if they are not killed instantly, writhe in their silent agony, tear grotesque holes in themselves, and haplessly emit vibrations that signal their distress. At the same time, punctured skin and muscle exude coded fluids. Warning signals for some fish ... and invitations to dine for others. These are all good reasons for underwater hunters to hone their skills and reflexes to the point where they can either be certain of delivering a quick, humane kill or forego the shot.

Sharks detect vibration in the water through tiny bristles embedded in gel-filled follicles and connected directly to their highly tuned nervous systems. The follicles extend from snout almost to tail with the greatest density concentrated on both sides of the snout.

It's a simple system. Balance the amount of vibration being detected equally between the bristles on each side of the snout, and the shark is pointing directly at the source of the vibrations. Neither turbidity nor darkness in any way impairs this system. Sharks can detect vibration well beyond the range of their optical vision. The sense of smell helps, too. Sixty percent of a shark's brain is devoted to interpreting smells.

At close range, vision adds to the stream of information directing the shark's movements. I'd seen plenty of photographs of white shark jaws, and I'd stared in creepy fascination at the life-sized fiberglass cast storming out of the wall in the Adelaide museum, wondering what I'd do if I was ever confronted by the real thing—and then dismissing the thought as just too horrible to contemplate. I didn't need the slack-mouthed gape of this four-meter beast to remind me which end posed the most risk.

Perry Gilbert of Cornell University put the Snodgrass gnathodynamometer to work to determine the jaw strength of a modest-sized shark. Three thousand kilograms-per-square-centimeter! Couple that with the razor-sharp teeth and ferocious head shaking, and it's easy to see how shark attacks shred and mutilate human flesh.

There's an anomaly, though. Humans encounter thousands of sharks every year. Despite this, there are, on average, only about 50 reported attacks on humans each year.

Great whites are considered the most aggressive and unpredictable of all sharks. Yet, they seldom attack humans on sight. There might be a number of reasons for this. Breeding males lose their appetite for anything except sex. Pregnant females don't feed until they've whelped their pups. Liver fats provide sustenance between widely spaced meals.

On the other hand, some research suggests that those constraints only apply to members of the core population. Outliers—sharks segregated from the mainstream activities of their species by age, disease, or geographic isolation—are not governed by the same constraints. Was this shark, many kilometers up St. Vincent Gulf from the open ocean, which is the natural home of the great white, an outlier? Would it behave erratically? Desperately? It was gone.

Brian Rodger had described to me the behavior of great whites he'd observed from the crow's nest of a fishing boat near South Australia's Dangerous Reef. The sharks circled the bait from a distance of around 50 meters. Then, having made up their minds to attack, they had accelerated in a direct line from that distance. Perhaps a ton or more of shark, homing in at 50 kilometers-an-hour.

In terror, I rotated as quickly as I could, both hands on the gun to overcome the drag of the water. Twice, three times. Four. Again. Nothing.

A light blotch appeared on the surface on the very edge of visibility. Transfixed, I swam toward it. I had to reestablish contact. No shark there, though. Just the lifeless white bellies of the 15 or so fish on my float. Red-speckled nylon cord billowed away from the float and terminated in kelp on the same patch of reef I'd started fishing who knows how long ago. I tugged on the cord, and the anchor combed through the kelp before it came free. As I began the long swim to shore, drag from the float skidded the cord through my loose grip until the anchor lodged in my hand.

Chastened and scared stiff, I spent most of the interminable journey swimming with my head down peering between my legs, expecting at any moment to see the living incarnation of the Adelaide museum cast homing in down the trailing float cord. Instead of skirting around the Horseshoe Reef, I headed directly for it, seeking some physical security and a lot of solace in the shallow waters immediately seaward of it. I knew I'd feel safe once I'd negotiated those shallows and passed over the drop-off on the inside of the reef.

As the reassuringly familiar bottom shelved up to greet me on the edge of the reef, one faint tug on the float cord signaled a dying convulsion from one of the fish I'd previously thought dead. Reluctantly, I turned back. Kicking fish spell trouble.

But the float seemed uncharacteristically light as I pulled in the cord to reduce the distance I needed to swim to reach the fish and dispatch it with my fish knife. There were no fish on it. No steel rod either. A sack full of fish had been taken in one headlong rush. Fresh-cut copper wire gleamed where razor-sharp teeth had sheared through metal with only the faintest tug of resistance.

With the sun rimming the western horizon, I lay face down in centimeters of water atop the reef and wondered where I would find the courage to swim over the drop-off and across the 100-meters of open water separating me from the beach.

Adrenaline rush: Streaking in from the blue distance, this silver-tipped whaler turned and charged at high speed directly at the camera. It's unlikely that it was intent on attack, but it's possible that a glint of light from my equipment, or some vibration I created, triggered its curiosity or stimulated some instinct to hurriedly check what might be a source of food. Fish, struggling on a hook and line, flapping on a spear, or just swimming abnormally as result of injury or disease, will be quickly attacked; but alien and bulky bubble-blowing divers are not natural prey. Most sharks, most often, are reluctant to get too close. As this one swiftly grew large in the view-finder, I thought I was going to have to bang it on the nose with the camera. It veered away, though, maybe spooked by the sound of the motor-driven shutter being released. Even sharks, superb predators that they are, have to be certain that they can remain unscathed during an attack. An injured shark, like an eagle with a broken wing, ceases to be a predator and instead instantly becomes prey. Great Detached Reef, Australia, 1986.

When Predator becomes Prey

Double bass plus one: More polite than the bustling shark, but probably just as hungry, these red bass gathered inquisitively in the Red Sea. Behind the scrutiny of those puppy-like eyes lies the enduring question in a fish's life; "Is this food?" It's only size and reputation that differentiate sharks from other carnivorous fish in the sea. Every meat eater will, in a flash, turn mercilessly on any creature unfortunate enough to be injured or vulnerable. Bass like these are no different. If one of this seemingly friendly little group was to be suddenly injured and incapacitated, its companions would tear it to pieces in a frenzy driven by the relentless competition for survival. Shaab Umm Kammar, Egypt, 1988.

No-one will ever notice! A small jack hides atop a stingray. Palancar Reef, Mexico. 2000

Later that same summer, there was one more encounter with a great white; this time with Ron, who had made it home for a long weekend. That year, for some reason, the shallow waters of St. Vincent Gulf seemed more densely populated with sharks than any of the local fishermen could remember and certainly more than we ever encountered in the years following. Over that summer, southern bluefin tuna, common in the open sea, surged in shimmering schools along Adelaide's suburban beaches. Countless red snapper, browsing their way like rambling herds of bison to the breeding grounds in the mangroves at the northern extremity of the gulf, detoured closer to shore and lingered in the shallows close behind the Horseshoe Reef. Wary of human hunters, they simply drifted out of gun range without interrupting their constant forage for shellfish, worms, starfish, and crabs.

Sharks came in close, too. Most of them were smaller bronze whalers. Cheeky and flighty. Guerillas, setting a solitary spear fisherman's nerves on edge by zooming in close then veering away. Creeping in unseen and immediately vanishing as soon as they were detected. Probing and testing defenses. And then, apparently satisfied that there was no danger and confident of success, they'd launch a frantic raid on a float full of speared fish.

One such pilfering attack, close to shore, with the small shark thrashing the calm surface into foam with its wildly flailing tail, attracted the attention of an astonished local journalist on the beach. Unable to differentiate between what's in the public interest and what's of interest to the public, he wrote his story, and we found ourselves reported in the newspaper the next day as "survivors" of a shark attack. We didn't feel like survivors. We were just disappointed that our hard-won fish had been shredded and rendered unfit for sale.

Shortly after this, we made our first foray off the rocky shore north of the new oil refinery at Port Stanvac. Three hundred meters from shore, we could hear the *thrum-thrum-thrum-thrum* of churning propellers and lifted our heads to watch as a tanker coasted past on its way to the refinery's deep-water mooring buoys. It was an impressive sight from our vantage position, low in the water and only 100 meters inshore from its path.

We resumed fishing. Minutes later, Ron let out a sharp cry of warning. "Shark!" He was 20 meters away and had his face submerged and his back toward me when I looked up. He was pivoting slowly, following the shark, which had cruised in from deeper water. Visibility was only about ten meters, so I couldn't see either Ron or the shark underwater. As Ron's measured rotation brought him to face in my direction, he lifted his head. He'd lost sight of the shark as it left him and moved across toward me.

It was a lean and gaunt great white, close to three meters long. After circling me once, it then swam back toward Ron. Twice more it repeated this maneuver. Slow, sluggish, perhaps sick, it made no aggressive movements toward us. It eventually disappeared silently into the haze to follow whatever lonely and hostile path fate had laid out for it, and we never saw it again. It left us with an enduring impression, though.

We sunned ourselves on the rocks for a while, looking out across the gulf, excitedly swapping the details of our shared encounter, and wondering if the zebra-fish, morwong, and snook we'd left hanging from our floats in the water close to the rocks, to prevent them from drying out, would draw this big shark back into our vicinity.

After half an hour, with a little trepidation, we clambered across the rocks that had been scoured by an ice-age glacier, entered the sea, loaded our guns, and headed out to the offshore reefs again. We'd been drawn into a rite of passage and we felt different—about ourselves, about each other, and about the sea. It was clear that we could find any amount of adventure, virtually just down the street from our homes.

7

Nerve of A Bandit

We called him Jeb; a contraction of his initials. Jordan Edward Bannon. He was wealthy. And compulsive.

"Strike me bloody pink! This has to be photographed!" he blurted out emphatically.

"But we don't have a camera," Dave said.

"We'll bloody well go and buy one," retorted Jeb.

"Can we finish this dive first?" I pleaded.

"Shops'll be bloody well closed by then," replied Jeb. "Come on!"

With that, he jammed his snorkel between his teeth and began splashing back the way we'd come. Across the water of the big pond. Water clear as air. Through the diaphanous screen of pale-green weed that hangs like a tattered curtain between the big pond and the smaller, shallower pond. Finally, to the rickety wooden causeway that lays flat the bull rushes crowding the shallows. We were at the Picaninnie Ponds in South Australia's most southeasterly districts.

His two-tone green Chevrolet Bel Air stood waiting in the dusty parking area; its engine still ticking hot from the overnight drive from Adelaide.

"We don't have an underwater housing either, Jeb," Dave pointed out.

"We'll bloody buy one of them, too. Come on." Jeb would not be dissuaded.

"In Mount Gambier?" Dave continued. "It's a country village."

"Come on!" Jeb commanded.

He tossed his fins, mask, and weight belt into the overly ample boot and squeaked across the driver's seat, dripping wet in his full-length wetsuit. Dave and I exchanged nervous sideways glances. We'd never sat in an expensive luxury car in our wet wetsuits before.

"Come on!"

We followed.

Jeb enjoyed these outings with the boys. His wife Deidre, heavy with their first child, didn't dive. A curious couple, really. Jeb was adventurous, with the nerve of a bandit. Deidre worried a lot. He'd embarrassed us all one night at his comfortable apartment when he'd violently lost his temper with her constant anxiety. His coal-black eyes blazed, and Deidre shrank back, beaten and scorched by the foul-mouthed heat of his rage. It had been difficult to carry on with a simple diving club meeting after that. Deidre went to bed; Jeb tried to laugh it off and rekindle enthusiasm for the weekend excursion we were planning. But in the darkly tense atmosphere, it was easier for us to excuse ourselves and leave.

Out here on the road, though, Jeb was liberated. He had a grin on his thickly bearded face as he sent the Bel Air swishing on its too-soft suspension across the limestone track, out of the Picaninnie Ponds, and toward the main road. His right hand slicked through his ebony hair, and the drops of water that had previously been sliding down onto his nose sprayed across the dashboard.

It was fresh water. Beneath the pounding wheels that were sending a plume of pale dust into the breathless blue sky lay the limestone bed of an ancient sea. Hard, mean, and sere, it supports little vegetation. Clumps of pinched, stunted mallees and expanses of coarse native grasses somehow survive as winter rains soaks away quickly, and endless summers burn away virtually all surface moisture. If only they knew.

Underground, out of their reach in the cool cavernous grottos that riddle much of subterranean South Australia, billions of liters of fresh water make their way to outfall in the sea. Farmers know about the water, of course. Rashes of irrigation bores puncture the limestone crust and pump life into fodder crops and milk into dairy cows.

Divers know about it, too. At Picaninnie and Ewens ponds, the water appears on the surface, just behind the sand dunes that hold the heaving Southern Ocean at bay. Sapphire jewels set within a fringe of emerald rushes. Elsewhere, the water can be reached in subterranean chambers. Either above ground or below, the visibility is breathtaking. Cold-filtered by the dense but porous limestone, the water carries virtually no particulate matter. Only rising bubbles of air give any hint of the presence of water.

At Picaninnie, newcomers often jerk with reflex fear of falling as they pass for the first time through the green curtain that screens the shallow rim of saucer-shaped Turtle Pond from the precipitous edge of the deep pond. Beneath them lies a 36-meter drop.

Jeb had thought he was going to fall. His eyes had popped, and in the lunar light of the blue deep where red has been washed from the spectrum, he saw picture possibilities. Jeb was a writer, about to turn, apparently, into a photographer.

And so, on a busy Saturday morning, we were standing in a camera shop in Mt. Gambier, in our wetsuits, waiting while Jeb tossed up between the most advanced Pentax or Nikon cameras that could be found in the town.

"I'll take the Nikon." With the decision made, Jeb heaved his wallet up onto the counter. It landed with a thud. I'd become used to the sight of that wallet.

Six or more months had passed since I'd first encountered Jeb and Deirdre. They'd been fooled by the sign that said "Boat Ramp" alongside the haphazardly angled slab of concrete jutting off the beach and into the sea at Christie's Beach.

Jeb had backed the brand new Bel Air down the ramp to launch his brand new yellow and white fiberglass Stebercraft, and the trailer wheels had fallen off the seaward end of the concrete. Lowered and still stuck fast to the trailer, the Stebercraft was taking waves over the stern and filling up; even more weight for the already overwhelmed and spinning Bel Air wheels to contend with. Deirdre, then newly pregnant, and saturated from the armpits down from attempts to lift the trailer, couldn't help.

A straining nylon rope tied between the lug beneath the Bel Air's Victorian-plated bumper and the tow bar on my old Holden helped sufficiently. Deirdre wept. Jeb was grateful and tried to stuff ten dollars into my hand. In those days, that was half my weekly wage. I declined.

"Let me at least buy you a beer mate. Come on … where's the pub?"

Deirdre didn't look as though she wanted to go to a pub.

"Come home and have a hot shower," I offered, and she looked most relieved.

Jeb, gregarious, beaming, still wearing his wetsuit, strode boldly through our front door, into the living room, introduced himself to my father and mother, and heaped praise on the assistance he'd just received.

Deirdre gratefully accepted my mother's offer of first shower, and then shyly confessed that she had no dry clothes. "We only came down for the day. We only moved here from Melbourne this week.", she explained. When she emerged, dry, happier, and pink, she was wearing one of my mother's dresses. Her wrung-dry dress and underclothes went onto a clotheshorse in front of the gas fire.

Mother was impressed by the sight of the Bel Air and its trailer-load of expensive plastic parked in the street outside our house. Perhaps the neighbors would be, too. "Would you like to stay for dinner … while you're waiting for your clothes to dry?", she asked.

Jeb stripped his wetsuit off in the shower, dressed, bounced back into the living room rubbing his hands together and said, "Right, let's go and get a few beers to have with dinner."

We went down to the hotel, and I had my first view of Jeb's wallet. It looked as though he were carrying the Melbourne Yellow Pages in it.

"S'truth! What kind of work do you do?" I was astonished.

"I'm a writer," Jeb explained as he swept up his change and grabbed the brown paper bag containing three bottles of Southwark beer. I made up my mind on the spot that I was going to be a writer.

Diving dominated the table conversation. Jeb was keen to learn about the local dive sites. "I'll pick you up on Saturday morning. We'll dive anywhere you want to take me," he promised.

Over the following months, Jeb joined our diving club. We'd waived the rules that sought to filter out neophytes; "This is an action club, not a teaching club." After very little debate, we concluded that anyone who owned a boat was clearly capable of learning quickly and should, therefore, gain automatic entry.

Jeb had never heard of abalone, the thick, muscular sea snail highly prized as seafood in Asia, but he became instantly interested when he learned that they could be freely collected by divers and sold to fish processors for nearly a dollar a pound. The need for licensing divers to protect the species and the fishery they support had not yet become evident.

A suggestion that a hookah—a boat-based compressor feeding two divers with continuous air—would enhance the amount of time we could spend on the bottom collecting abalone led immediately to the Compton Street dive shop. Here, Jeb paid cash for a bright red Tecumseh compressor, two Seabee regulators, and 100 meters of yellow reinforced air hose.

Jeb would write during the week, and dive with us on weekends. Writing was his security. "I grew up poor as a church mouse, and I'll never be poor again." Diving was his release. Wealth gleaned from writing; diving to relax. However, Jeb seemed to relax more when we were collecting several hundred dollars worth of abalone each weekend.

Jeb's simple passion for living resonated deeply within us. We were as poor as church mice, too, and we didn't like it. Perhaps Jeb's path was wide enough to take us to where we wanted to be!

Late one Saturday afternoon, heavy groundswell rolled across the reefs off Maslins Beach late one Sunday afternoon. We were spent. There were three of us, lying in Jeb's boat, resting in the last glow of afternoon sun before weighing anchor and heading for home. Eleven people aboard a small cabin cruiser waved as they motored past. Moments later, they'd inexplicably navigated from deeper water into the shallows within the surf line of the reef.

Tumbling surf slapped the cruiser over sideways and then inverted it. As the first wave passed, the cruiser lay upside down and awash; bow just breaking the surface, outboard motor bumping on the reef below. One child struggled for life in the upturned cabin. An elderly man clawed at the keel with the torn fingernails of one hand while he fought to keep his free arm wrapped around his infant grandson. A heart attack forced him to surrender the child to the sea.

We were there by then. Jeb had ordered the anchor line cut and skimmed the Stebercraft across the reef top shallows. One diver in the water, one in the boat, and Jeb gunning the motor and watching the oncoming, rearing waves.

We took the infant first; alive, but terrified and choking on the water he was swallowing. Dave's strong arms heaved him up out of the water and over the gunwale and dumped him like a poled tuna on the deck. Then his arms were there again. Hands outstretched. Ready.

"Stand clear! Stand clear!" cried Jeb. He took one desperate backward glance to be sure that the people in the water were clear of his propeller and then rammed the throttle forward.

Howling, the outboard plunged deep and bit. Spray punched out from the bow as it speared up the face of the wave and slapped through the tipping lip. The stern came up out of the water as the hull pivoted on the wave crest, and the motor wailed like a siren in protest as the propeller spun in free air. Jeb had the wheel hard to starboard even before the bow crashed down into the following trough. He was on his way back to the doomed cruiser almost on the back of the same wave.

"She's in the cabin!" A mother's helpless plea, gasped breathlessly as her head, wreathed in swirling sodden blonde hair, bobbed up from under the blanket of cold sea foam.

Screaming uncontrollably, eight or nine years old, her daughter was trying to force herself upward into the peak of the bow. Even this small air pocket gurgled away each time a breaking wave pounded over the sunken cruiser. As each wave passed, and the cruiser wallowed upwards a little, the pocket of air drained back into existence and released the frantic little girl from total immersion. Greenwater light soaked dimly through the cabin windows. Safety lay less than a bodylength away, but it was downward, and this little girl could only think of struggling upward.

Eventually, we were able to get up into the cabin to release the foredeck hatch, and the girl—screaming, fighting, kicking—was part stuffed, part sucked through the hatch and into open water. Everyone survived; even the elderly man.

We were interviewed on television news—in our wet suits, of course. Jeb reveled in the glory. "Great story in all this!"

Now here, some months later, Jeb's view was that there was clearly a story in the Picaninnie, too. But there was a complication.

"Nice camera," Jeb said. "Now, what about an underwater housing?"

The salesman looked blank. Jeb dismissed him. "Never mind. Where's the nearest sports store?" That's where he bought an elliptical Australian football rubber bladder and a new dive mask.

"Scissors?" he demanded. While the sales assistant and we watched, Jeb cut one end out of the bladder, placed the camera inside the bladder, stretched the open end of the bladder over the glass faceplate of the mask, and snapped the mask's retaining ring into place to complete the seal. The black rubber carcass of the newly purchased mask was left on the counter as we strode out of the shop and boarded the Bel Air for the trip back to the Picaninnie.

Focusing was a problem. So was composition. Most cameras require the eye to be placed against the viewfinder to accomplish those tasks. The fact that there was no aperture in the rear of his makeshift rubber housing to allow him to use the viewfinder didn't seem to worry Jeb at all.

After lots of peering down into the bladder through the faceplate and fumbling with distance settings through the flexible rubber membrane, he seemed satisfied and held the camera out in front of his face with both hands. He squinted at us through one eye while using the screw holding the retaining ring in place as a sort of open gun sight. We dived and surfaced in front of him, and he squeezed the shutter release and groped for the film advance lever through the rubber. Then, the bladder emitted a bubble.

With more conventional underwater housings, streams of tiny bubbles give early warning of leaking seals; signals to surface before the camera suffers inundation. Jeb's housing only emitted a solitary bubble. Just one.

Jeb emitted a loud gruff noise through his snorkel. The volume of the solitary bubble equaled the volume of the bladder. The camera was completely flooded. Hypnotized, we all peered down at the falling faceplate. Invisible one moment, then flashing reflected light back to us as if it was a bright slice of the sky sideslipping into the depths. Brilliance sinking. A small puff of silt 30 meters beneath our feet released the spell. Jeb shrugged, rewound the film, opened the camera under water, extracted the film, and let the ruined camera drop. It spun quickly downward, open back flapping in the slipstream, and created a larger puff of fine black silt when it landed on the edge of a ledge close to the bottom. I stared down at its last resting place. That would have been five or six weeks' wages for me.

When Jeb had the film processed in Adelaide, there were three or four frames exhibiting blurred dark blobs.

"Is that my fin?", asked Dave.

"Looks more like Jeb's."

Next week, expensive Perspex sheets, all cut to shape, lay scattered on Jeb's polished wood dining room table. Acrylic glue tinged the air with the pungent smell of solvents. There was a new camera. The Perspex would form the underwater housing for it. Depth squeezed the new housing. It didn't leak, but the flexing sides jammed the controls and rendered them useless.

"No problem," said Jeb, and a motorcycle tire valve was tapped into the housing and glued in place. Before his next dive, Jeb pumped additional pressure into the housing. "That'll keep it in shape," he smugly confirmed. One hot day, though, Jeb's over-pumped housing stood steaming in the sun while we prepared for the dive.

Eventually, the inner pressure became greater than the Perspex walls and seals could withstand. The housing exploded with a sharp crack. Jagged Perspex and carefully machined control glands went whizzing through the air in all directions. One dull metallic *clunk!* followed, and there was a dent in the door panel of the Bel Air.

Jeb didn't seem to care. Lately, he'd been worrying that we weren't fishing enough abalone from the seabed. He started diving for them during the week. He camped for days at Robe and Victor Harbour; he bought a caravan and parked it at Victor Harbour so he could work reefs we'd found between Wright Island and the mainland. We'd join him there on weekends.

Deidre, now a mother, had disappeared from Jeb's conversation. The child, "the kid," was seldom mentioned, either. Abalone diving became his consuming passion.

Frustration bubbled over during one long weekend at Victor Harbour. Strong winds and lashing rain rocked the caravan. We read and reread the stockpile of diving magazines. Jeb hurled his magazine across the caravan, his eyes blazed in anger, and he declared, "I need a bigger boat. We could work in this weather then." Within a week, he had gone. "I'm going back to Victoria to have a boat built", he'd said. "Thirty-footer. I'll be back by Christmas."

He never returned. Christmas passed. Letters went unanswered. Weeds grew under the caravan at Victor Harbour. Nearly a year later, the police pounded on my parents' door. They had a photograph. It was Jeb. Different name. No beard. But it was him, "armed and dangerous." Names and addresses of the members of the diving club had been found in a notebook in the caravan. The police visited us all.

"Have you seen him recently?"

"No ... why?"

He'd escaped from Pentridge jail in a laundry truck.

Jeb was no writer. The Bel Air and the Stebercraft and the compressor and the caravan and everything else had been paid for with the proceeds of armed robberies of the banks at Bairnsdale, Sale, and Orbost in Victoria. His return to Victoria had been intended to refill the coffers. Armed, and with Deidre disguised as a man, they'd forced their way into a bank manager's home in the early hours of the morning. Deidre remained in the house and menaced the man's family. Jeb took the manager to the bank at gunpoint and asked him to open the vault.

All the money Jeb could have ever wanted was probably right in front of his eyes. When he entered the vault to reach out for the money, though, the manager stepped back and slammed the vault door shut. Like the child in the capsized cabin cruiser, Jeb was trapped. But for him, there was no way out. He was captured and jailed.

Months later, a carelessly guarded laundry truck offered free passage, and Jeb took it. We had police watching our house for some days, but he never appeared. When he was finally run to earth, the judge described him as a menace to society and sentenced him to 30 years. Judging by the newspaper reports, Jeb hadn't said a word about his role in the rescue at Maslins Beach. Brilliance, sunk.

48   Thirteenth Beach

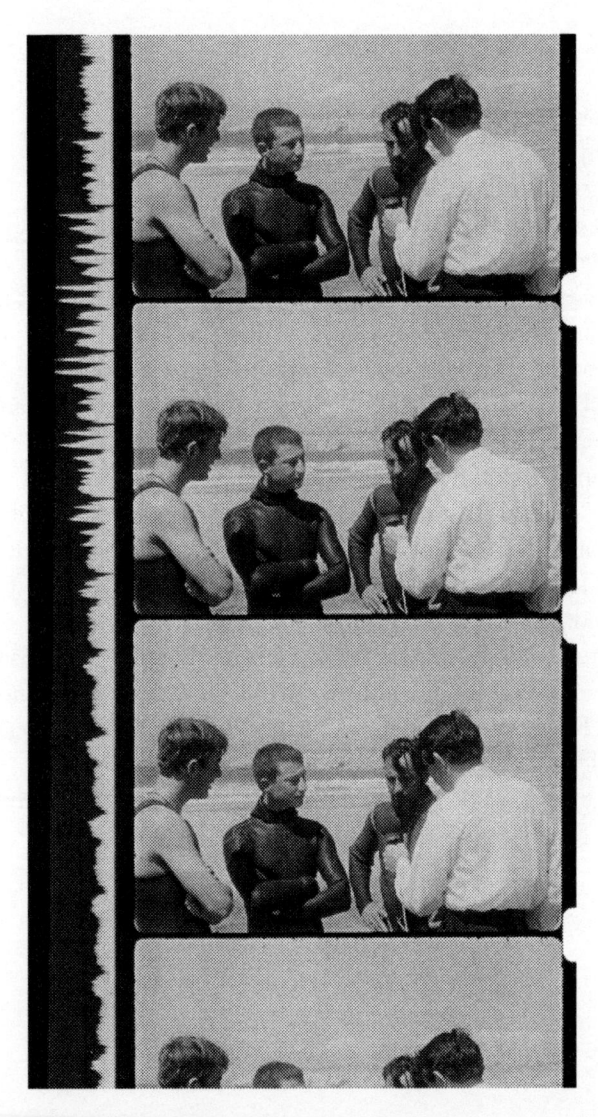

Only Jeb knew what the real scoop was! A clip from the film of Dave Bennett (left), me (center), and Jeb being interviewed for television news by David Flatman after we'd rescued a family from the sea off Maslins Beach, South Australia, in 1967.

8

Gung-ho!

After enduring some persistent ribbing from other competitors about the quaint name of our small club—the *Sea Sweepers*—Ron and I joined a more adventurously named club, Trevor Hayman's *Dorsal Fin Spear-fishing Club*. We then finally came up with a name that we thought could not be considered to be sissy in anyone's language and formed our own club with Neil Wehlack and Herb Ilic: *Gung-Ho! Divers!*

Under this banner, we explored as much of the coast of South Australia as we could, spearing fish and reveling in the reputation we earned when we decisively won the South Australian Nemrod competition. Arrogantly, we elected to fish in only one of the three heats, amassed a huge score, and then didn't bother to turn up for the other two heats. We still won the trophy—but few friends—by a wide margin. We swam the reefs off Robe and Port MacDonnel in the southeast, gathering abalone and lobsters in the absence of fish. We swam out of every cove we could reach by car and foot between Hallet Cove and Victor Harbour, dived at night during the week at Port Noarlunga, Rapid Bay, and Second Valley, and explored Yorke Peninsula from Edithburgh to Port Victoria.

Brian Rodger and Rodney Fox introduced us to the Althorpe Islands, Wardang Island, Baudin Rocks off Robe, and the Tipara Reef off Wallaroo. When holidays or long weekends permitted, we'd head for the more distant reefs of Eyre Peninsula from Wanna, just south of Port Lincoln, around to Streaky Bay.

On one such trip, after our car continued to overheat, we were stranded in Port Augusta at the head of Spencer Gulf. Freddie Hellsinger, a wool presser I knew, owned an old boat here. We dropped in, and he was good enough to ease our disappointment by puttering us down to the Port Augusta power station. Here, in the deep water of the coal-unloading berth, locals fish for the snapper that are making their way from the sea to spawn in the mangroves that tangle the uppermost reaches of the gulf.

Ron, Neil, and I went over the side into almost zero visibility and dived repeatedly for half an hour toward the mud ten meters below. We rested the noses of our spear guns in our left palms alongside our faces, right arms extended behind us, thumbs on the trigger, hoping to blunder into an unsuspecting snapper—quite clear proof that youthful enthusiasm sometimes clouds judgment! When that, not surprisingly, failed to produce any fish, we drove out of town down a dirt track to reach the muddy shore and swam through the mangroves, hunting and hoping to find snapper hiding in the eerie brown stillness within the roots of these trees. Once again, we returned snapper-less.

Ron and I offered to write a weekly skin-diving column for Adelaide's *The Advertiser*, South Australia's major daily newspaper. We were astonished when this was accepted, and we began to be paid for putting words on paper … perhaps Jeb had been right after all! On the basis of the fame that would surely follow, we even managed to somehow convince a salesman from a South Road boatyard that four salt-encrusted, piratical adolescents, zooming around the reefs, brandishing spear guns in a boat boldly painted with the boatyard's name, would help him sell more boats. He loaned us a five-meter aluminum Quintrex with a 20-horsepower engine on a trailer for all the spearfishing competitions that summer.

Demands from the editor of *The Advertiser* for photographs to illustrate our columns helped lead us into underwater photography. Ron began his photographic exploits with an amphibious Nikonos. I eventually followed with a twin-lens Yashica, which was fortunate enough to remain dry despite being encased and submerged in a succession of highly imaginative, but generally unsuccessful, homemade underwater Perspex housings.

Cameras calmed our hunting instincts. We still speared fish, but not as frequently. And if we thought that hunting fish with a spear gun was difficult, hunting them with a camera was doubly so. As the 1960s drew to a close, the guns stayed home more often than not, as we began to acquire better cameras, and spent more time underwater using scuba.

Gung-ho! 51

One of the foggy bottom boys: Southern Australian waters are rich in nutrients, so poor visibility often results. But there's abundant life waiting to be discovered. Here, Neil Wehlack approaches a gorgonian coral in the Gap at Pt. Noarlunga, St. Vincent's Gulf, 1990.

9

Down the Sinks

From ground level, it looks like a circular manhole, roughly chiseled through the limestone rock of a South Australian cow paddock.

From where we now hovered, in gin-clear water close to 60 meters below the surface, the manhole became an aperture admitting a shaft of sunlight that speared down through the darkness like the pale blue beam of a searchlight.

Con Penglis and Graham MacKenzie had led us here. First, to the farmer's house to gain permission to enter the property, and then across the paddock to the manhole, where they'd secured a rope ladder to a steel spike that had been hammered into the rock. We were by no means the first to dive here! Graham dropped the rolled-up ladder through the hole, and we heard a faint, hollow splash as it hit water somewhere beneath us.

As each of us squeezed down through the manhole on the first few rungs of the ladder and paused to allow our eyes to adjust to the deep gloom underground, we found ourselves suspended in the roof of a bell-shaped cave, six or seven meters above the surface of a wide subterranean pool.

We lowered the scuba tanks down on a rope and ferried them across the 20-meter-wide pool to a ledge that ran, at water level, around one side of the cave. This was where we kitted up. Nobody had said "Sssshhhh!" But we spoke in echoing whispers, hushed by the ethereal presence of the shaft of bright sunlight angling down into the unbelievably clear water.

"We'll swim down the shaft, but don't follow it down past 60 meters. If you don't want to go that deep, stop at the top of the rock pile and wait there," Con had said as we slid off the ledge and swam on the surface across the inky dark water to the turquoise patch where the sunlight hit and penetrated the surface.

It was surreal. A line of four divers, following each other headfirst down in loose formation, with only the quicksilver streams of air bubbles from our regulators betraying the presence of water. Graham's distinctive and polished twin stainless steel tanks flashed like mirrors as they caught the sun.

Many years earlier, one of the land owners of this property had decided that the manhole was a convenient place to dump loads of the fragmented lumps of limestone rock that litter the ground here and play havoc with agricultural machinery. He must have worked tirelessly for a long time, because there were a lot of rocks down there this day. They lie across the top of a small natural plateau, about 30 meters below the surface and cascade down the steep slope that drops away on one side of the cave to depths probably greater than 200 meters. As it happened on this day, the shaft of sunlight struck the slope of rocks close to the limit we'd set for the dive. We all hovered there, absorbing the hauntingly theatrical impressions of this doorway to the underworld.

Time ran out quickly for us. Five minutes after leaving the surface, we were all heading up the shaft of light again to avoid lengthy decompression. It had been a short but entrancing dive.

In 1973, four divers succumbed to the entrancement and died in the Shaft. That set off a flurry of noisy protest among bureaucrats and understandable anxiety in the mind of the landowner. This led quite quickly to the Shaft being closed to divers. This also led to the formation of a voluntary cave divers association, which worked hard to try to prevent politicians from legislating away the freedom to dive. To a degree, the association was successful and, thanks in no small measure to the generosity of the landowner, the Shaft is now being dived again.

But, in my opinion, the association is now the bureaucracy it fought so hard to prevent. This is not meant to be criticism of the association. It offers exceptionally high levels of training and guidance; none better. It's the system underpinning the association that worries me. There is no choice. The association stipulates a lengthy and prescriptive list of conditions for equipment, experience, and behavior. Divers who are not members of the association can not dive in the Shaft. Even those who are, must dive in the presence of a supervisor endorsed by the association. There's even a tax; a fee to be paid to the supervisors to compensate them for travel and expenses and to protect them from any lapses of their own forgetfulness or carelessness that result in them losing or misplacing items of their personal equipment. What originally drew divers to the Shaft and brought it to the attention of the world—the excitement of managing risk in pursuit of discovery in the natural world—is no longer available.

There have been no deaths in the Shaft since the 1973 tragedy. While this might, or might not, be attributable to the intervention of the cave diving association (there were no deaths in the Shaft before the 1973 tragedy, either, and the association did not exist then), what I think has been killed off is another freedom and the basic human right and obligation to accept accountability for our own actions. Surfers, kayakers, and climbers would never put up with such levels of paternalism eroding the pure spirit of their sport, and rightly so. Why divers submit so readily is a mystery to me.

But that's now. Back in the 60s, free from these impositions, Ron and I would often dive in caves at night. They are perpetually dark anyway, so we reserved the daylight hours for diving in open sinkholes, such as the Shaft, Kilsby's, and Picaninnie Ponds.

On one cool and windy weekend in 1969, we made two night-time visits to what was then known as Sinkhole 91. This site was also known as the Pines, because it was one of the first to be discovered extending its labyrinthine passages and chambers under an extensive plantation of pine trees.

Collapsing surface rock had created a shallow crater in the ground at the edge of the pine plantation. At the bottom of this crater lay a small pool of water, deceptively covered with a layer of floating aquatic weed. Beyond the weed, and under the lip of the rocky entrance, lay the startlingly clear water.

Late on Saturday night we returned for our second dive of the weekend. While the forest of pines creaked and sighed in the gusty wind, we shivered into our wetsuits—cold and damp from the day's diving—and heaved our tanks onto our backs. After several strong tugs to test the knot of the stout cord line we'd tied off on a large rock to guide us home from our dive, we swept aside the floating weed and eased ourselves into the water.

Flashlight beams sliced whitely through the pitch-black darkness to reveal an elongated submerged chamber from which led several passageways.

As with many of these sinkholes, fine dark-brown silt stirred immediately wherever we touched the floor or walls or swam too close to rocky outcrops. In places, the constrictions within the passageways meant that the diver in the lead had clear water ahead, but the diver following was burrowing in zero visibility through a dense suspension of brown murk, with only the leader's paid-out safety line to guide them. We'd also face this murk whenever we turned to retrace our path.

The Pines, or at least the sections that we knew about then, was not a particularly deep dive; no more than ten or 12 meters in most places. But it was underground all the way, and the only way out to the air above was the same pool through which we'd entered. In caves such as this, a well-managed safety line offers the only safe passage out.

On the previous night, we'd crossed the first chamber and explored a passage off to the left. On this second night, we were going to probe a smaller passage off to the right. Ron headed off in the lead, paying out the line and flicking his flashlight across the walls and floor ahead of us. As he neared what we expected to be the entrance to the passage we'd decided to enter, he stopped, puzzled. When I joined him, I was puzzled, too. An observer watching from a distance would have seen our flashlights rotating through the darkness like beams from a lighthouse. Silently we questioned ourselves, "Had we swum the wrong way? Isn't that the entrance to last night's passage? Wasn't tonight's passage just to the right of it? Why don't we remember this pile of white rock?"

On the floor of the chamber lay a pile of angular, chalk-white rock. It was big enough to be a landmark in the cramped cave, but neither of us could remember seeing it before. We shone our flashlights on it, then on the walls of the chamber around us, then back to the pile of rock, then on each other. Ron mimed scratching his head—and then, as if a germ of an idea had taken root, slowly raised his flashlight to illuminate the roof above us.

"*Blurckbbbbs*!!!" Above water, and without the impediment of a regulator in the mouth, that would have been an expletive! There was no doubting the jigsaw puzzle matching of the angular rock below us with the angular cavity above us. The rock on the floor had been rock in the roof when we swam through here just 24 hours previously.

Seeping water, wind flexing the pine trees' grip of the ground above, maybe an earth tremor, or our own air bubbles—who knows—something had caused these few tons of rock to loosen their last hold in the roof and fall to join the others that had fallen over the years and gradually darkened as silt settled into their porous surfaces.

It is amazing just how quietly and quickly it is possible to exit a cave when the motivation is there.

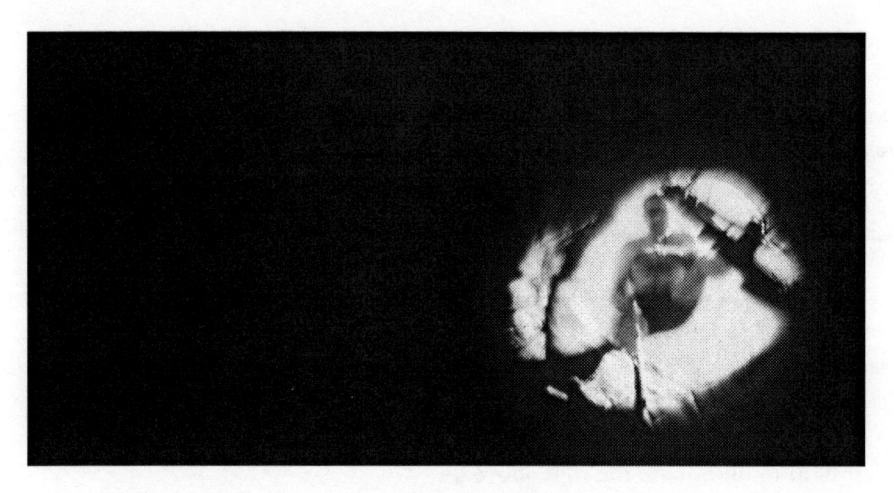

Water clear as air. Looking back up towards the sunlit world from a meter or so below the surface in The Shaft. 1969

1970s

10

In the Dam Black

In 1899, a gang of workmen hacked their way through scrubby pink gums and native pines, down a rough slope, and into the rocky bed of Yettie Creek, just north of Adelaide in South Australia. They were there to begin the ambitious task of building the then largest dam of its kind in Australia. The Warren was to be a thin concrete, concave dam, 27 meters high. Disused tram rails reinforced the concrete. Local rock, disintegrated with explosives and sledge hammers, yielded the aggregate for binding the cement together.

Three kilometers over the ranges, another gang began tunneling into the solid rock near the South Para reservoir. Their job was to divert surplus water from the South Para to the Warren reservoir since Yettie Creek carried insufficient flow to fill this monumental dam.

Seventy-one years later, Neil Wehlack and I groped our way down the face of the Warren toward an outlet valve about 20 meters from the surface of the reservoir that the dam now contains. Decades of tannin build-up, released by decomposing vegetation, had stained the water burgundy-black. No sunlight could reach us. Dense, swirling silt smothered the last centimeters of visibility and rendered useless any attempt to use a flashlight, so we had to work by feel in total darkness. As we neared bottom, we found a sharp thermocline and sank the last few meters in numbingly cold water.

Our task was to disconnect the valve-control rod from an articulated knuckle sitting atop the valve and within an aging and corroded cylindrical bronze sieve. The sieve, one-and-a-half meters high and about the same width, was designed to prevent sticks and other detritus from entering the valve whenever it was opened to allow water to pour from the dam. Its design also made it extremely difficult for a diver to get close enough to the knuckle to remove a pair of fist-sized hexagonal nuts from the threaded end of the massive locking bolt and then slide the bolt out.

We'd accepted this underwater laboring job, drawn by the excitement of becoming commercial divers. But after a series of frustrating and exhausting descents into the frigid, lightless waters of the Warren, the gloss was starting to wear off the idea—and there were still two more sieves to go.

Con Penglis had offered us the work as back-up divers when he'd accepted the job as lead diver with a local underwater contracting firm, Aquasalve, run by Ron Hooper. We were more used to following and learning from Con in the gin-clear water of submerged caves in the South East of South Australia, but we'd jumped at this chance to work with him replacing the old sieves.

On the first day of the work, Hooper had ruptured an eardrum. I'd stepped in to act as second diver for Con, and Neil had come up from Christie's Beach to act as our number three. In the end, the cold above surface and below, the sheer heavy laboring, and the depth, meant that we were all rotating regularly and sharing the load as much as we could.

The old sieves needed to come up first. That meant burrowing down through a deep layer of oozy muck around the base of the sieves to locate the nuts that were clamping the sieves' lower flanges to retaining bolts bedded in the concrete. Surprisingly, once we'd actually located the bolts and managed to get meter-long spanners onto them, they screwed off quite easily. More difficult, was getting at the valve knuckles inside the sieves.

Memorized drawings of the sieves, the knuckles, and control rods were the only guides we had in the water. It took several conferences on the bleak, wind-chilled dam top to deduce that someone would have to wriggle their head, arms, and torso into the sieve through the same slot that admitted the connecting rod. That would have to be done on his back, under the connecting rod. Then he'd have to reach up around both sides of the thick steel rod to get spanners on the locking nut and bolt head—all this while shivering in the pitch black, and trying to shut out the realization that, if the compressor hammering away on the dam top and forcing air down to us failed, it would take a very cool head to extricate ourselves from the sieve alive. "Hooper," we asked. "Tell us again how much we're all getting paid for this?"

When the sieves were first installed, most likely the workmen had simply stood on the concrete base, casually chatting away and enjoying the simple pleasure of working outdoors in the scented Australian bush. They were probably wielding long spanners from outside the sieve, and finished connecting the rods and knuckles before morning tea. For us, deprived of sight and having never even seen the thing we were trying to disconnect, there was no alternative—aside from unemployment—to attempting some spectacular, yet invisible feats of underwater contortion.

We took turns at this. One of us was doing this sort of clumsy reverse limbo dance, head first and upside down into the sieve. The other was doing his best to ensure that the air hoses, that he couldn't see, didn't get snagged on anything he couldn't see and didn't know existed—all the while trying to determine whether the complicated series of muffled metallic banging and clanging coming from the sieve contained any of the predetermined signals to "let in more hose," "pull it out," "take the weight of the connecting rod," or "is it lunchtime yet?"

Not that lunch was much to look forward to. We'd usually retreat from the dam wall to the edge of the surrounding bush to try to get out of the keen wind. We'd dine on meat pies and cans of Coke, fetched in a cardboard carton from nearby Williamstown by one of the Board of Works blokes who were supervising the job. By the time we got to consume them, pies and cans were both usually at the same tepid temperature. Unemployment started to look more attractive after the third straight day of this!

One consolation was that one of the sieves was in only three meters of water. The visibility was only marginally better, but the shallower water was just dismally cold, not nearly freezing, so we alternated between the deepest and shallowest sieves to spread the misery.

As soon as we had all three old sieves free and loose, they were winched up by the three-man Board of Works crew occupying a small pontoon moored just off the dam wall. The men on the pontoon would then use a small, manually operated crane to swing the new sieves out over the water and begin lowering them down to their final resting place on the concrete blocks supporting the valves. The first sieve to go down revealed to us another opportunity for innovative problem solving. The sieves had to be placed precisely on the concrete blocks to enable the bolt holes in the lower flanges to fit over the existing retaining bolts.

We had some help from the unseen but thoughtful engineers who had designed the new sieves. Foreseeing the difficulty that divers would face as they attempted to position the sieves in zero visibility, the engineers had replaced the original sieves' precise circular bolt holes with more forgiving elongated slots. Even so, aligning the slots with the bolts proved to be extremely arduous and challenging work.

With no accurate indicators to guide them, it was impossible for the work crew on the pontoon to lower the sieves with any precision. We attached a small buoy to the valve knuckle to provide some idea of the center point. Beginning with the sieves hanging directly over the buoy, the crew could lower the sieves over the valves, but that was only a rough approximation of where they needed to be.

Aquasalve was a low-cost contracting operation, so there were no voice communications between the divers down on the sieves and the crew on the pontoon. Instead, we decided to rely on pounding the steel winch cable with spanners to direct upward and downward movements of the winch, as we tried to heave and jostle the half ton or so of sieve centrally over the valve and with the slots directly over the retaining bolts. One of the work crew rested his hand against the cable topside, waiting for the signals to come pulsing up the cable, and ready to relay the instructions to the winch operator.

Down on the sieve, we had one diver sitting on top, holding the cable in one hand and a spanner in the other. His legs were dangling down the side of the sieve, close to where the second diver was trying to judge the height of the sieve above the bolts with one hand and tap instructions onto the leg of the signal diver with the other.

What had seemed like a good idea at the time didn't seem to be such a good idea in practice. Clearly, meaning was being lost somewhere in the translation, and the sieve would sometimes dangerously lurch up or down a few centimeters without warning. Crushed hands became a distinct possibility. Tempers boiled, despite the dead chill of the deep water. Late one afternoon, Con erupted like a hooked trout through the surface of the water alongside the pontoon and, from the center of a widening pool of agitated ripples he wildly berated the work crew for their inability to remember "two—up!! … three—down!!!" But it wasn't their fault.

Early the next morning, we were back, padding in our wetsuits through the mist that was welling up from the silent reservoir and creeping across the damp concrete walkway of the dam. In our arms we each carried lengths of light steel tubing. About a meter long, and just a slightly larger diameter than the bolts, the tubes could be pushed through the bolt slots and located onto the upper end of the protruding bolts while the sieve was still safely half a meter or so above the concrete.

We could then signal for the slow and steady lowering of the sieve, and use the tubing as levers to wrench the sieve around into alignment with the bolts. With the sieve in place, the tubes could be wiggled backward and forward to free them, and the nuts could then be threaded home onto the bolts. More limbo dancing and tortured arm and shoulder muscles followed as we worked to reconnect the control rods. Eventually, after nearly 40 wearying dives in six days, all three new sieves were in place, bolted down and reconnected. We were done.

As we'd done many times before, we slowed our final ascent to soak in the relatively warm water just below the surface. After the dreaded cold below the thermocline, this surface water literally felt like a warm bath. Blood-red light, the last feeble remnants of the sun's spectrum able to penetrate any distance through the tannin-laden water, welcomed us to the final meter.

As soon as we broke surface, Hooper killed the compressor, and the deafening clatter that had rattled incessantly across the reservoir every day for nearly a week ended abruptly. Sighing gently, compressed air excused itself from the surge tanks and regulator hoses, and left to rejoin the wind. We could hear birds and rustling leaves. The pressure was off.

This had been another fascinating aspect of diving. We understood now that commercial diving demanded far more than ability to dive. It demanded engineering and technical skills beyond any that we had, or wanted to learn. Diving was simply the vehicle for delivering those skills to where they were needed. The idea of becoming commercial divers had passed.

11

Skeleton in the West

Nostalgia for Western Australia, alluringly fronting the Indian Ocean and basking in the sunny reputation of its relaxed, Californian life style, proved to be irresistible. In 1970, Neil and I stowed our spear guns, aqualungs, and dive bags into the cargo hold of a Pioneer bus in Adelaide, and climbed aboard for the 2400 kilometer odyssey to Perth.

In the three years since Ron and I had pounded his car across this same highway, much of the dirt section had been paved, but it was still a wearying journey, and almost as soon as we arrived in the western capital, we were on the road again, driving another 1000 kilometers, towing a boat, north to Coral Bay with West Australian friends John Butler and Dave Innall.

For Neil and me, this was our first excursion into tropical waters. Blinking in the harsh white sunlight, doubly dazzled by the hard brightness of coral sand, we walked out onto the beach and stared in delight across the protected bay. Rimming the western horizon, too far away for us to hear, creaming rollers crashed silently into the Ningaloo barrier reef and defined, in a long streak of foam, the boundary between the competing blues of the great deeps and the vaulting heavens. Coral Bay was a gem of glittering turquoisel, set in the parched limestone bones of a remote desert coast.

We didn't wait for the boat to be launched. Wearing only masks and fins, Neil and I set off on a lengthy reconnaissance swim, just to marvel at the first live coral we had ever seen. Staghorn coral thickets, each living tip dipped in blue-violet, enmeshed the sandy bottom of the bay like thick leafless briar patches.

Safe in their proximity to these concreted entanglements, hosts of blue green chromis hovered in the slight current, flitting nervously for the shelter of the staghorn as we approached, and blossomed out into open water again as we passed.

Large, vividly colored parrotfish mooched across the sand. We saw our first tropical butterfly fish, banner fish, spectacularly adorned angelfish, and our first northern snappers. Swirling color and exotic species of fish intoxicated us and dominated the excited conversation around the camp fire that night.

We were out of our smelly sleeping bags in the brief coolness of dawn, fanned life into the near-dead embers of the fire to brew hot tea and cook breakfast, and prepared our guns and cameras for the first foray into the waters beyond the outer edge of the reef. Out there, where the reef tumbles into the deeps, massive brain and plate corals predominate and the open water is patrolled by marauding schools of bigeye trevally and other jacks, samson fish, Spanish mackerel, and ever-present sharks.

We speared only what we needed to eat, managed to keep the majority of what we caught away from the audacious sharks, and spent most of the time just swimming round in a heightened state of excitement, recording what we could capture on film, and indelibly imprinting many more images in our memories.

In Skeleton Bay, identified in local legend as the site of a mysterious grave which revealed human remains of unknown origin as the entombing sand dunes eroded, we found the most vibrant coral garden. In this sheltered nook, tucked in under the protective arm of Point Maud, but fed with food—bearing currents, the delicate corals thrived. We had no compressor for refilling our aqualungs so we divided the precious air between two dives: one on the outer barrier and the other in Skeleton Bay.

These were days and dives that forged an enduring attachment to the waters of Western Australia, and within a couple of years, both Neil and I had both retraced the route across the Nullabor Plain to settle and live in Perth.

12

Images on the Wall

My fascination with Western Australian marine life also led me to my wife. Robyn entered my life like an uncharted reef suddenly discovered in familiar waters. She worked in a bank that I had been into many times, yet we had never noticed each other. On one visit though, that changed. It would have saved me a lot of heartache, hangovers, escapes from irate protective fathers, and a futile engagement, if we had met earlier.

There was an inevitability about that first meeting with her that saw me return afterwards to my pokey little apartment with my head spinning. Her bubbling laugh, the sheer joy of life in her eyes, and her surefootedness in what for me was a clumsy first encounter, transfixed me.

I made the bed that day for the first time in three months. The kitchen was more of a challenge but, by the time I'd convinced her that there was a pleasant evening to be had dining on chili con carne, with a bottle of wine, and watching a couple of trays of underwater slides, I'd chiseled and scraped most of the accumulated splattered fat off the wall behind the stove, hauled all my diving gear out of the lounge room and stowed it in the trunk of my car, and managed to repel virtually all the mold that was advancing in seemingly endless whiskery gray strands from the grout in the shower recess.

Overlooking the sinuously waving fronds of brown algae in the throat of the WC did create somewhat of a setback, and she was a little bemused by the number of wrong number telephone calls that I had to answer while she was there, but all things considered, that first evening went well.

I'd promised to introduce her, in person, to the fish and other creatures whose images had briefly colored my white-painted apartment wall, and she had accepted. I took her for her first tentative snorkel swim off the tiny beach on Carnac Island, west of Fremantle. There, in just a couple of meters of protected water, Robyn tensed, then squealed with delight as a young sealion casually rolled over on its back, lay on the sandy bottom directly beneath her, and blew a ring of bubbles up towards her. I could have kissed that sealion!

Although it took some effort to consummate the relationship after that, Robyn and I have been soul mates ever since.

13

Tail of the Typhoon

"Your launch will be waiting at Mersing to take you in speed and comfort to Pulau Tioman."

That reassurance in the glossy brochure clinched the deal. "Speed and comfort" had been the summarized version of Robyn's non-negotiable terms and conditions as we searched for a location for our first overseas diving trip. When we first met, Robyn was a dedicated beachgoer, but not a diver. She had willingly but tentatively taken up snorkeling and quickly became comfortable with that. Knowing that husbands should not attempt to teach their wives to drive, I applied the same principle to diving to safeguard our fledgling marriage. I enrolled her in a diving course as a birthday gift.

Robyn had passed that course easily but, on the Sunday evening when she'd completed her final open-water checkout dive, she made it very clear that her future dive sites would be characterized by easily recognizable similarities. "Warm water, calm water, clear water, someone to carry the heavy gear—that will be you, Wade, if no one else is available—and close proximity to creature comforts, such as a hot shower and a clean bed." There have been some notable exceptions, which Robyn has endured without complaint but for which I'm still paying, but essentially those same conditions prevail today more than a quarter century after they were first declared. Consequently, I chose our first overseas destination with exceptional care.

Tioman sits in the South China Sea about 30 kilometers off the east coast of the Malay Peninsula. Its most striking feature—the dragon's horn—is the twin volcanic plugs of Nenek Si Mukut and Batu Sirau, which stab 690 sheer meters up through the dense jungle at the southern end of the island. Parts of the film South Pacific were filmed here.

At the time we visited, only one small single-story hotel had been built on the island. Subsistence fishing and farming were still the way of life for most of the people living in the few small villages dotting the indented coastline. It seemed an ideal choice.

We left Singapore by road before dawn, crossed the causeway, and headed north through Johor Bahru and Kota Tinggi. First light revealed the patchwork coverage of rubber and palm oil plantations that quilt the lowlands of the Malay Peninsula.

A few chickens scrabbled in the dusty street that led down to the dock in the small harbor in Mersing. Whining mangy cats, all with crooked and broken tails, pleaded at our feet as we unloaded our diving gear and luggage at a grimy open-sided shack that doubled as cafe and departure lounge. Cats' tails are traditionally broken in Malaysia in the belief that this prevents them from jumping.

A quick scan of the boats moored against the thicket of leaning piles confirmed that our launch had not yet arrived and that there was time for breakfast. Poached eggs, toast, and marmalade. Then Dilip arrived. He was the Mersing-based travel agent who had arranged transport and accommodation for us at the hotel on Tioman.

"Mr. and Mrs. Huggs? You're launch is waiting. Please follow me."

We'd been watching the mangrove-lined inlet while we ate breakfast and had seen no gleaming launch sweep into view and tie up at the dock, so we were surprised by the news. But we were happy enough to be on our way and followed Dilip out the door.

He led us down a rickety wooden walkway that bridged the mudflats and led to the pier. Ahead, we could see a typical local fishing boat. It was quite large, probably 15 meters. Sharp, upward-jutting bows fell back to low gunwales amidships and a slightly raised square stern. A deckhouse, painted dull green and red, squatted in the center of the vessel. Bedecking the topsides was a chaotic cargo of cardboard and wooden boxes, red plastic fish bins, white plastic floats, bamboo marker poles topped with black rags, and several lines of freshly washed clothes hanging out to dry.

"Doesn't look like much of a launch to me," Robyn murmured darkly. We stepped aboard, entered the deckhouse, and met the strong, sweet smell of last night's curry.

"Hey! We're here for adventure! This will be fine," I countered as I turned to enter the forward section of the deckhouse.

"No please. Straight on." Dilip corrected my course.

"Straight on? To where?" Only the open air lay straight ahead. I could see that through the doorway on the port side of the deckhouse.

"No. Please. Straight on." Dilip waved his arm to keep us moving as I uncertainly turned to him.

When I turned back to face the open door, there was another arm waving to us. It belonged to a friendly Mersing fisherman beckoning us toward him. We could see his face, too. It was barely visible over the gunwale. He was standing on the roof of the deckhouse of his own boat that was moored alongside the boat we had just boarded.

"This, is a launch?" Robyn asked as we peered down at the diminutive but bright blue-and-red craft rubbing against the hull of the larger boat like a whale calf nuzzling its mother. "This isn't what was in the brochure." Dilip came to my rescue with a gentle but insistent "Please. Other passengers waiting."

Assisted by the strong brown arm of the genial fisherman, we slithered down onto the roof of the deckhouse and then onto the narrow gunwale of his little boat. From there, it was just a step down into the deckhouse and the cramped seating area just forward of the wooden-walled engine compartment.

Six other people, all Malays, were sitting patiently on the benches lined along either side of the hull. Between their feet lay string bags of potatoes and other vegetables, an assortment of boxes and suitcases, and, very shortly after we arrived, our dive bags and luggage. Greenish light filtered in through a few smeary glass portholes set just above the benches. Fumes reeking of dead-fish, fresh paint, wet dogs, and diesel fuel seeped up from the bilges. And it was stifling hot.

We were soon getting underway. Loud clattering from the antiquated engine made conversation a little difficult, but, as far as Robyn was concerned, that was a moot point; she did not intend to speak to me for at least a week. Everything went well, though, at least until the mooring lines were cast off and we began to move down the inlet toward the sea. By then, pale blue smoke had seeped through the cracks in the engine compartment wall, and the atmosphere in the deckhouse became really uncomfortable.

We then nudged out of the inlet into open water. Less than a week earlier, a typhoon had spun across the South China Sea. Its tail had only flicked Mersing, but lines of low, greasy swell were still rolling up from the southeast. Our boat lurched and dipped like a drunk on a unicycle.

About an hour out from Mersing, a small red bucket caught my eye. It was jammed in under some sacks of vegetables. I managed to grab it during one of the periods of weightlessness when the boat fell suddenly into some gaping hole in the sea, and all the passengers and cargo floated briefly free, before crashing down with a nauseating thud. Nausea was why I *needed* that bucket.

When my head emerged from between my knees after from my first use of it, a look of horror appeared on the gentle face of the Malayan woman sitting opposite me as she recognized the straggly remains of a poached egg white dangling from my left nostril.

Robyn opened one of the small portholes to ventilate the now even more malodorous cabin, but, along with gusts of welcome fresh air, it also allowed sloshes of seawater to cascade in every time the boat stumbled and rolled into an oncoming trough. The prospect of sufficient water pouring in to sink the boat seemed to be quite appealing to me by that stage, but the other passengers were clearly becoming tired of my retching and the periodic drenching of sea water. With some difficulty, I managed to time my move with a dizzying downward slew and spiral of the boat, and emptied the bucket through the porthole.

Fresh air tasted like nectar, so for the remainder of the voyage, in the depths of despair, I knelt on the hard seat with my face plugging the porthole. This enabled direct ejection into the South China Sea of what was left of the breakfast, followed in succession by alarming quantities of bile, lumps of stomach lining, what looked like a kidney, some small change, and finally, the innersoles of my Reeboks. All this detritus was flushed away as our launch rolled over and buried the porthole—and my face—into the steep swells that continued to roll endlessly up from the wildly dipping and rearing horizon.

Unpleasant as these frequent dunkings were, they did at least offer my face momentary shade from the sun that had risen into a clear sky, and was now pouring its radiant scorn down on our blighted passage.

We finally landed at Tioman, nearly six hours after we'd chugged in a cloud of blue gas out of the inlet at Mersing. Every part of my face forward of my ears was glowing red from radiation sickness. Salt-caked and evacuated of any form of nutrients, I was barely able to totter down the jetty and into the reception area of the hotel, which resembled a Dayak longhouse.

"If you get seasick, why didn't you take the plane from Mersing and fly here?", inquired the helpful receptionist. She recoiled as I slowly raised my eyes from the hotel register, in which I was attempting to legibly write our names, and in gave her the same blood-shot, malevolent gaze that Jack the Ripper probably reserved for his victims.

"There's a plane ...?"

"Er ... yes ... every day. Very comfortable. It takes just 20 minutes. Dilip can book for you."

I risked a sidelong glance at Robyn to confirm what I immediately suspected. Dilip was dead man walking.

Sitting under a tree is the best cure for seasickness, and Tioman has an abundance of those. Jungle cloaks the inland, and coconut palms fringe the shores. As soon as our bags were stowed in our bungalow, we headed toward the idyllic, picture-postcard beach and its graceful waving palms.

Thud!

"What was that??", Robyn asked. The answer rolled to a stop not far from her feet.

"Falling coconut.", I offered weakly.

She looked at me as though I'd just said, "I wish I'd married your sister" and then cocked her head to one side to inspect the tree we were almost under. It was heavily laden with fat green coconuts. So was the one next to it, and the one next to that. Every tree on the beach was in the same fecund condition.

"Why don't you sit under the tree. I'm going to sit in the cabana", Robyn said as she strode away, her tropical silk sarong swishing like a short, exasperated sigh with every stride.

I followed, trying to stay just far enough behind her to ensure that the heat throbbing and pulsing from my face didn't burn her back.

Dappled sun bathed the cabana. We sat there in shade and safety looking out over the sheltered bay and its offshore reef, ordering piña coladas and snacks from the small hotel beachside cafe when our appetites returned, and generally starting to feel at peace with the world. Late in the afternoon, when a few thunder-clouds gathered and spattering rain dimpled the sea, we rose and headed back along the beach toward our bungalow.

"What on earth??" Robyn was staring at commotion in the shallows over the reef.

Grebes are interesting birds. They are designed for diving and, like penguins, their webbed feet are placed well back, close to their tails, to enable maximum propulsion when they're pursuing their food underwater. When they're courting potential mates, they direct that propulsive force downward and, by paddling furiously, they're able to lift their entire bodies out of the water and skim across the surface on the very tips of their toes. It's a very impressive display. This is even more so when it is emulated by humans. Two snorkelers, who had been patrolling a hundred meters out to sea, were now performing this very feat right in front of us.

As we watched, they thrashed their way up and out of the water on the outer edge of the reef and flailed their way across the reef top. Finally, half way across the beach, they ran out of energy and crashed headlong into the sand, chests heaving and legs bleeding from the scratches and gashes created by their spectacular passage through the coral.

"Shark!" Gasp ... heave ... "Shark!" was the only answer we could get from them.

Robyn gave me one withering glance as an afternoon thundershower burst over our heads, and a sheet of hissing rain grayed the jungled slopes and sent us sprinting for shelter.

Early next morning, we hired a local fisherman and his small boat to carry us a short distance northward around the coast to a secluded cove.

"Will this get us away from that shark?", Robyn asked as she stared over the side, and watched patches of coral slide past beneath us.

"It will definitely get us away from those two snorkelers," I muttered.

Granite boulders guarded the entrance to the cove. Jungle shelved steeply down from the mists above, almost to the high-water mark at the back of the tiny, crescent-shaped beach. We spent the first half of the new day here, snorkeling in clear water among muted coral gardens.

Only one larger fish, a timid hump-headed wrasse, came into sight. It streaked away in panic as soon as it saw us. These large fish often survive, where nearly every other large reef-dwelling fish has been fished out of existence, because wrasse are known by the local fishermen to be frequently toxic. Their dietary habits create this unwitting protection. Hump-headed wrasse are among the very few fish that can safely dine on creatures with high levels of natural toxicity—puffer fish and sea hares, for example.

Wrasse also often carry the mysterious ciguatera fish poison, which is rife in many tropical predatory species. Ciguatera is generated by one-celled dinoflagellates that inhabit coral colonies. As the coral polyps are eaten by coral-eating fish, small doses of ciguatera toxins begin to accumulate in the food chain. Larger predatory fish, feeding and growing by eating the coral eaters and the fish that eat them, eventually carry sufficient ciguatera to render themselves inedible to humans. There's no warning other than awareness of the risk; the toxin is tasteless and does not affect the appearance of the flesh. Cooking doesn't kill it; neither does freezing. Ciguatera poisoning is rarely fatal, but a bout of it can leave the victim nauseous, cramped, and with chronic diarrhea for months. There is no certain cure.

"Isn't mackerel a predatory fish?", Robyn asked suspiciously as the fisherman generously and unexpectedly handed us our lunch—small mackerel he'd caught while we'd been poking about the coral, barbecued on his boat's rusty-blackened griddle, and served with a slice of papaya on broad, glossy green leaves plucked from a tree overhanging the cove.

Any whole fish that can fit on a dinner plate is probably safe to eat. At that size, it hasn't been alive long enough to eat a big enough dose of ciguatera to cause problems for humans ... but we waited until the fisherman tucked into his own serving before we began eating our own.

"Good enough for him, good enough for me, Robyn said happily." Fresh and moist, skin curled and crisped, it was delicious.

Wherever we snorkeled or dived here, it was much the same; the sea is the major source of food for the villagers of Tioman, and the reefs had been heavily fished. At low tide, exposed outcrops attracted the attention of villagers armed with axes and mattocks. They chopped away at the soft coral rock to reveal and extract worms and small crabs that were living in burrows and fissures.

Our fisherman friend took us out early every day, guiding us to spots he thought would be good diving, happily puttering off to somewhere else when a quick dip over the side revealed nothing but dead coral and few fish. Occasionally, in protected nooks, we'd find vibrant coral colonies, bustling with the color of basslets and butterfly fish. Turtles and stingrays made fleeting appearances.

Lunch every day, as it had been on the first day out, was fresh fish and papaya, eaten either onshore or on the boat, but always in an impossibly beautiful blue, turquoise, white, and green setting of sky, sea, sand, and jungle. We'd stay out until the daily gathering of afternoon thunderclouds rumbled their electric discontent over the island and blocked the sun. One nervous shark, no more than a-meter-and-half long, sniffed tentatively into sight as we swam back to the boat in bronze light late one afternoon. It zipped away before I could point it out to Robyn. Seen through our western, holidaying eyes, this was indeed paradise.

One of the villagers knocked gently on our bungalow door one evening. He'd been one of the passengers on the trip out from Mersing. He was a teacher who lived in Kampong Tekek, the closest village to the hotel. The next day, he was leading his children on their first hike across the island from Tekek to the largest village on the east coast, Kampong Juara.

He spoke faltering English, which was immeasurably better than the two words of Malay that we'd picked up (three if you count "thank you" as two words). He wondered if we would like to accompany them on the hike. This was an extraordinarily kind gesture; he'd walked nearly three kilometers to make it, and we readily accepted.

At first light next morning, we set off from the hotel to meet with him, his wife, and two children at Kampong Tekek. Our inability to speak Malay meant that we could only offer his family a smile and a "good morning," which sounded awkward and out of place against the exotic backdrop of weathered wood and rusted iron houses swaddled in the lush and vivid foliage of their gardens—or the jungle; it was difficult for us to see where one ended and the other began. Nevertheless, we were made to feel welcome.

It was a six-hour hike each way. We left Tekek, passed through the village's small vegetable patches, and followed the lower reaches of the Ayer Besor River for some distance before beginning the steep climb through the jungle toward the ridge which divides the eastern and western zones of the northern section of Tioman.

Only Robyn and I wore shoes; our teacher-guide and his wife were barefoot and more surefooted than we were over the stones of creek crossings and on the slippery mud where springs seeped water from the rock across the dirt trail. Midway up the ridge, the teacher took a couple of pot shots with his small-gauge shotgun at a reticulated python he'd spotted in some low-hanging branches. He missed, and before he could reload, the arm-thick snake had disappeared into the undergrowth.

On the ridge, in the depths of the jungle, we encountered an elderly couple. Our teacher-guide led us to them to pay our respects as we crossed their property. Wrinkled like walnuts, stooped but not frail, they'd lived here all their married life, first hacking out and then planting and tending a small rubber plantation. Japanese soldiers had failed to penetrate this far inland during the Second World War when Japan seized Tioman as a refueling base for the invasion of Malaya. The couple had simply stayed here, high on the ridge, out of sight and safe, stockpiling the latex from their rubber trees. When the war ended, they had many bales of latex to take to market and could have bought for themselves a comfortable house on the coast. They preferred to stay in the simple but scrupulously clean home they had built for themselves on the mountain.

We learned all this through the translation of our teacher-guide as we sipped strong and sweet black coffee and nibbled on, of all things, Arnott's milk arrowroot Australian Bush Biscuits while sitting on the polished linoleum floor of the furniture-less living area of their two-roomed house. When we asked, through clumsy sign language, if we could take their photograph, they rose from their cross-legged squat, disappeared into their sleeping area, and emerged a few minutes later in their best clothes. I photographed them sitting proudly in the entranceway of the red and blue house and finally, after a delightful hour or so, we parted with many handshakes, toothless smiles, and "terima kasihs".

We skirted around the neat rows of their rubber trees, all oozing trickles of dirty-cream latex from the chevrons of lacerations scarring their outer bark into small cups suspended against their trunks. Their natural rubber is less valuable now. The Japanese strangulation of natural rubber supplies during the Second World War occupation of Malaya forced the world to develop a synthetic alternative derived from petroleum. But, for as long as these kindly people lived, they'd continue to harvest the latex, roll it into sheets through a manual wringer, dry it in smoke from a wood fire, and then watch as the young men from Tekek came up to carry it away to market for them.

With one last wave, we left the open, orderly shade of their plantation and again entered the dark, chaotic abundance of the surrounding jungle.

Gracious hosts; They spoke no English, we no Malaysian, but we were warmly welcomed into their home. Tioman, South China Sea, 1979

14

One Last Dance

Two old-wives slowly circled in a sad dance. One of them was pitifully sick. Tassels of dead skin streamed from its body. Patches of peeling scales were erupting on its flanks. Its tail and pectoral fins were rotting, perhaps from the effects of what appeared to be a dirty grey mold extending out along the rays from the base of the fins. The other seemed perfectly healthy; plump, boldly striped in black and white, sharply angled dorsal fins spiking pertly upward. But these two fish were inseparable.

On this Western Australian reef, fifteen meters down in open water, a few meters away from the overhanging limestone ledge where most of the members of their school were milling around, they continued their circular ceremony. One dying; one watching. Few other fish seemed to be paying them any attention, but I watched them for 20 minutes, trying to detect some underlying reason for their behavior.

Fish have few face muscles, so it is difficult for humans to discern any visual signs of emotions. They have no voices that we can hear. They don't need tear ducts to prevent their eyes from drying. Happy or sad, angry, comfortable or in agony, their faces retain the same stoic, distant aloofness.

So was this a heart-wrenching farewell? Was the healthy fish apprehensively herding the sick one away into exile to avoid contagion for the whole school? Was it waiting for the right time to move in for a feed? In the end, I could only interpret what they were doing from within the context of my human experience. I retreated, and left them to their last afternoon together.

1980s

15

Cathedral Deep

o o o o o o o o o o o o o o o o o o o o o o o o o o o o o o o
"A lunar light revealed waving sea whips and circling fish."

—*William Beebe*

"The deadly fascination of deep water."

—*Ron Moon*

Storm swells thump onto the reef and, through the application of sheer blunt force, reveal weaknesses in the reef structure. Massive coral bomboras—clumps of limestone veneered with living polyps but only secured by slender coral stems—succumb to the wave assault and tumble down into the delicate latticework of the reef. Pulverized, and at the same time pulverizing, these natural autogenous grinding mills reduce stately coral structures, and themselves, to rubble and elemental sand.

Quietly, invisibly, billions of creatures bore into the coral, collectively excavating tons of limestone sand every day. Parrotfish, armed with beaks of fused teeth, add to the erosion by gnawing away at living hard corals, digesting the protein and expelling the gritty skeletal remains.

Sluiced and sorted by waves and currents, some of the sand and rubble washes across the reef tops. Fans of bleached reef alluvium create shallow lagoons behind the bulwarks of the reef. Sand abraded from the face of the reef heads in a different direction, down into endless night …

In dim blue light, 70 meters down a deeply striated vertical wall in the Coral Sea, constant rivulets of sand wriggled off a ledge and trickled down into the blue-black abyss. Spindly colonies of black coral, gaunt like the leafless twigs of dead trees, waved slowly under the invisible hand of the slight current. A solitary adult queen angelfish, robbed of its color by the blue monochrome light, bustled across the barren reef face and stared at me. Out in the deep, a single shark. Below me, even deeper, Peter. Ice calm. Deliberate.

This is dangerous territory for divers breathing air. Oxygen toxicity is a possibility. Nitrogen narcosis is inevitable. At this depth, as the second stage of our regulators adjusts to feed us air at the same crushing pressure as the enveloping water, eight times more nitrogen than at the surface was flowing into our lungs with every breath.

Our blood is always saturated with nitrogen, but it does nothing to sustain us. At normal atmospheric pressure, nitrogen passes in and out of our lungs and dissolves in our blood and tissues with no effect. Breathed under pressure, it causes nitrogen narcosis—"rapture of the deep." In warm water, the sensation is pleasant enough. Jack Daniels or Johnny Walker, in moderation, creates the same mellow sense of well-being and loss of inhibition. Unlike its alcoholic equivalents, though, narcosis falls away as the pressure is relieved—and there's no hangover.

Narcosis is probably the result of dissolved nitrogen impeding communication impulses in the fatty tissue of the brain and central nervous system. But narcosis' friendly comfort can kill like a smiling assassin. Euphoria leads to deadly dismissal of vital indicators, such as elapsed time and air consumption. Cavalier indifference leads inevitably to the other dangers of breathing air under pressure; oxygen toxicity, bends, and embolism. Death.

Peter and I had committed to this dive well aware of the risks. One bounce dive. One peep into the abyss. Plunge to 60 meters and begin the slow and staged ascent all within five minutes. Minimum time at depth. Maximum time in staged decompression, even though, in theory, there should be no need for lengthy decompression.

It was interesting. And, in its own way, quite profound. Of course, it didn't in any way approximate the abyssal revelations of Beebe and his bathysphere. At 70 meters in clear tropical water, we were still within the twilight of the euphotic zone, where there is sufficient light to allow photosynthesis to continue. This process by which marine plants and other organisms, such as diatoms, miraculously convert light into food dwindles with depth and water clarity.

Here in the Coral Sea, the diffuse boundary separating the euphotic zone from the deeper dimmer disphotic zone, where photosynthesis is not possible, probably lay another 50 meters or more below us. True abyssal darkness would probably only begin another 150 meters below that. Another 300 meters or so beyond that lay between the unreachable bottom and us. So our "peep into the abyss" was a delusion.

Yet, swimming free in the cathedral deep of the ocean on the seaward fringe of a continent is something few people experience in a lifetime. But there is significant risk.

I can remember staring at my watch and being unable to register the elapsed time. My pressure gauge made no sense. But the preset red bar in my depth gauge did. The needle of the gauge had pushed it past the planned 60-meter mark to around 70 meters. That number held hypnotic attraction.

We'd sunk deeper than we'd anticipated, and yet that discovery only mildly disturbed me. A problem I could solve, but I wasn't sure how, but I'd get around to it. Laws of physics don't have a pause button, though.

Invisibly, the human body breathing air at that depth is precariously close to the limits of oxygen tolerance. Oxygen, that life-giving gas, is toxic in the extreme to mammalian life. It is only our cells' natural antioxidant defense systems that enable us to safely use oxygen to support life. Under double atmospheric pressure, pure oxygen is poisonous and will cause cell and lung damage—convulsions and death in extreme cases. Diluting oxygen with nitrogen by breathing compressed air and not pure oxygen pushes the safe limit deeper, but there's still a limit. English scientist John Dalton had it worked out in 1801. His law of partial pressures states that the total pressure of a gas mixture equals the sum of the partial pressures that make up the mixture.

Under this law, the gases in a mixture of gases behave as if there are no other gases in the mixture as pressure changes. This is the main reason that the so-called safe limit for sport divers breathing compressed air is considered to be around 40 meters. At this depth, the concentration of oxygen in a lungful of air is hovering near the same concentration of pure oxygen breathed at ten meters.

Press beyond this fuzzy limit by going deeper, and the risk of oxygen poisoning increases significantly. But, in a mind befuddled by nitrogen narcosis at 70 meters, articulate recollection of Dalton's Law is impossible.

Arching my back allowed me to gaze up toward the sun. Blue-haloed, tiny wraith-like figures lay silhouetted on the transparent surface; snorkel divers peering down at us. Neil Wehlack hovered watchfully at 50 meters. Always thoughtful and reliable, he pointed to me and then tapped his watch. A silent reminder that time was passing quickly.

Underwater, weightlessness diminishes as air cavities within the human body, cellular neoprene in wetsuits, and inflated buoyancy vests compress under rising water pressure. Left unattended, this process can rapidly spiral a diver into terminal descent, with narcosis increasingly anaesthetizing the brain to the risk. The invisible hand of the abyss will draw the foolish and foolhardy into eternal blackness.

Happily numbed and distracted from the passage of time and the consumption of air, we'd drifted into a delicate predicament. Too little air to stop for decompression at 20 meters, ten meters, and then finally at three meters as we'd planned. Chastened, we began the ascent.

Brightening light. Shallower water. Clear head. And a sense of relief as the pressure came off. But, like our peep in the abyss, the relief was illusory. With only about 20 percent of our air remaining, we were still 50 meters below the surface.

Popular mythology told us that, during a short bounce dive, the body absorbs nitrogen quickly but not in sufficient quantity to create the need for lengthy decompression. Providing the rate of ascent is slow and measured, the cells and tissues of our bodies free themselves safely of the limited accumulation of excess nitrogen. Maybe.

Now, 50 meters below, we were confronted with the inescapable consequences of our actions. Maybe the need to decompress remained. Maybe it didn't. Like drinking drivers who wish they'd been more sensible when the flashing red-blue light of a police car chills their revelry, we reluctantly resigned ourselves to the only option available to us and settled for a slow, sustained ascent to three meters.

Once there, we clung to a knob of coral to avoid drifting away from the reef or bobbing to the surface and remained as motionless as possible to conserve energy and air. I kept my legs and free arm as straight as possible to give any bubbles of nitrogen free passage through my joints. I'm not sure if that helped or not, but it made me feel better! Of course, joint pain is the least concern for divers at risk of the bends. Nitrogen dissolves most readily in fatty tissue. About 60 percent of the human nervous system is constructed from cells with high fat content. Bubbles accumulating there can cause catastrophic damage. We eked 40 minutes from our remaining air at three meters.

That night, as *Challenger* lay peacefully at anchor behind the reef, I lay on my bunk staring up at the darkened ceiling. Ron Moon's observation about the deadly fascination of deep water floated to the surface.

In the late 1960s, Ron and I had spent an Easter weekend on our first trip to the crystal-clear freshwater sinkholes in the southeast of South Australia. We'd met two other divers doing the same thing. In the hotel one night, they'd been telling us about that day's deep dives and their plans for the next. Late the next day, they were found dead 50 meters down in a hole known as Kilsby's.

Diving is an inherently safe sport. But when there is a tragedy in deep water, it is quite commonly a dual fatality.

No one can be sure why. One possibility is that one diver becomes affected by narcosis and starts to behave erratically or rashly—perhaps stripping off and discarding vital pieces of equipment. Intervention by the companion diver requires extra exertion … and exertion accelerates the onset of narcosis. So then there are two divers under the influence, perhaps locked in a grotesque giggling embrace as they sink into oblivion. This is literally a fatal flaw in the buddy system.

Out in the Coral Sea, though, with the hull of *Challenger* rising and falling gently beneath me like the breast of a sleeping giant, my latest exposure to the deadly fascination of deep water gave me pause for thought. Seventy meters, breathing air, is indeed taking a foolhardy risk. I resolved never to do that again.

Edge of a continent: On only a few days a decade the Pacific Ocean swell drops sufficiently to make it possible to safely drop divers from a boat onto the outer edge of the Great Barrier Reef. Here, the reef, rimming the very shoulder of the Australian continent, plunges away into a thousand meters of water. (That is a large shark. Visibility was around 100 meters, and the shot was taken with a 17mm lens. The shark wouldn't approach any closer, though). 1987.

16

Coconut Logs

"He said for some reason that the *schnellboot*—the fast boat—is not available. We have to get up now and go." I shielded my eyes and peered down at my watch. It was three in the morning and the flashlight being held on our faces by some unseen figure in the darkness was both disorienting and extremely irritating. Robyn groaned. "I knew it … we're going over on one of those coconut log things … I just knew it."

We were on the island of Bathala in the Ari atoll of the Maldives, near the equator, southwest of India. This was the beginning of the end of our Maldivian adventure, but it was the start of a voyage that gave us fresh appreciation for the oceanic wanderings of migratory peoples in dugout canoes and balsa rafts. Bathala had been developed as a diving destination by German divers—hence the promise of a *schnellboot* to speed us on our way home.

There was another sleep-deprived couple making the same passage. Jeremy and Brenda were honeymooners from Dublin who, like us, had expected a smooth and rapid transfer to Malé much later in the morning aboard this fabled, but not yet seen by anyone we could find, *schnellboot*.

In the predawn darkness, the two Maldivian crew members fussed over us somewhat. Light from their lanterns splashed a safe path for our feet as we stepped down from the dock, sensed the now-familiar smell of fish oil and diesel fuel, ducked under the framework of the shade canopy, and felt the motorized dhoni dip under our weight. Without a word of English, they gently and politely organized us so that we sat two people on each side of the dhoni, properly stowed our dive bags forward, and offered us slices of papaya and bottles of water.

A third Maldivian was asleep in what must have been discomfort—in a fetal position on the boards that braced the stern of the dhoni. He remained motionless and comatose, occasionally swept by the beam of a flashlight, while the other crewmembers jerked the engine awake with a hand crank, cast off the mooring ropes, and swung the dhoni around toward the channel that led from the lagoon, through the reef, and into the open sea. We mused on the reason for this third crewmember being here.

"Must be to help unload the baggage."

"Maybe just a local passenger heading to Malé."

"I wonder if he's okay; might be ill?"

"He'd be a lot better if the *schnellboot* was here ... and so would I!" Robyn fumed.

We were in deep water as soon as we'd transited the short natural channel connecting the lagoon with the open sea and passed over the steep slope of the island's fringing reef. All 1,200 Maldivian islands sit atop coral reefs that have grown, and are still growing, on the gradually sinking basalt mountain peaks of the Chagos-Laccadive ridge—a rumpled spine of volcanic rock squeezed like toothpaste out of a tube from a southerly drifting puncture in the earth's undersea crust.

Upwelling molten lava cooled, hardened, accumulated in staggering amounts, and created north-south ridges extending over 1,500 kilometers and reaching close to the surface of the sea, if not through it. Warm-water coral polyps, drifting free across the ocean in their larval stages, found these basalt ridges ideal territory for starting a family and began the speck-by-speck process of building massive reefs from their limestone secretions. As basalt continued to accumulate, the sheer weight of it caused the earth's crust beneath the ridge to slowly sink. But the corals kept building upward toward the sun and the surf at about the same rate as their foundations were subsiding under them. Every thousand or so years, the corals built a few centimeters of new reef.

Today, pure coral deposits 1,200- to 1,400-meters-thick encrusting these basalt ridges create the chains of islands we know as the Laccadives, Maldives, and, at the extreme southern end, Chagos. This is why the beaches of the Maldives are so blindingly white; there is no rock other than pure chalk-white coral in these islands for the sea to grind into sand. None of the islands is higher than three meters above sea level. There are no hills, no valleys, no rivers, and therefore no silt to run off and cloud the water—so we'd had some wonderful experiences here.

The first came at dawn on our first morning. After landing at Malé late at night, we'd been assigned a temporary room on the island of Furana, just across from Malé International Aiport, itself a small coral island extended to yield enough area to accommodate a runway. Lights blazing in the moments after takeoff, our Singapore Airlines jumbo thundered low overhead as we puttered across to Furana in a small dinghy. In the morning, we were to be picked up by a boat that would take us the 60 kilometers to Bathala.

As soon as it was half light, I couldn't lie in bed wondering. I grabbed snorkel gear and walked the ten meters from our bed to the water, scattering fiddler crabs in sideways panic as I crossed the gently sloping beach.

It was a relatively long swim across the coral-rubble littered lagoon. Without stopping to lift and peer under slabs of rubble, there wasn't much to see, either. A few small parrotfish. A pair of silvery jacks, patrolling the early morning calm of the shallow clear water. An occasional juvenile clown triggerfish bumping its nose down into holes in the sand in search of food.

It was the drop-off of the reef that I wanted to see, and I kept plodding quietly along staring into the pale blue horizon between the transparent surface of the lagoon and the creamy-gray bottom. Deepening indigo gradually replaced the pale blue as the open sea beyond the reef edge started to fade into view. Silently, but in just the same way that the low thumping bass raises excitement and anticipation before the opening act of a rock concert, the intensifying color acted as a spur to my eagerness, and I dug my fins in hard to speed toward the reef edge.

Riotous color and activity drew a gasp of disbelief from me—the full scope of life on a Maldivian reef backdropped by the rich blue of deep water shot with the first rays of the sun. Blue and yellow tangs, purple fairy basslets, silver jacks lined in iridescent mauve, a small black and white manta, swarms of sardines, lavender and lemon butterfly fish, and countless colorful reef fish that I'd never seen before milled in erratic kaleidoscopic disarray.

"Robyn! ROBYN!" I raised my head, spat out my snorkel mouthpiece, and called to her across the lagoon. Warm yellow sunlight was starting to gild the tops of the frayed fronds of the coconut palms that clothe Furana, as they do most of these classic coral islands. I couldn't help but try to call her out to share this moment, but the distance was too great and her jet-lagged slumber too deep for her to hear me. Solitude in the sea is, for me, time to be treasured, but it comes distant second to sharing time and experience with my life's traveling companion. I called again, but when her familiar form didn't emerge from the beachfront bungalow, I returned to my solo swim along the edge of the reef, consoling myself with the knowledge that there would be another week of mornings like this.

Bathala was even more spectacular. Nearly 60 kilometers away from Malé, it had seen fewer people and less development. It is small. We swam around the whole island in one lengthy snorkeling session several times. We took air cylinders from the small dive store and dived deeper along sections of the island's reef.

We paid local boat owners to take us to more distant dive spots amid the maze of coral islands that sprinkle this remote tract of ocean. Everywhere we went, we were confronted by the same vivid and animated profusion of life.

Strong currents sweep through the atolls of the Maldives. With care, though, it was usually possible to intersperse exhilarating drifts with the current along deeper reefs with quiet and private exploration of delicate coral gardens tucked into nooks in the lee of the reefs. On days when the currents eased, we could spend more time exploring individual tila—coral formations rising from the seabed. Undercut and perforated with fissures and caves, tila create rich habitat.

Our diving logbooks record eels thick as my arm sharing deep-shaded crevices with exquisitely delicate porcelain crabs and even smaller, wisp-thin shrimp marked in lavender and cream. On the shoulders of the tila clustered enormous stinging anemones, bulging, baggy bags in pinks, oranges, and blues, each with their own families of immune anemone fish living safely within the crowns of waving tentacles. Scorpion fish lay motionless among the corals, heavily tasseled and disguised, waiting for their next unsuspecting meal to come along. All the while, swirling blizzards of sleek blue and yellow rainbow runners and flighty fusiliers circled and dipped, veered and swarmed all around us.

On one occasion, a large rainbow runner dropped out of its school and braked to an abrupt halt right in front of me, mouth open, gills flared, just centimeters from the sandy bottom. It was instantly attended by two tiny cleaner wrasse, fearlessly picking and nipping away at irritating parasites in the runner's mouth and gill rakers. Their flitting dance had flagged the presence of their cleaning station to the passing shoals of fish. In some mysterious way, the runner had interpreted their signals and zoomed in for a service. Job finished, the wrasse flicked out of the way like mechanics in a Formula One pit stop, and the GT Runner accelerated away like a silent McLaren to rejoin the race for food and survival.

Robyn saw her first shark here. Silvery bronze, a whaler of some kind, it swept in from out of the blue behind us, slowed to swim alongside us, and then fluidly accelerated until it had disappeared ahead of us. A beautiful fish, barely dipping into its reserve of power and speed to leave us behind. Robyn spent the remainder of that dive mastering the art of swimming with her arms tightly folded and her knees positioned neatly under her chin. Every attempt I made to pry loose a hand that I could hold was firmly resisted.

In the pleasant cool damp of first light, we often walked barefoot to the beach to watch the departure of fishing dhonis, which had sailed soundlessly into the tiny harbor sometime after sunset. Softly billowing in the breezes that barely ruffled the water, their triangular, lateen sails crept the dhonis forward toward their daytime fishing grounds. These were scenes out of history.

Arab seafarers first reached these waters probably 2,500 hundred years ago, when they began trading with the original Indian and Ceylonese settlers of the Maldives. It is difficult to consider such a sprawling archipelago to be a crossroads but, strewn as they are across the main sea trade route connecting Africa, India, and China, it was inevitable that the Maldives would evolve from a blend of cultures. It is certain that early Chinese warrior-merchants knew these islands, and there's some hint that the Romans did, too. But it is the Arabs who made the most permanent impression, and the dhonis, closely related to dhows and feluccas, are evocative reminders of the Arab heritage of the Maldives.

No one knows when the first coconuts came ashore here, either as cargo or as flotsam, cast adrift from a beach somewhere in the western Pacific. Like the corals millions of years before them, they found ideal conditions, and proliferated in the high humidity and well-drained sands of the Maldivian beaches. In abundance, they yielded materials for trade, food, and shelter. Preserved from sun and water by applications of fish oil, their tough and fibrous trunks also proved to be an ideal resource for the skilled boat builders of the atolls.

Gracefully inefficient, built simply from local and familiar materials, embracing the wind, gently pressing their hulls through the sea, enabling modest yet sufficient catches, dhonis, like the coracles of Ireland, the kayaks of Greenland, the Polynesian outrigger canoes, and even the couta boats of southern Australia, seem to me to be the embodiment of harmony between people and their natural environment.

This is pure romanticism, of course. We couldn't survive in our billions if we could rely only on such unsophisticated technology. Harmony, as we travel inexorably toward our future, will depend on our human capacity to learn, innovate, and adapt.

Virtually every commercial fish stock in the world is in some degree of collapse through over fishing. Fish farms, automated and insulated from the natural world, will most likely become the means of feeding the global village with fish protein. There are problems associated with fish farming—the introduction of antibiotics, pollution from fish-farm effluent, escape of genetically changed farm stock. But, by reducing the cost of production, fish farms will also probably be the most effective means for protecting what remains of the wild fish stocks. Handicapped with uncompetitive high costs of production compared with fish farming, industrial wild-stock fishing will probably be unable to justify the current levels of government subsidies that today keep the big fleets afloat. If that happens, open sea fishing will then largely vanish as a way of life, just as meat and hide hunting vanish as land-based agriculture develops. In the meantime, there's time to appreciate the insight into historical harmonious exploitation of the Earth's resources that the Maldivian boat builders bequeath us.

It seemed that the motorized dhoni we were now in, heading back to Malé, would benefit from the attention of one of those boat builders. Copious amounts of water gushed rhythmically into the sea from a length of black plastic piping, around ten centimeters in diameter snaking up from under the floor boards and twitched into position over the gunwale with a cinch of rusty wire. Gamely attempting to be heard over the pervasive thump of the diesel, the unseen bilge pump signaled its efforts to propel the water through the plastic pipe with a reassuringly metronomic *tic-phut-tic-phut-tic-phut-tic-phut-tic-phut-tic-phut.*

We'd only pieced all this together after we'd been at sea for a couple of hours and the sun had popped up above the horizon ahead of us. We'd noticed the radio first. It was one of those handheld walkie-talkies, swinging on its leather strap from one of the cross members of the shade canopy. Glistening crystals of salt crusted its body. Green corrosion had ominously erupted, long ago, from its battery compartment.

Motivated by this discovery, our eyes had then gone exploring for more calming sights, and settled on the compass. It was a dry-dome type, although it hadn't been designed like that. Domed compassed are usually filled with light transparent oil, which allowed the compass card to rotate freely so that it can accurately indicate the desired course as the bow of the boat swung to and fro. All the oil had drained from the compass of the dhoni and the card was tilted and stuck in one fixed position.

Not that the skipper was paying much attention to it anyway. He was sitting against the port gunwale, one bare foot tucked under his buttocks, the other resting on the tiller handle, staring vacantly down at the floorboards. His foot countered every swell that threatened to divert the bow of the dhoni from whatever course he could see inscribed in the floorboards. Long brown toes curled around the tiller when it had to be drawn toward him and stretched out when it had to be pushed away. No land was in sight anywhere. He was steering literally by the seat of his pants, feeling the rhythm of the swells and the kiss of the breeze and sun, drawing on long-imprinted memory of the recurring patterns of wind, wave, and light underlying the apparent chaos of the open sea.

Three or four hours out from Bathala, the sea began rising, not threateningly but sufficiently to underscore the diminutive size of the dhoni. Overhead, between us and the lines of small, cumulus cloud-streets striping the stable airs of the upper atmosphere, a sagging lump in the canvas canopy revealed the resting place of the second crewmember. Despite being grilled by direct exposure to the sun, both he and the third Maldivian, still comatose on the stern boards, slept on. Heat, monotony, hard seats, thumping diesel, soporific rolling of the dhoni all pressed down on us and forced us deep into our own thoughts.

Commotion, however, broke out amongst the crew when the *tic-phut-tic-phut-tic-phut-tic-phut-tic-phut-tic-phut-tic-phhhhhhhhhhhh.* suddenly stopped. This was when we discovered the purpose for the mysterious third Maldivian crewmember. Unable to be awakened by the clatter of the diesel, all the chatter among passengers and crew as we'd left Bathala, and the searing sunshine, he was instantly awakened and electrified into motion by the absence of noise from the bilge pump. He had the floorboards covering the bilges up, and a rusted metal bailing bucket swooping down to gulp in its first load of water, almost in one motion. His labors held the undivided attention of everyone on board. Deep water swirled in front of him. Responding vigorously to the loud and urgent exhortations of the skipper, and first mate who had somersaulted down from his hammock on the canopy, he was shifting a lot of water, but it didn't seem to make much difference to the amount in the bilges. Freeboard, that highly desirable distance between the upper edge of the gunwale and the surface of the sea, slumped from about 50 centimeters to almost zero when the fretting peak of a wavelet slopped up against the side.

"OH, DANNY BOY, THE PIPES, THE PIPES ARE CALLING!!! FROM GLEN TO GLEN AND DOWN THE MOUNTAINSIDE...!!!" It was Jeremy. Blaring into song.

Despite being wide awake, and continuously calculating the relative volume of water inside and outside the dhoni, we all jumped, startled at the sudden outburst and sheer volume of his voice. The Maldivian desperately bailing got such a fright that he leaped involuntarily upward like a startled cat.

"He always sings about home when he's worried," his wife yelled as Jeremy lustily sang his heart and fears out, wide eyes sweeping the rolling hills of Indian Ocean blue as if he were expecting, any minute, to catch his first mist-shrouded glimpse of Slieve Donard towering above the Mountains of Mourne.

Maldivian culture is rich in folklore. One legend among the islands' seafarers tells how angered and mischievous spirits will take control over a dhoni and cause it to sail for hours and hours in the same spot. At the same time, the spirits will litter the sea close to the stricken dhoni with floating dead bodies.

For hours, although the aquamarine lacework of our wake rising and falling on the swells astern indicated that we were moving forward, it had seemed that we were pinned in the center of this rough and tumbling watery blue disc, rimmed all around by an unchanging circular horizon. By the time Jeremy had launched into his seventh or eighth encore of "Danny Boy", I was starting to think that an offering to the spirits of an additional dead body for use elsewhere might be one way of releasing us from their grip, and allowing us to end this seemingly endless voyage.

Singing, though, is apparently, ineffective protection from the evil spirit of seasickness. "Oh Danny Boy ..." eventually gave way to "Oh Gorrrrrd" and a reasonable imitation of the now-extinct bilge pump's former glory. Looked at in different light, seasickness clearly offers an effective cure for bad singing.

Silence, apart from the pounding diesel, the scraping and splashing of the tirelessly manned bailing bucket, and occasional groans from Jeremy, settled again on our vessel of coconut logs as it made its interminable passage to Malé and the waiting airplane.

The day's work begins: Maldivian fishermen set out at dawn to troll for tuna, jacks, and other pelagic fish. Despite the calm sea, the waters of the atolls are swept by strong currents and demand expert seamanship for safe passage. Bathala. 1984

17

Raine Island Moon

Convicts came early to Raine Island. This low limestone hump lies at the natural northern entrance to Australia's Grand Canal, a natural, amethyst waterway snugged between the Great Barrier Reef and the northeast flank of the continent. Convicts hewed the limestone into blocks and built a squat, round tower that stands as a national monument today.

A shipping beacon was desperately needed to protect mariners from the deadly tantalus of Wreck Bay. South of Raine Island, this embayment opens its arms and promises safe passage through the thumping surf, which pounds almost incessantly on the outer barrier. But there is no passage here. Just a deep indent in the tracery of reefs.

Seafarers who fell into the embrace of Wreck Bay under the press of a spanking easterly were dead men sailing. They would have watched as their ship appeared to sail safely in blue water though a wide passage in the reef, with tremendous surf breaking to their right and left. Realization, and the cold dread it spawned in their hearts, would have risen slowly. They would have had lookouts shading their eyes and straining to see lethal lumps of isolated reef in time for the ship to avoid them. One of them would have looked farther, in toward the mainland, and seen the unbelievable. Out of the indigo deep rose the dun reef and heaving breakers they thought they'd left behind. Ahead of them in an unbroken line. To port and starboard, too.

Sheer luck might have cast some into narrow channels and through them into the calm water behind the reef, but most would have been hurled onto the reef like eggs against a wall. Cargo and lives would have spilled out of ruptured hulls to be strewn across the signless wastes.

Captain James Cook's lips tasted the salt mist of death not far from here in 1770, as he worked his way up the eastern coast of this then-mysterious southern land. He ran out of wind, just off the reef, and his ship, *Endeavour*, began an inexorable drift out of the open sea and toward the reef. In the depths of his crisis, Cook stood on deck with a thousand meters of water beneath his keel, but, just a few yards of his port beam the raging surf of the reef-top. He was bitter that he and his men had come so far from their homes in England, just to die anonymously at an unmarked speck on a blank chart.

But Cook was a master mariner. His fatal lapse of reason and tolerance wouldn't be triggered until, in Hawaii, he collided with another culture as strong, proud, and determined as his own. On this day, he was only confronting the elements. One slight gasp of breeze wafted across the reef. Cook seized it and used it to breathe hope into *Endeavour*. His men gave everything their straining muscles could deliver. Lethargic canvas tautened. The gap between coral and copper-sheathed hull slowly stretched.

Later, Cook's quill indelibly inscribed "Providential Channel" on the chart. A gap in the reef had beckoned just as the tide turned. Zachary Hicks went ahead in the long boat. Sounding. Testing. Cook hauled the *Endeavour* around and followed Hicks and his long boat to safety. Captain William Bligh had cleaved the same waters in his long boat after being expelled by the mutineers on the *Bounty*—an open boat journey that rivaled Ernest Shackelton's polar rescue voyage in the *James Caird*. So these are rich waters to test personal courage.

Challenger lay at anchor under a full moon in the lee of Raine Island. By nine o'clock, all the night divers had returned.

Robyn waved me off from the marlin board. No flashlight. No camera. More than a hundred meters of water lay under the stern. After swimming 30 meters, I could see the steeply shelving thickets of stag horn coral beneath me. Phosphorescence twinkled like stars at my fingertips as I pulled myself forward into a dive and purged water from my regulator. Another hundred meters, and I'd crossed the sloping flank of the reef and turned onto the vertical wall that Raine offers to the open sea.

We'd dived at night here a year before. Deep on this wall we'd seen prolific life. Turtles ghosted overhead on their way to the beach and their torturous egg-laying exertions. Sharks, befuddled by the bright lights, blundered blindly into our flashing flashlight beams. Tuna, reflective as mirrors, streaked along the reef face.

Few other anchorages on this section of the Great Barrier Reef offer easy access to open water at night; the wall on Raine drops vertically for 300 meters.

I had a simple plan. Descend quickly down the wall to 30 meters, stabilize buoyancy, test the current. If there was negligible drift, swim out from the wall into open water. And hang suspended over the void. To drift free. Like a spirit. Deep in fathomless ocean. At night. Alone. Chris Newbert, author of *Within a*

Rainbowed Sea, does this all the time in 3,000 meters of water off the Kona coast of Hawaii.

From 30 meters, I could still see the brilliant moon dancing, wraithlike, through the limpid surface. Turtles passed overhead, soundless silhouettes guided by unknown navigation systems. In the cool of night, thousands of them come in from the open sea to lay their eggs in the sands of Raine. But now it was time to swim out into the black.

It didn't seem possible. Something was holding me back. Nothing physical. Here, on the wall, where the mind picture held for a year, had become a reality, it suddenly didn't seem to be such a good idea. In the gloom, the wall at my back offered security. Swim away from it, and I'd become the center of the universe. Perhaps the center of attraction for a big cruising tiger shark.

We'd found a turtle on the island last year, bleeding and mutilated, still trying to haul itself up the beach. Sharks had taken two flippers. It would be a long swim back to *Challenger* without at least two legs.

I turned and put both my hands on the wall. I had learned something. This wall wasn't just the outer edge of Raine Island anymore. Imagination and irrational apprehension had defined it also as the outer edge of my courage.

Overhead, the dancing moon beckoned me to the surface.

Beacon of safety: Convicts built this tower on Raine Island in 1844. Standing remote and isolated 120 kilometers east north east of Cape Grenville, on Cape York Peninsula, at the outer edge of the Great Barrier Reef, it offered mariners the second known shipping beacon to be built by Europeans in Australia; the first showed the way into Sydney Harbour. It was designed to indicate safe passage from the open Pacific, through the coral maze, into the protected waters of the Australian "Grand Canal"—the two thousand kilometers of natural coastal channel lying between the Australian shore and the ramparts of the Great Barrier Reef. Inscribed on the interior wall for the early sailors is "Fresh water at 7 ft."

Buried at that depth to protect the barrels from the ravages of the tropical climate, the water provided some hope of life support for shipwrecked sailors. Poignantly, a solitary headstone marks the passing human life. Annie Eliza Ellis, wife of tower-keeper George Ellis died, aged 52, in 1891.

Raine Island supports the largest breeding population of green turtles in the world and is the most significant seabird breeding ground on the entire Barrier Reef. The unique landscape of Raine makes this dual occupancy possible.

Turtles, heaving themselves laboriously out of the sea and heading inland under the cool cover of night, encounter low but steep limestone ledges running parallel with the shore. Many of these ledges were created by the convicts quarrying stone for the tower. The ledges spell disaster for some turtles as they attempt to clamber over them, overbalance, and topple over backwards. Graceful in the sea, but pathetically clumsy on land, they cannot lever themselves upright again.

As long as they can draw breath, they never stop trying to right themselves. But it is hopeless. Their massive bulk pins them down, and their flippers flap futilely in the air. Grunting and puffing, full of the eggs they came to lay, they await their last dawn. When it comes, it brings their horrific doom. Blistering tropical heat stews them alive in their shells.

The Queensland government is reluctant to intervene by demolishing the ledges because the ledges help ensure that bird-nesting areas are not completely overrun by nesting turtles. Artificial barriers, designed to dissuade rather than condemn to unnecessary and inhumane death, could achieve the same result. Raine is, after all, an altered environment. It is not wilderness.

One hundred kilograms: A potato cod cruises overhead, looking for food at the famous Cod Hole off Queensland, Australia in 1986. This is a tourist dive, but it is well worth it. Don't keep food hidden in your buoyancy vest pocket, though!

18

Diving in the Desert

Umm Kamar blocked our view of the helicopter gunship, but we could hear it throbbing low across the water toward us. It was getting close to curfew, and we were probably being treated to a testosterone—laced reminder of the order to be back in harbor by four o'clock. We were anchored in the lee of Umm Kamar, a sere island, a wedge-shaped chip of desert, flaked off and deposited on the Egyptian Red Sea coast near Hurghada.

In a downward gale of hot air, scented with fumes of burned kerosene, the chopper finally *bat-bat-batted* into view above the sun-bleached island, sand-blasted a few of the roosting storks into ungainly and angular agitation, then hovered deafeningly above us. Clearly visible, were the rivets in the fuselage and the streaks of grime slipstreamed back from some leaking oil or hydraulic line in the undercarriage. So, too, was the door-gunner, helmet visor down, leaning forward to scan our bedraggled boat over the barrels of his machine guns. Our waves were not returned but, apparently satisfied that we represented no threat to peace in the Middle East, the pilot pivoted the chopper, dropped the nose a little, then batted away like a bellicose dragonfly to menace another boat anchored a kilometer or so away.

A turbaned Egyptian crewmember, bare brown feet splayed for grip on the deck, heaved on the anchor line, and we were soon on our way back to Hurghada. With tensions high in the whole region, there were two kinds of civilian vessels in the Red Sea after 4 o'clock every afternoon. Those safely berthed. And targets.

About six percent of the world's coral reefs occur in the Red Sea. In many ways, they're comparable to coral reefs anywhere else in the Indo-Pacific zone; you'll certainly encounter many of the same types of fish and corals. But one of the things that make the Red Sea different is where it is. Gunships, and the constant real but unfathomable tensions aside, this is an exotic and romantic location. Surface, in turquoise water above an exquisite coral garden vibrating with color and life, face the shore, and you're confronted with the starkest of contrasts. Shimmering sheets of dry brown sand bake in the unbelievably hot sun. Weathered and worn hills of bare rock frown down on the shore. Silence. Nothing moving. Not a hint of vegetation anywhere. Behind the hills, hidden, lie the parched wastes of the Western Desert. And the heat. Intolerable, suffocating.

"Ancient" is a word that sits well in this worn and arid landscape. The Red Sea first came into being about 30 million years ago, when the Arabian Peninsula splintered away from Africa and allowed the sea to flood into the gap. Its age is one of the reasons it holds so many species of fish and coral; there's been plenty of time for species to accumulate there.

We saw lots to interest us both above and below surface. At Shaab Umm Kamar, four lionfish crowded together upside down against the roof of tunnel. It was a passageway that passed through a series of roomy chambers in the coral before emerging on the seaward side of the reef. Three of the lionfish exhibited the usual pattern of black and white stripes, but the fourth, smaller than the rest, was jet black. It was a juvenile.

Beyond the lionfish, crammed together into a dense mass, was a school of bright pink Cryptic cardinal fish, no more than two centimeters long. Nocturnal carnivorous feeders, they spend most of the daylight hours cloaked in the safety of darkness in deep caves and ledges. When they emerge onto the reef at night, they go hunting small crabs and shrimp. They slowly parted to let me through as I pressed forward into the tunnel.

Hidden safely behind them was a much larger fish, deep bodied. Solid. Sixty or 70 centimeters long. Silhouetted against the pale light seeping in from the seaward end of the tunnel, it hung warily, midway between the roof and the sandy floor. It was facing me, but, with no flashlight to scare off its shadowy anonymity, I couldn't clearly identify this fish. I jumped when it surprised me with a headlong rush—not at me, nor the dense mass of cardinal fish, but at the group of lionfish behind me.

As it bustled past my face and into the light of the tunnel mouth, its distinct spots and disproportionately small head revealed it to be a polka dot grouper, also for some obscure reason known as a panther fish. In the entrance to the tunnel, I watched as the battle of the catfish played out; panther fish against lionfish.

Lionfish are members of the Scorpinidae; relatives of the stonefish. There are several species. Delightful and delicate, spectacularly striped in black, white, and sometimes red, arrayed with oversized and plumed fins and spines, they actively hunt smaller fish and crustaceans. As with their cousins, the stonefish, lionfish depend on venomous spines for their defense. They've become amazingly adept at maintaining their foremost dorsal spines pointed directly at any approaching threat.

I have first hand experience of that ability. One tiny lionfish, no more that four or five centimeters long, huddling under a protective ledge on a reef at Bathala in the Maldives, had flicked upside down and pricked the end of my index finger. I had tried to bring my hand up underneath it to ease it out into clearer water to photograph it. My finger throbbed for two hours, and the fish remained unphotographed.

As the grouper attacked here in the Red Sea, the four diminutive lionfish resorted to the same effective defense. Whichever one was under most immediate threat from the grouper stood its ground and, with unflappable poise, deftly pushed its poisonous spines erect and forward. The grouper, 20 times the size of the lionfish, lunged several times. Each time it stopped short of its intended prey, clearly recognizing the danger in those spines. I wondered how it knew that they were to be avoided.

Grumpily, clearly defeated, the grouper eventually swished in a tight turn, bustled back through the scattering cloud of cardinals, and resumed its hungry vigil in the deeper recesses of the tunnel. The four lionfish looked as though they couldn't care less and continued to float in a composed group, upside down, waiting for evening when it would be their turn to become predators.

We had a number of experiences with creatures showing uncharacteristic fearlessness in approaching us. Moray eels abound in the Red Sea. Of the hundred or so species of moray, most of them could probably be found here. Like all the eels, morays undergo a planktonic larval stage, floating free in open water. In the sea, this results in widespread distribution by oceanic currents until the larvae grow into juvenile eels and find a reef on which they can settle down and call home. We'd seen many species in Egypt, ranging from pencil-thin mottled snowflake morays, burgundy, black, and white zebra morays, and, in one cramped chimney-like hole in a reef, five vivid yellow-headed morays intertwined like plaited rope, all watching us intently with beady blue-tinged eyes. And, of course, the giant moray of legend—green-brown, massive gaping jaws lined with needle teeth designed to very effectively hold slippery flapping prey, and staring, unblinking, merciless eyes.

It's this appearance that give morays, in general, their bad rap,. They're not helped by the niche they fill in their ecosystem. Secretive, nocturnal hunters, they lurk in the shadows of the reef, away from bright sunlight. Nature has compelled them to continuously open and close their mouth in a threatening gape; that's how they pump water carrying life-giving oxygen over their gills. But, they're not generally aggressive towards humans. Most people who do manage to get themselves bitten by morays have antagonized the animal, either deliberately or accidentally as they've pressed forward into the eel's lair in search of lobsters or other cave-dwelling life. Whatever the cause, though, a moray bite can result in a savage wound. It is to be avoided.

All this was going through my mind as I first leaned back on my knees, and then tried to squirm slowly to one side, to allow one of these giant morays to get past me. I'd settled on the sand in a gutter on Carless Reef and leaned forward, into the gloom of an underhang, to see what might be there. A big moray was what was there! As soon as it saw me, it eased forward; not aggressively, but deliberately, persistently. As thick as my leg, and close to three meters long, it didn't seem to be anxious to get away from me. It certainly didn't seem intent on lashing out with its ferocious teeth, but it did seem to want to occupy the space that I was in, whichever space that I moved into. Its face was constantly in front of my own, its elastic throat ballooning and shrinking as each successive gulp of water coursed in through its mouth and flowed out the dark circular gill openings behind its head.

When I inhaled a chestful of air to lift myself slightly off the bottom, and pushed my hand into the sand in front of me to move myself slowly backward out from under the ledge, the moray followed me into the open water. Out on the Great Barrier Reef, I had seen one moray attack another. The victim of the attack had been swimming across a reef face, and the aggressor struck from the refuge of a ledge without warning. Knotted in writhing combat, they'd stirred up a cloud of sand and silt from which they both eventually shot, in different directions, probably both grievously wounded. I think that, if this eel in the Red Sea had been frightened or angry enough to strike, that is how it would have happened. Curiosity, in this case, is what seemed to create the common bond that held us in this strange encounter. Although, of course, there's always the chance that this eel was a member of the cargo-cult of sea creatures that have been fed by divers they've encountered earlier and now consider any future encounters to be opportunities for handouts. Whatever the reason, this was very different behavior from that of the wild morays we've encountered elsewhere.

The eel, seemingly probing for deeper insight into the alien form confronting it—or simply trying to find the food—sometimes s-bended back on itself, swayed from side to side, then again moved forward toward me at a slightly different angle. At one stage, although I was careful not to deliberately touch it, it was arching its upper body against mine as I leaned backward; someone observing from a distance might have described two mismatched dance partners performing a sort of slow, liquid, interspecies shimmy.

Eventually, the moray tired of the close-range inspection, sagged downward a little, then slowly swirled around in a graceful spiral back into the privacy of the ledge, treating me to a passing view of the wide slab of its mottled flanks as it did so.

Less pleasing, on a later dive on a colorful wall on the Shaab Abu Ramada, a hump-headed wrasse approached me head-on and hovered directly in front of me. This surprised me. On the Great Barrier Reef, and in Thailand and Malaya, these solitary fish had always been exceptionally flighty; dark bulky shadows on the edge of visibility. I'd never been close enough to see the detail in the bright blue lines around the eyes that earn this fish another of it popular names—Maori wrasse. This one, weighing around 30 kilograms, swam so close to my camera that I could not bring the lens to focus on it. I backed away a little, and the fish followed. I backed away again and held up my left hand—as though expecting the fish to recognize a "hold it there" signal.

"*Crunch!*"

It snapped its tail, lunged forward, and bit my hand. Equipped as they are with bony-plated mouths, hump-headed wrasse easily crush heavily shelled mollusks. Fortunately, I didn't taste as the fish had expected, and it quickly released me—spat my hand out really—and swam away, now disinterested. Stout cotton gloves prevented damage to my skin, but my bruised hand felt as though it had been squeezed in a slamming door. I spent the rest of the dive trying unsuccessfully to lure the wrasse close to me again in the vengeful hope that I could club it to death with my camera housing.

Days on the Egyptian reefs often began with up to two hours on a slow boat belting its way out to sea against strong breezes that whipped up steep, sharp chop. On exposed reefs, the boat danced uncomfortably as soon as we anchored. On the days we were able to anchor in a protected cove in flat water, the temperature soared as soon as we were out of the breeze. Sweat streamed off our bodies and faces until we were able to step off the boat into the blood-warm water. But the diving, and the unique backdrop of the desert, made the discomfort worthwhile.

Apart from the four o'clock curfew, which denied us access to the reefs in late afternoon and rendered night diving impossible without the risk of being depth-charged, the high levels of security were visible but unobtrusive. I pitied the sentries patrolling on foot the runway at Hurghada airport, without shade, in the full sun of the Egyptian summer. They were paying a high personal price to guard visitors from the threat of the extremists who were committed to driving foreigners from Egyptian soil.

With diving behind us, there was time for a few days in Luxor. It is touristy, but that's because it contains some of most impressive architectural treasures of ancient Egypt, and is an easy point of departure for the Valley of the Kings and Tutenkahmen's tomb. After the heat and grit of the Red Sea coast, Luxor offers shade and greenery, nourished by the lifeblood of water from the Nile.

Giant human-gods carved from rock stand at the ruined entrance of Luxor temple. Beautiful still, despite the windborne sand abrasion spreading like cancer across their polished faces, they stare mutely, serenely out over the Nile and the desert beyond. Five thousand years of Egyptian history have unfolded before them. Robyn and I saw them for the last time from a small felucca—an Egyptian sailing vessel, similar in many respects to the Maldivian dhoni. There was no curfew at Luxor and, in the early evening, we were able to convince the owner of this cargo boat to untie from his berth and sail us aimlessly and romantically first up and then down the Nile.

Lulled by the gentle flapping of the loosely billowing sail, and the creak of rope against wood, we watched as the last rays of the sun struck the temple and then sank from sight behind the City of the Dead.

Diving in the Desert 105

Snake tales: Neil Wehlack angling for a portrait of an olive-brown sea snake at Wishbone Reef off the far north Queensland coast in Australia. Venomous enough to kill a horse, air-breathing sea snakes like this pose little risk for divers. Curious as cats, they'll often wrap themselves around the arm or leg of a diver. If they're handled gently, they show no sign of aggression and quickly get on with their ceaseless hunt for food that they can get their teeth into. 1986.

Food? A curious potato cod asks the perennial question. Lizard Island, Australia. 1987

Sea of Eden: Robyn sets off with Wayne Osborn to explore a bountiful reef at Palau. 1990

Streamlined and graceful: A whaler in a late afternoon sweep across the floor of a lagoon. Ashmore Reef, Coral Sea, 1987.

Diving in the Desert 107

Turning water into stone: Exquisitely sculpted by nature, fixed but ferocious predators, plate corals like these can be found throughout the world's tropical and warm temperate seas. In their billions, they extract calcium from seawater and deposit it speck by speck, to build massive coral reefs. Great Detached Reef, 1987.

19

Torn Along the Dotted Line ...

As the rays of the sinking sun tint the low sand dunes on Cape Dombey in southeastern South Australia, they strike the protruding corner of a buried and deeply rusted heavy iron plate. One edge is knobbed with rivet heads, spaced a few centimeters apart and long since fused inseparably with the plate by more than a century of corrosion.

This is the site of the old jail, which used to serve the coastal township of nearby Robe. The iron plate once hung as a sturdy door on the now demolished limestone cellblock. Quietly disintegrating, hidden by the sand and the straggly coastal bushes, it now lies fittingly attended by the continuous rumbling of surf on the rocky shore of the cape, and the murmur of the sea wind.

Fittingly, for this iron plate was not originally made to be a jail door. In 1857, amidst an inferno of smoke and sparks, it was cast and rolled in an English mill and later, in the clattering Scottish shipyards of A&J Inglis, on the muddy banks of the River Clyde, it was hammered into its place in the hull of the screw steamer *Admella*.

Australia's European-based maritime history is rich with accounts of tragic shipwreck. Many are famous: *Batavia, Gilt Dragon, Tryal,* and *Zuytdorp* on the first-discovered west coast; *Pandora, Loch Ard,* and *Cataraqi* on the east and south coasts.

Less known is one of the most fascinating; the 1859 wreck of the *S.S Admella*, on Carpenter Rocks, halfway by sea between Adelaide and Melbourne. This shipwreck rates as one of the most moving stories of human suffering, compounded by greed, political penny pinching and bungling, and unsurpassed heroism.

As a dive site, the wreck of the *Admella* is difficult to reach ... and it is probably hardly worth the effort. Shallow, broken up by salvors and gales, pounded by heavy surf almost every day of the year, it offers little visual interest. In the 1960s and 70s, several mates and I made visits to the shore, hoping to be able to at least swim over the historic site, but weather and sea conditions always defeated us.

Idle hours, spent waiting for wind and waves to abate, provided ample time to learn and appreciate the depths of the wreck's history. So, while I can't take you for a dive here, I can at least recount the tale ...

Melbourne; August 1859

"The Victorian government dug its political grave one foot deeper today when the Premier refused to agree to a request from merchant James Henty and financier Henry Miller for an extra insurance premium to be paid by the government before dispatching the Henty-owned vessel *Lady Bird* to the wreck of the *Admella*.

"Premier, Sir John O'Shannasy claimed that he had no constitutional power to spend public money without obtaining the prior consent of parliament. Whether the incensed public will allow him sufficient time to redress his outrageous and cold blooded vacillation remains to be seen."

So raged the newspapers of the day. The *S.S. Admella* was the pride of intercolonial shipping. In 1859, this vessel provided the equivalent of modern day intercity jet travel.

Admella was 59 meters long, eight meters wide, and weighed in at 395 gross registered tons. Elegant and sleek, with interchangeable 100 horsepower steam engines driving its twin-bladed propeller, *Admella* could cleave the water at 17 knots. Additional economy and efficiency came from the sails straining against the three masts. Passengers and cargo were carried swiftly and comfortably between coastal ports in South Australia, Victoria, and Tasmania. *Admella* became a famous and highly desirable mode of transport.

In the uncertain waters of southern Australia, the ship carried the certainty of safe passage. Like the giant *Titanic*, which would set out on its maiden voyage across the Atlantic 53 years later, *Admella* was designed to be unsinkable. Two lateral bulkheads divided the ship's hull into three watertight compartments. It was believed that *Admella* could remain afloat even if two out of the three compartments were flooded.

But a fatal flaw was hidden from designers, passengers, and crew as the *Admella* set out on August 5, 1859 from Port Adelaide, and headed south down St. Vincent's Gulf, bound for Melbourne with 113 people, a cargo of flour, copper, and lead in the holds, and six thoroughbreds, including champions Jupiter, The Barber, and The Shamrock, stalled on deck.

In 39 voyages between Adelaide and Melbourne, there had never been cause for alarm aboard the *Admella*. Never any need for lifeboats or life belts. The vessel's only captain, Hugh McEwan, was a cautious and capable master mariner.

Australia's southern coast lies like a ragged net thrown across the prevailing westerly winds. Holes in the net—those passages between the reefs and islands of Bass Strait—offer a maritime highway for passengers and trade. But in the 19th century, weaving a ship through those holes, hindered by primitive navigation aids, incomplete charts, and poorly understood currents, was a dangerous practice. Crews and passengers alike viewed with trepidation their turn to "thread the eye of the needle."

Late in the afternoon, off Cape Willoughby, on the extreme eastern end of Kangaroo Island, *Admella* was rolling heavily in a westerly swell. One of the horses, Jupiter, lost its footing and fell to its knees.

Captain McEwan turned the *Admella*'s bow to the sea to ease the vessel's rolling while the difficult task of hauling the horse to its feet was completed. An hour later, *Admella*'s bow was turned back to the southeast.

Evening fell, and darkness cloaked the long lines of marching swells. *Admella* became a fragile island of light and warmth amidst bleak desolation. Up on deck, shrouded in fog on a cold, calm night, with neither stars nor lights to guide him, Captain McEwan had no way of knowing his true position. Safe and secure in their warm bunks, the passengers slumbered beneath his feet. Gentle rumbling of the *Admella*'s twin 100 horsepower steam engines merged with the *shoosh* of the sea against the iron hull. Reassuring, comforting sounds.

But a silent enemy was at work in the water around the hull. An uncharted current, welling from the bleak wastes of the Southern Ocean, was sweeping the *Admella* toward the coast. While Captain McEwan thought he was cruising safely 40 kilometers offshore, his ship was plowing toward a reef from which it could never escape. There was no warning.

At 5 a.m. on August 6, a gentle swell lifted the *Admella* over a reef offshore from Carpenter Rocks. The vessel trembled slightly and seemed to hesitate as the hull grazed the deeper rocks.

Admella regained momentum before settling gently atop the reef and into the trap that the uncaring and unknowing sea had set for it. Human ingenuity now became an accomplice in the death and dismay that was to follow.

The rivets fastening the watertight bulkheads to the hull created the fatal flaw. As the swell that had carried the vessel to its grave retreated, the *Admella* settled with the bow and stern sections overhanging the rock platform. Forces unimaginable to the vessel's designers built up in the hull. Finally, the strain was unbearable, and *Admella* broke into three sections—sections literally torn along the dotted lines of the watertight bulkheads' rivet holes, which girdled the hull.

Some passengers died then; hurled from the ship into the swirling water. Daylight soaked through the darkness and revealed the full horror to the sodden survivors. Nearly two kilometers of tempestuous surf separated them from an uninhabited and dismal stretch of coast.

Wind-torn cloud scudded low across the sky as the weather began to worsen. Barometric pressure dropped. Gray combers, hissing with energy stolen from Southern Ocean storms, tripped over the reefs of the Carpenters and relentlessly battered the dismembered hull of the *Admella*. Heroically, burly Adam Purdon, a fireman, volunteered to swim ashore to raise the alarm. He drowned within minutes.

Crueler death awaited Danish seaman Soren Holm. He swam to one of the *Admella*'s upturned lifeboats and scrambled astride the keel. With a piece of board as a paddle, he made laborious headway toward shore.

Spirits lifted aboard the wreck as they saw him near the shore. But fate was playing with him in the way a cat plays with a mouse. As Holm neared the beach, his clumsy raft drifted into a rip—one of the vagrant currents that drains water from a surf pounded beach. Holm began an inexorable and final journey out to sea. Helplessly, he passed within hailing distance of the wreck. Exhausted by his exertions, he could do nothing except lie across the keel of the lifeboat and stare at the beach he had almost reached. When a cat tires of playing with a mouse, death comes swiftly and terribly; one seething breaker tumbled down and swept Holm from view.

On the wreck, survivors watched, agonizingly pierced by the cold jaws of wind and sea. Everyone except for James Whittaker. He refused to come out on deck. Stowed under his bunk was the small chest of gold bullion he'd been carrying to Melbourne. James Whittaker, elderly and frail, feared exposing himself and his bullion to the savage sea. In the end, the sea came looking for him.

Whittaker's tilted cabin wall faced the open sea. Tons of crashing water were ramming this blunt barrier several times every minute. Eventually, the irresistible forces of nature triumphed. The cabin wall caved in, and the hungry sea swarmed in to swallow Whittaker—and his gold.

Two sailors, Leach and Knapman, finally made it through the surf and arrived exhausted on the beach. Ahead of them lay a 50-kilometer barefoot march across rough coastal limestone heath to Cape Northumberland lighthouse at Port MacDonnell. Suffering terribly, they marched on through the night, knowing that the lives of every remaining soul aboard the *Admella* depended on them getting to that lighthouse. When they arrived, crippled and breathless, they could barely recite their tale of catastrophe.

After such heroic deeds, what was needed, of course, was swift and decisive action to mount a rescue. The people of both colonies—Victoria and South Australia—looked to their governments for such action. But none was forthcoming.

Victorian Premier, John O'Shannasy, said it was a South Australian problem; the South Australians claimed to lack the resources to mount an effective rescue. In those days, each state maintained its own navy; there was no central federal government to coordinate such things as sea rescue. O'Shannasy's Victoria had naval vessels available, but he refused to commit them.

Meanwhile, out at sea, deadly peril lay ahead of the mail steamer *Bombay*. En route to Melbourne from Suez, this 1,100-ton ship was forging across a moonlit sea, directly toward the reef that had snared the *Admella*.

Hope rose in the hearts of the *Admella* survivors as they watched the lights of the *Bombay* draw closer. Perhaps this was an attempt to rescue them.

With no lights, the *Admella* was invisible in the darkness. Hoarse shouts rose from the salt-caked throats of the survivors. Perhaps the *Bombay*'s lookout heard them and took them as a warning. Perhaps the lookout glimpsed the lines of foaming breakers in the wintry moonlight. Whatever the cause, the *Bombay* suddenly seemed to sense imminent danger and sheered away.

As the lights first shrank, then disappeared, so did all thought of rescue in the hearts of the wretched people aboard the *Admella*. Utterly cold and dejected, they huddled hopelessly on the sloping deck of their dead ship and wondered if they would live to see the dawn.

Calmer weather and bright sunshine next morning brought meager relief. *Admella* lay in two distinct pieces; the bow section perched precariously awash nearly 20 meters away from the larger, safer stern section.

Captain McEwan recognized that there was no hope for the people trapped on the bow. The stern section was the safest, so lines were thrown across the gap. People tried to cross this dangerous bridge. Some succeeded. Others did not.

A father desperately seeking salvation for his two tiny daughters, tied them to him and moved nervously out onto the slippery ropes. When he fell, he took them screaming to their deaths in the surf. One woman refused to be moved from the bow. A falling mast had broken her legs. In her arms she clutched her dead baby. When the tiny, pathetic corpse was pried gently from her grasp and dropped into the sea, her will to live left her. Without speaking, she rolled off the wreck and disappeared into the surf.

The public howled in rage at their elected representatives' callous incompetence. Common people swiftly organized what politicians, with all their power and influence, could not—funds to mount a rescue. A public appeal raised the required money almost immediately. In the meantime, a hero was striding the beach at the wreck site.

Captain Benjamin Germein was lighthouse keeper at Port MacDonnell. He ordered repairs to be made to one of the boats that had been dashed ashore from the wreck. With a crew of men who had gathered at the beach, he made attempt after attempt to take the fragile craft through the waves and out to the wreck—but only after forcibly removing Leach and Knapman from the boat. Despite their exhaustion and deeply lacerated feet, the two men had been determined to take part in the rescue.

The steamer *Corio* hove-to off the wreck and launched its pilot boat under the command of coxswain Louis Thomas. Thomas was an ex-whaler. He was fearless, but the seas defeated him and his crew. After being swept stern-first through a gap in the reef, Thomas and his crew found themselves in the relatively calm water between the wreck and the shore. Thomas' experience told him that his puny boat had no chance of penetrating the surf pounding the wreck and the reef to rescue weak survivors. And there was no chance of returning to the *Corio*. Thomas retreated to the beach to join Germein.

Many of the men on the beach viewed Thomas' attempt with disdain, but Germein saluted Thomas's courage and wisdom and then pointed to the need for a lifeboat. A proper lifeboat. No other craft could reach the imperiled survivors in such conditions. There was, however, such a vessel in Portland, 80 kilometres by sea to the east.

Built at Williamstown near Melbourne in 1857, the Portland lifeboat was the most technologically advanced vessel of its kind. Self-righting, self draining. It offered the only hope for the few remaining survivors on the *Admella*. In fearful weather, and under the command of Captain James Fawthrop, this boat was towed from Portland to the wreck site by the steamer *Ladybird*.

Off the wreck, and in company with a whaleboat from Portland, Captain Fawthrop and his men went into action. The plan was simple. The whaleboat would anchor clear of the reef and pay out a line attached to the lifeboat as the lifeboat rowed through the surf toward the wreck. Once the survivors had been taken off, the men in the whaleboat would haul on the line to assist the lifeboat crew on their hazardous voyage out to sea from the wreck.

Twelve unsuccessful attempts to reach the wreck continuously swamped the boat, splintered oars, and pummeled the lifeboat crew—but they kept trying. Eventually, they were close enough to fire a rocket carrying a line across the wreck. James Johnstone, Portland's quietly-spoken schoolmaster, stood in the bow holding the rocket in his bare hands—there was no rocket launcher aboard.

His first rocket was aimed truly, but the weakened survivors were unable to snatch up the line it carried. His second rocket exploded in his hand and shattered it. Despite his injury, Johnstone managed to hold another rocket and fired it, but again, the survivors could not hold the line it carried.

A towering wave swept the lifeboat across the reef and ripped away the keel. Oars were lost. Foaming water cascaded over the boat. Fawthrop and his men were in extreme danger, but, true to its design, the lifeboat righted itself, and the water drained away. But the crew was helpless. With injured men aboard, and few oars, they could only signal to be hauled back to the anchored whaleboat, and then returned to the *Ladybird*.

Once again, the survivors were plunged into despair, and they were forced to endure another night—the seventh—without food, water, or shelter. Ten more people died in the darkness. The bodies of all except one were washed into the sea. The remaining body, that of James Hare, a steward on the *Admella*, was held and tied to the rail. Unbelievable suffering had taken the few remaining survivors to the brink of cannibalism. When it rained in the night, a few men sucked the fresh water from the hair of the corpse.

The next day, the weather abated, although a heavy sea still pounded the wreck and reef. Rested and desperate, Fawthrop and his men were ready for another assault on the wreck, as were Germein and Louis Thomas. They all knew that failure today spelled death for the few souls who had survived the night. Dreadful suffering had taken its toll of the survivors. Only one woman, Bridgette Ledwith, was still alive. Every child had perished. Every horse was dead.

The final rescue attempt began from both sea and shore. Germein reached the wreck first and, in wildly tossing water, took off three survivors, including Captain McEwan. These were passed across to Thomas' more seaworthy pilot boat, and Germein returned to the wreck. One more survivor slid down the rope Germein had attached to the wreck before he was forced to turn for shore, fearful that his damaged boat would founder. Heavy surf capsized him near the beach. Germein was lucky to escape drowning; the man he'd risked his life to save was not so fortunate. Too weak to withstand the tumbling foam, he drowned within a few meters of the beach.

Meanwhile, Fawthrop and his crew had reached the wreck from the seaward side. They were unwelcome. Numbed and irrational through the fear and privation of the eight days on the wreck, and resentful that Fawthrop had retreated on the previous day, some of the survivors declared they would sooner perish than ride with cowards. They refused to move.

Fawthrop stood firm and proud. His stentorian voice, rising above the buffeting wind, lashed them from their apathy and soon, wearily, tentatively, pathetically, 19 emaciated people, including Bridgette Ledwith, slid down the ropes into the lifeboat. Of 113 people aboard a week earlier, only 24 had survived.

While the survivors recuperated at Mac's Hotel in Portland, the citizens of Adelaide and Melbourne rejoiced. In Melbourne, though, relief soon turned to revenge. The population turned savagely against the supine O'Shannasy government, and threw it from office. Political pressure also mounted and swept aside the delays in establishing more lighthouses along the southern coastline. At last, light was shining through the eye of the needle.

Fawthrop, Germein, and their dauntless crews were all awarded medals for heroism. The old lifeboat was withdrawn from service in 1915 and was displayed in Portland's Botanic Gardens as a memorial to the men who served in it. And there it lay, slowly rotting.

In 1991, I was working for the local aluminum smelter, Portland Aluminium, under the leadership of Wayne Osborn and the late David Judd. Together, we were able to create numismatic history by devising and funding the minting of 1,000 facsimile *Admella* gold medals by the Royal Australian Mint. Using technology available only in the United States, the mint's senior engraver, Horst Hann, created the first facsimile medal ever struck in Australia. It is faithful in every detail to the original medal used to create the mold. Funds generated by the sale of the facsimile medals enabled the lifeboat to be moved into the temporary protection of a small shed. Here, at last protected from the elements, nesting birds, and neglect, the boat could undergo preservation work in preparation for more appropriate public display. It remains today as the oldest surviving seagoing vessel in Australia. The balance of the funds helped move the boat again, this time into permanent display in a purpose-built gallery in the distinctive Visitor Information Centre on the Portland foreshore. For some years in the 1990s, members of the Portland Surf Lifesaving Club—led by Andy Murrell and Robyn, and supported by the Victorian Surf Life Saving Association, Glenelg Shire Council, and several corporate sponsors, including Portland Aluminium and Carlton and United Breweries—staged the "*Admella* Surfboat Marathon," a grueling surfboat race from the Portland Harbour out to Lawrence Rock and back. Members of the winning crew each received one of the replica *Admella* medals, and these were as eagerly sought as the prize money.

Fawthrop's grave can be found in the old North Portland cemetery. Mac's Hotel is still in business.

As for the *Admella*, salvors quickly moved in on the wreck and recovered most of the copper. Timber washed ashore was put to use in construction of buildings along the coast. Iron hull plates were hauled to Robe for use in the new jail. Port Adelaide's maritime museum displays an interesting collection of artifacts from the wreck.

Out on the Carpenter reef, several tons of copper ingot remain unsalvaged. Judging by accounts of divers who have visited, the ingots, jumbled and dispersed by innumerable storms and corroded and buried by shifting sand, have merged with the reef. They're only traceable with electronic metal detectors. The site is protected, as it should be by the state government of South Australia, so nothing can be recovered from it without permission from the state's Receiver of Wrecks. If there's truth in the legend, though, there's something more valuable than copper out there in the tumbling surf. No one has ever reported finding Whittaker's gold.

20

Similan Nights

Deep crimson. Lustrous, like hard-glazed porcelain. Boldly sculpted plates and tubes, superbly integrated with sealed, flexible joints. Massive. Strong and squat, this was a heavyweight crab. One muscular claw extended upward; pincers open and ready to snap shut in crushing defense. Tucked safely under the other claw, supper. A small, lifeless, silvery sardine. Color and form discovered and drawn from the enveloping jet blackness by the warm amber cone of Robyn's flashlight.

It was close to midnight, and the *Andaman Explorer* slept at anchor, safe in a sandy cove amid the granite tors of the Similan Islands. Its gleaming-white mast light was the only sign of human presence; the only light that challenged the stars twinkling above us. Eighty kilometers to the east lay the mainland coast of Thailand.

We had swum on the surface from the yacht, toward the dark bulk of Elephant Head; a low granite islet, about 60 meters away from our anchorage. A solitary insomniac gibbon had called *hoo-hoo-hoo* from the dense rainforest rearing behind us. Earthy scent from the invisible forest, swirled down by the gentlest of breezes, hung in the moist night air. This is wilderness.

Thai government foresight has protected the Similans from settlement. No loggers harvest the forests here. Fishermen are now excluded, and reefs and coral are healing from decades of indiscriminate dynamite fishing.

Soft gasps escaped from our buoyancy vests as we deflated them and began our descent, wreathed in the bubbles of our exhalations, toward the jumble of massive boulders and scattered coral lying in the night below us.

Our flashlight beams shone vertically downward, probing for contact with the boulders we'd seen during the day. We encountered the top of the first, large as a house, at ten meters and followed its rough, round bulk, bristling with patches of stunted hard corals, down to its base, buried in the steeply sloping bottom at about 20 meters. Beyond this point, the bottom shelves deeper and eventually lies 45 meters down, but we'd planned to go no farther.

Now, within moments of my fin tips stabbing gently into the coral rubble, my flashlight beam spotlighted the first stonefish. Grotesque and motionless, it was lying in a small cleft between the base of the granite boulder and another smaller slab of rock. Stonefish are common here. They are the natural landmines of the sea. Time spent learning to recognize their highly camouflaged form is time well spent. They will not readily move from their chosen resting place. Premature movement can reveal their presence to prospective prey. A clumsy or careless diver risks agonizing injury, and perhaps death, from the dozen or so highly venomous dorsal spines arrayed down the fish's backbone.

Stonefish are members of the Scorpinidae. Scorpion fish. They are well named for their capacity to deliver a shocking dose of venom from bulging sacs squeezed between the muscles of the upper back. They also have venom sacs lodged at the base of their pelvic and anal fins. This is pure defense, though—disincentive for any marauding predator that could be unfortunate enough to detect a stonefish and attempt to eat it.

Stonefish lie motionless and wait for their meals to come to them. Only the occasional flickering rotation of an eyeball offers the faintest signal of danger. Small crabs, shrimp, and fish that venture close enough to the apparently harmless stone are suddenly engulfed as the inert lump convulses forward and transforms into a gaping cream maw aswirl with tasseled fins. Momentarily, as it flares its pectoral fins to brake its forward rush, the predator reveals brilliant reds and oranges streaked where fins join body. Then, like a plump chicken settling after ruffling its feathers to trap warming air close to its body, the stonefish gathers up its fins and composure, merges again with the weed and stone of the seabed, and awaits its next meal.

As if to remind me that aggression would be folly, the spines of the stonefish before me in Thailand became erect and revealed the intense red, yellow, and orange membrane that stretched between the bases of the foremost spines and the sides of the grooves that seat them. Gorgeous, hidden color; unsuspected given the drab mottle of the fish's outer skin.

I moved on and discovered a jumbled collection of small earthenware pots strewn down the slope of the reef. Spotted with algae and early coral growth, they'd been here for some time. They're evidence of the effectiveness of the Thai military patrols against dynamite fishermen. These pots were to have been bombs, thrown over the side and detonated to kill fish. They were either confiscated and dumped harmlessly over the side by one of the patrols or perhaps frantically abandoned by a dynamiter attempting to elude discovery and arrest by on oncoming patrol boat. Now, empty and randomly stacked, they're providing ideal and comfortable housing for many of the fish that they would have needlessly obliterated from the reef. One pot, though, came with me as a souvenir.

Shiver-inducing cold water suddenly licked around me; a small whirling eddy of a current welling up from the depths of the Indian Ocean way to the south. It is common here in the Similans. Above the surface, tropical heat and humidity belie the chilly blobs of water that curl away from the mainstream of the current, swirl their way through the depths, and wash over thinly insulated divers like clouds passing over the sun. In daylight, it is possible to see them; wraithlike patches of colder, denser water, gradually mixing with the surrounding warmer water, diffracting light and distorting visibility like flawed glass. At night, they just swirl up unannounced out of the darkness.

And then there had been the waving flash of light from Robyn as she signaled for attention. She'd found the crimson crab midway through its supper. How do crabs catch sardines? They don't. People do.

Like a low-flung constellation of bright stars, the trawlers of the Thai fishing fleet spangle the horizon off the Similans every night, sieving the sea for sardines. Like trawlers everywhere, they kill more than we need to feed ourselves. Millions of tons of inedible or unsaleable fish—by some estimates up to ten million—are unnecessarily dragged from the oceans of the world and killed every year along with the 95 million tons of fish that we want to eat. We call this wasted tonnage "by-catch". It is a term we can live comfortably with because it doesn't conjure up the images of the appalling despoliation that we cause through our growing appetite for protein from the sea.

Politics and economics of global fishing have no meaning for the crimson crabs of Elephant Head, though. For them, spillage from the decks of the Thai trawlers brings a windfall supper.

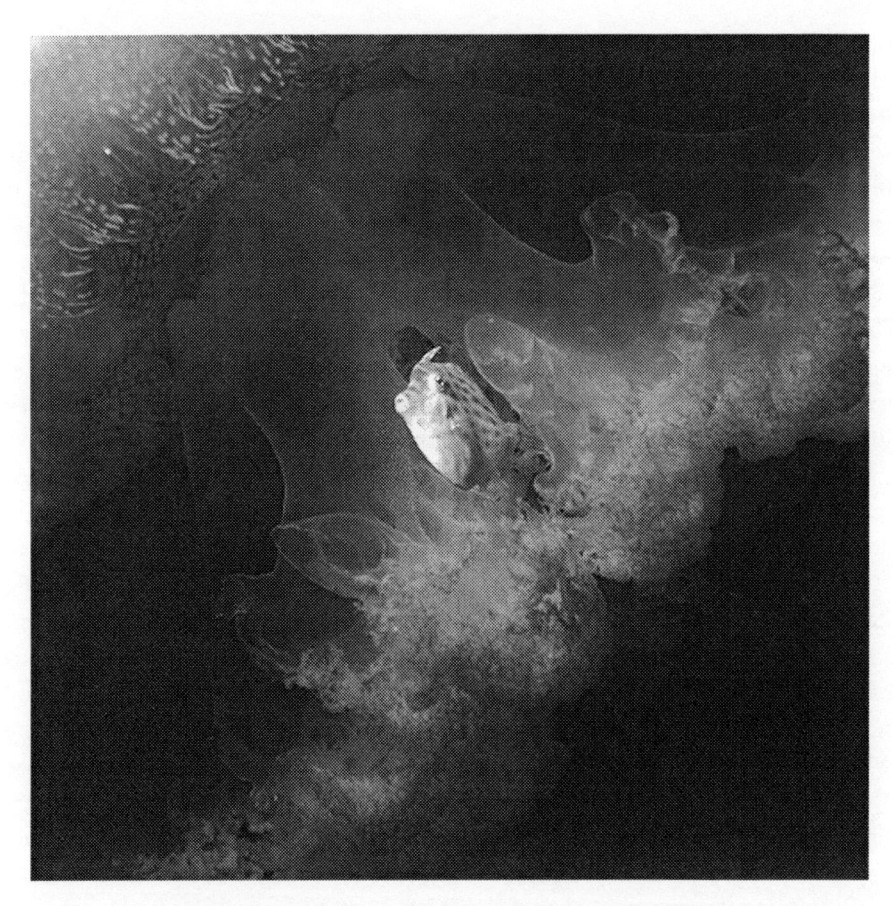

No fixed address. This juvenile trigger fish has tenuous accommodation in the folds of a free-drifting jellyfish in the Indian Ocean. Halls Bank, Western Australia, 1973.

21

After Ataturk

Gallipoli, on the shores of the Aegean Sea in Turkey, was the scene of almost nine months' bitter trench warfare between troops of the British and Turkish empires. Gallipoli holds special significance for Australians and New Zealanders because it was here, in 1915, that their combined forces created the legend of the Anzacs; the Australian and New Zealand Army Corps. So fierce was the fighting, so bloody and shocking the hand-to-hand combat, the shared horror of it all forged enduring respect and friendship between the opposing Turks and Anzacs. Anzac Cove, the quiet, picturesque little bay in which the first shots were fired as the Anzacs stormed ashore to tackle the entrenched Turks, is again quiet and remote. Bathed in warm Mediterranean sunshine, nestled at the base of an arid limestone ridge, passing peacefully through a timeless rural summer, Anzac Cove eerily reminded us of home on the south coast of Australia.

Ghosts. All around us. Ghosts in khaki, floating in the cool, sky-blue antiquity of the Aegean Sea. Faceless ghosts, drifting back and forth across colorful beds of sea-smoothed pebbles. Lifting and subsiding in the gentle swell. The same gentle swell that was rocking us. Only the hushed rush of transparent wavelets lapping over the pebbles disturbed the silence. In 1915, torrential steel rain had thrashed the surface of the sea here. Those same pebbles had been soaked in human blood.

It was here that Australian and New Zealand Army Corps troops invaded Turkish soil. It was an invasion conceived by the British warlords to plunge into the "soft underbelly of Europe," force open a sea route to Russia through the straits of the Dardanelles, and hence bring a speedy conclusion to the First World War. There was one problem. Courageous and resolute, the Turkish troops offered no soft underbelly. The Anzacs, along with British Empire and French troops, landed elsewhere along the Gallipoli coast and marched into a firestorm.

Recollections of C. E. W Bean's description of the firestorm, heard from a distance, popped into my mind. Bean was a war correspondent. He said that it sounded like someone tapping a wooden box. *Tock-tock-tock-tock-tock-tock.* Imperceptibly, that noise crept from the imagined past and became real. The silence retreated. The ghosts dissolved in headlong flight.

Tock-tock-tock-tock-tock-tock. It was very loud. Very close. Behind me. Goosebumps rose on my skin. Goosebumps that had nothing to do with the chilly water.

A quick glance. A haunting coincidence. A small Turkish fishing boat. Wooden. Low to the water. Red. Its diesel motor going flat out. *Tock-tock-tock-tock-tock-tock.* Just like someone tapping a wooden box. Two fishermen returned my wave. A third just looked. Wrinkled Turkish faces. Leather-brown. Momentarily clad in illusory brown serge and soft-pointed hats. Staring over the parapet of a trench instead of the gunwale of a boat.

I turned and started to swim for the shore. Just below the mirrored surface, a silver-shrapnel burst of three, maybe four, small fish flashed past my face. The only ones I'd seen here. Like most of the eastern Mediterranean, the Aegean has been denuded of fish stocks by millennia of human exploitation. As far as marine life goes, swimming underwater here is akin to swimming in a wonderfully landscaped but barren swimming pool. Molten summer heat sears the world above the surface. Blue sky. Bronze-metal sun. Glossy green scrub clothing scarred, frowning, hills that stab abruptly upward behind the thumbnail of a beach.

Off to my left, a gentle splash came from Robyn as she went duck-diving, looking for a memento of our visit. Immediately, she found a corroded .303 rifle cartridge case. Gallipoli was a dangerous place to be in 1915. It can still be dangerous to travel there.

We hired a car and driver in Istanbul. The driver seemed perfectly normal until we swung out of the hotel and into the clamorous cyclone of Istanbul's traffic. Back in 1915, the Turkish leader and master of the Gallipoli Peninsula, Kemal Ataturk, told his men, "I do not order you to attack—I order you to die!" Our driver was still trying to obey that order.

Our guide book claimed that the 170-odd kilometer journey from Istanbul to Gallipoli is, "an interesting one which threads its way through the scenic coastal districts of the Sea of Marmara then dog-legs inland through some sere rural areas and finally skirts the rocky spine of the Gallipoli Peninsula by winding along the shores of the Dardanelles."

After surviving the first-wave assault of the city drivers, we embarked on that interesting journey. But the most memorable impressions were created by old but surprisingly agile Turks abandoning terrified donkeys and flocks of panic-stricken goats in desperate attempts to get out of our way. We got to Gallipoli at the same speed that artillery shells did. When the driver triumphantly announced our arrival, "Gelibolu!" and the car ricocheted to a halt, I risked a peep through my fingers. We were in the wrong place.

Oh, we were in Gelibolu all right. But that's not where the action happened. The battlefield is nowhere near the village. It's another 50-odd kilometers farther down the peninsula. Robyn hinted that we could walk the rest of the way. But the driver ignored the hint and aimed us in the general direction of the Gallipoli that we wanted to see. Our heads snapped back as he rammed the accelerator to the floor.

Marble and bronze monuments mark the skyline at Gallipoli. Neat and clipped lawns, set with rank after rank of memorial plaques, have healed the wounds of the trenched and tortured ridge-top battlefields. Peace and dignity have long since replaced death and obscenity. The atmosphere is almost indistinguishable from any other war cemetery.

We were disappointed. I stepped down from the ridge, moved away from the manicured memorials, and stood alone in the raw scrub of Shrapnel Gully. There, the atmosphere of Gallipoli began to assert itself. Heat. Dust. Humming flies. Clawing, chest-high scrub. Vulnerability. Nowhere to hide.

For the invading forces, it was a hopeless quest. The strategic military importance of the Gallipoli Peninsula has been recognized since the time of Xerxes the First nearly 500 years before the birth of Christ. It lies at the very crossroads of history and culture; a stepping-stone between Asia and Europe. It controls the sea road from the Mediterranean to the heart of Eastern Europe.

For all their suicidal and unimaginable bravery under misguided and incompetent British leadership, the invading troops, fighting for *land*, were confronted by the insurmountable obstacle of Turks who were fighting for their *country*, and doing so from virtually impregnable positions and fed by limitless supply lines. Gallipoli achieved nothing but the premature and violent deaths of around 140,000 soldiers on both sides.

Hidden beneath the scrub, shallow redoubts remain as evidence of frantic digging—digging that sought to build protection and built a legend at the same time. Digging there today would probably unearth bones of some of the thousands of men who lie in unfound, tumultuously excavated and churned graves.

Standing at Gallipoli enables the events described in the history books to be set against an authentic backdrop. But there's no sense to be made of this. This is simply one of those many places on Earth where the youth of nations have seen their duty in stark black and white and accepted the risk of death and mutilation as the price to be paid for honorably discharging that duty. There is a curious legacy attached to all this, though.

We stumbled across that legacy as we made our way into Turkey aboard the *Istanbul Express*.

Almost as soon as we'd boarded that train in Germany for the journey across Eastern Europe, the sense of romance conjured by the name of the train quickly evaporated. It soon became apparent that this was no "express". This train lumbered slowly, and stopped at every station along the line.

At every station there were poor and disheveled platform vendors offering greasy sausages to hungry passengers. Not for us, though. Earlier in the afternoon, we'd dismissed with disdain these horrid, oozing slugs of animal offal. We were waiting for the gentle chiming that would signal dinner was being served on tables laid with white linen and silver cutlery in the dining car.

"I'm going to have a crisp, chilled Riesling tonight," Robyn had mused. Unfortunately, there was no dining car. There was no food. There were just the vendors, with their few awful twitching sausages, for which increasing numbers of passengers were starting to compete. Before night fell, we'd joined the competition and elbowed our way through a jostling crowd to snatch a sausage each.

That other basic of life and travel—sleep—also generated some curiosity. We'd wondered, when we'd first entered our carriage, and found four additional people sitting in our sleeping compartment, where they were going to sleep. As soon as night fell, we had the answer; in *our* sleeping compartment. Embarrassed and apologizing for unintentional contact with semi-bare and sweaty bodies, we all wrestled our bunks down from the walls and ceiling and interlocked them into a couple of layers of communal beds. Sleep did not come easily. Quite violent rocking as the train clattered along its poorly maintained tracks, frequent jolting stops and starts, oppressive heat, and the dead-rat-in-a-drainpipe effects of the sausages, kept us awake. And then there were the border crossings.

Every border required two stops, two searches, two inspections of papers and passports; one in the country we were leaving, one in the country we were entering—although, to be fair, we weren't forced to submit to fingerprinting, as we are now on entry into the U.S. As we crossed into what was then Yugoslavia, jackbooted thugs in uniforms boarded the train and strutted and shouted at sleepy passengers to produce their papers. Those who moved too slowly were roughly pulled aside for even louder harassment.

We approached the Bulgarian/Turkish border in pre-dawn darkness. It was here that we were forced to leave the train for immigration formalities. Robyn and I joined the throng of a thousand or so bedraggled fellow passengers and stood there, waiting our turn at the anemically lit window at the end of the platform. We were well back in the line. It was going to be a long wait.

Machine-gun toting Turkish soldiers patrolled up and down the line, asserting their authority every now and then by demanding, "Passpot! Passpot!" One caught me staring at him, and he immediately demanded to see our papers. I handed him our passports and he riffled through them.

"Australiani?" he asked. I nodded, and he immediately beckoned us to follow him. We'd boarded the express without visas, and it seemed that we were about to pay the penalty for taking that risk. Instead, though, the soldier led us to the front of the line, roughly elbowed aside the person about to step forward to the window, placed our passports on the counter, and barked out a stream of explanation to the clerk.

Immediately, the clerk extended his hand to us, warmly shook our uncertainly offered hands in response, and stamped our passports. The soldier then escorted us back to our carriage and offered his hand in friendship. The Turks, it seemed, were still following another call of their warrior leader, Ataturk.

Long after the battle, Ataturk composed a speech. It was an extraordinary speech, given the ferocity of the fighting and the fundamental differences that underlaid the conflict between the Christian and Muslim armies. An excerpt from that speech has been carved into a stone monument at Anzac Cove, and it explained the foundation for our friendly reception. It says, "Those heroes that shed their blood and lost their lives … you are now laying in the soil of a friendly country, therefore rest in peace. There is no difference between the Johnnies and the Mehmets to us where they lay side by side here in this country of ours … You, the mothers, who sent their sons from far away countries wipe away your tears. Your sons are now lying in our bosom and are in peace. After having lost their lives on this land they have become our sons as well …"

On this bleak railway station, we'd become beneficiaries of the legend that the Anzacs and Turks had forged as they slaughtered each other at Gallipoli. And, when we submerged ourselves in the transparent waters of Anzac Cove, the ghosts of that legend flooded in with the tide.

126   Thirteenth Beach

Crossroads at Istanbul: European and Asian cultures have mingled over the waters of the Bosporus for nearly three thousand years. Today, this 24 kilometer waterway is also a major route for tankers carrying oil from the Black Sea to the western world. Turkey frets over safety and environmental issues as upwards of 5500 tankers a year tackle the narrow, twisting passage.

Not all shipwrecks are time capsules of death and destruction. Robyn approaches the *USS Mahi*, an old minesweeper, deliberately sunk on a bare sandy bottom off the west coast of Oahu, Hawaii. The ship now serves as an artificial reef in an area where the natural reefs have been shaved clean of most of their inhabitants by over fishing. 2001.

Meanwhile (below), in the chilly waters of Gibraltar—the British colony on the southern tip of Spain—a sunken barge is similarly, slowly, becoming a cavernous reef. 2001.

Free falling: Robyn sinks into the Blue Hole in Palau. 1990.

Deep stars: It's not only fish that proliferate in the cold rich waters of the Galapagos. Fifty meters down off Cousin Rock, colonies of sea stars spangle the drab volcanic rock. Although they lie close to the Equator, these sea stars are washed by the chilly waters of the Humboldt Current. Welling up from Antarctica, the Humboldt enriches the waters of the Galapagos with nutrients not usually found in equatorial waters. As a result, marine life abounds, although the water is too cold to support prolific reef-building corals. 2000.

1990s

22

Two Men in A Leaky Boat

The phone shrilled insistently. It was Wayne. Calling from Kununurra. Two thirds of his way through three months long-service leave.

"G'day!" I said, "How's it going?"

"Great! Are you coming up to meet us in Coral Bay?"

"Of course. Where shall we meet?"

Wayne holds a degree in electrical engineering. He also holds a master of business administration. He works in the mystical and rarefied atmosphere of industrial upper management, where his mind is called upon to mesh smoothly and synchronously with complex engineering and commercial issues. Everything he does is carefully calculated and painstakingly planned. An ideal background, one would think, for the successful completion of a long-distance call from a public telephone box.

"We'll pick you up at … hang on … the light's flashing!"

There came the sound of frantic searching. A couple of coins clunked into the green box.

"Right. Where were we?"

"Where will we meet?"

"That's right … hang on! The bloody light's flashing again … it's okay, Ben's got some change. Ben! Ben! BEN! Come here!"

At this point, Wayne's son Ben obviously trotted up and surrendered some pocket money. Five cents went into the green box, and the light stopped flashing.

"Now we're right mate. Sorry about that. We'll pick you … Stuff! The light's flashing again! Exmouth mate!" Click … silence.

So, I caught the plane to Exmouth a week later, discovered Wayne and his family waiting hopefully at the airport, and traveled with them the 150-odd kilometers south to Coral Bay.

Camping is now quite comfortable at Coral Bay. Since my first visit in the 1970s, camper parks have been developed to offer neat serviced sites, grassed with hardy saltine lawn and shaded by droopy, gray-green casuarinas. On the day we arrived, a two-story block of self-service units opened. We settled on a quiet site, screened from the rest of the park by the ubiquitous casuarinas.

Next morning, Wayne revealed even more of his engineering background just before we went diving. Everything was ready. The boat was inflated and loaded down with gear. We were both in our wetsuits. And the cameras were loaded. Well, my cameras were loaded. Wayne was about to load his.

"Why do you need to use a calculator and a slide rule to load a camera?" I asked.

He gave me one of those looks which said, "Obviously you are not an engineer!" and then he said, "I'm going to calculate a new set of exposures for my flash unit because I'm using a different ASA film!"

"Okay. I'll wait for you."

With that, Wayne huddled over the hood of his car and started furiously scribbling into his spiral-bound notebook.

The day wore on. Sweat dripped from his nose. At one stage, I stole a quick glance over Wayne's shoulder at the computations that were consuming so much time and space in the notebook. It looked something like:

$$\text{aperture} = (\cos b \times \sin a) + (\tan X - r2h) \times (ASA\ 1 + .000002 \times ASA\ 2) \times (Pv1 - Pv2)$$

---

a couple of beers at the bar.

Finally, triumphantly, Wayne declared the answer. "f8.1076946539085341112!" and all was ready, and we were able to cast off and head out to sea. This was an indication of the attraction of Coral Bay and, in fact, the entire Ningaloo Reef National Park.

We were heading off from the mainland to dive on a barrier coral reef. Our transport was a three-meter inflatable, loaded with a mountain of tanks, cameras, and other equipment. And that's all you need. It's even possible to swim out to the reef from the shore.

With clear water zipping past under the rubber pontoons, the sun beating down and warming our bodies, and the prospect of several hours underwater before us, life seemed to be replete.

Then Wayne spotted my heath-robinson electronic flash diffuser; a short piece of second-hand sewer pipe, capped with a piece of translucent Perspex, and held in place on my strobe with a rubber band. I'd decided to introduce electronic flash to some of my underwater shots, but I wanted it to be weak and heavily diffused. There was nothing commercially available to help me achieve the results I wanted, hence the piece of second-hand sewer pipe.

Peals of laughter greeted this device as soon as it appeared from my camera box. Frankly, it did look somewhat bucolic alongside the eloquently engineered Nikonos gear that Wayne uses so well.

But then, suddenly, his attitude toward my "pathetic light bucket," as he called it, changed. This change in attitude coincided with the realization that air was getting out of our inflatable boat, and water was getting in.

At that moment, we were beyond the reef, near a breaking bommie. The distant Coral Bay shore was a thin sandy line on the horizon.

As the boat began to demonstrate the flotation characteristics of a soggy Kleenex tissue, Wayne realized that my "pathetic light bucket" was the only bailing implement we had on board. He developed an instant affection for it, and, armed with this pint-sized lifesaver, he proved yet again that a frightened man with a bucket can outperform the best bilge pump ever invented.

Just audible above the roar of the torrent of water he was sending over the side were his wild-eyed suggestions that I should "pump some bloody air into that bloody pontoon ... bloody quick!"

It turned out that the pontoon air-valve cap had worked loose, possibly—only possibly, not certainly—because I'd been absent-mindedly twirling it back and forth on the way out to the reef. But with the water out, air in, and the valve tightened, dignity returned, and we were able to drop anchor in a narrow gutter just inside the reef.

We kitted up, gave each other a confirmatory nod, and rolled over backward from opposite gunwales of the boat. As the bubbles cleared and fingers of cool water wriggled their way into my wetsuit, Wayne became the ideal partner on a photographic dive; he checked me out, gave me the okay sign, waited for a sign in return, then turned and swam away. I turned in the opposite direction and headed for the bottom in six meters.

Visibility was about 20 meters. On both sides of the gutter, large bommies reared up from the bottom and reached to within half a meter of the surface. Coral growth was profuse in patches.

I'd first dived near this very spot about 20 years before, and then again about ten years later, so I spent some time contrasting the scenes today with those of my memories. Fish populations have been decimated. No kaleidoscopic abundance. Just small numbers of isolated fish wandering around the reefs like cleaners in a deserted football stadium. Few big fish. No sharks.

Subsequent dives reinforced this view. We trekked north towards Point Maud to swim in Skeleton Bay, firmly expecting to find the abundance and beauty that Neil Wehlack and I had encountered in the early 1970s. To our dismay, the corals were dead. Many of them still stood, but there were all grotesquely draped in death-shrouds of filamentous green algae.

Coral Bay and the Ningaloo Reef have suffered the combined effects of a series of environment-changing events. Human line-fishing pressure has been increasing and relentless for 40 years or more. Early waves of shell collectors literally left no stone unturned as they searched for, and stripped out, attractively housed mollusks.

Twice in the late 1980s, the corals themselves created massive fish kills when their spawning coincided with hot days and low tides. Corals, anchored as they are in their limestone homes, can't go wandering in search of a mate. Instead, simultaneously stimulated by the full moon in early autumn, entire reefs of coral eject their sperm and eggs in billowing pink clouds.

Sperm and eggs mingle in a rich broth of life and, all being well, are washed out to sea as fertilized eggs. Billions and billions of them. Most will be eaten or die before they've completed their free swimming phase and settle, perchance on the reef, to begin a new veneer of life on the skeletons of the previous generations. This is how one of the world's smallest creatures builds massive reef structures over the millennia.

But when low tides and hot days stagnate the waters of the reef, the clouds of fertilized eggs perish. Rapid decay sucks oxygen from the water, and the reef's fish suffocate in their masses.

Cyclones, such as the one that thrashed the Ningaloo reef in March 1999 with wind speeds up to 108 kilometers-per-hour, piled up additional damage.

There's also the coral-destroying activates of the *Drupella* snail. Between 1987 and 1989, these snails multiplied dramatically and consumed up to 75 percent of the live coral over nearly 300 kilometers of reef. Since then, the coral has staged a patchy but encouraging recovery.

Still, nature is resilient. Strewn across the long lagoon, which runs for kilometers along the coast behind the reef, are healthy and luxuriant coral gardens full of interesting fish and other life. In the course of a week, we both spent hours engrossed in these coral gardens. They're in shallow, protected water, so they're also ideal for kids and beginners. Close to the shore, schools of spangled emperor have been hand-fed for some years. Now tame and game, these fish will approach any diver to see what's being offered.

Judging by the numbers of Spanish mackerel coming in on boats that had been fishing the deeper water behind the reef, there are also still larger schools of fish out there.

Our dives, in the shallow waters behind the reef, often lasted for more than two hours. On one occasion, I drifted around an upturned clump of staghorn coral—inverted testimony to the power of a cyclone—and discovered Wayne lying some distance off in a narrow cleft, waiting patiently for a small fish to emerge from a hole in front of his camera.

Settled and comfortable, free from the need to think about air consumption and decompression limits, he'd become part of the environment; a man-fish, oblivious to my presence. I let myself sink gently onto the coral rubble, and lay watching him.

Seawater, probably as close as we can get to a universal solvent, has the power, over time, to dissolve almost any other substance. But in some mysterious way, it also has the capacity to crystallize the bonds between those kindred spirits who draw adventure and inspiration from its restless surface or the calm of its depths.

Wayne, lying there, as at ease as he would have been reclining in his home strumming blues, was the embodiment of that special quality shared by all my diving partners over the years. A quality that seems to have welled from a common source. "Mother, mother Ocean" indeed, as Jimmy Buffet sings.

After ten minutes or so, I retreated quietly, and left him to complete his solitary creative vigil.

Late on the last day, as I swam on the surface across the glass-calm lagoon, Wayne was already in the boat, warm and dry and finishing off the last of the food. He reached over and took my camera from me and said, "You know what mate?"

"What?"

"When we get the chance, we ought to go down on the old submarines off Barwon Heads together. I think you'd enjoy that. We'll go out in the *Cossack Kid*."

"Sounds great. Let's do it." If only I'd known....

23

Cossack Kid

Wayne and his brother Glenn were on their hands and knees, poring over the circuit diagrams and electronic components strewn across the forward thwart of the wildly pitching *Cossack Kid*. Shrieking wind and hissing graybeards made it almost impossible to hear exactly what they were saying, but, from the snatches of conversation that did manage to swirl past me before being hurled away in the maelstrom, it was clear that they were into heavy electrical and electronic diagnoses. I might not have captured all the terms accurately, but it seemed that we were confronted with a tricky problem.

"Could it be the inverted dispersional transhedral accumulator?" Wayne pondered.

Glenn rubbed his chin, slowly shook his head and offered his view. "More likely the transpondentially arrayed accelerated impedance arrestor ... although the farradazical horizontally opposed hertzcube could be intermittently squaring."

"Hmm. Yes. Hadn't thought of that."

This was the second attempt to find the submarines.

Midway between Port Phillip Heads and Barwon Heads, a couple of kilometers out into Bass Strait, lays the Ship's Graveyard; a now-disused scuttling ground for ships and submarines that had reached the end of their merchant and military service.

Our first attempt to dive there had been sunk when the five meter long *Cossack Kid* almost became a dive site as we tried to cross the bar of the Barwon River and an enormous wall of green water had come in over the bow. Standing abreast behind the low windscreen, Wayne, Glenn, and I had all been totally swamped by the green cascade and the clumps of floating seaweed it carried. Years of pounding across the swells and chop of Bass Strait had flexed and dented the *Cossack Kid* into a casual accumulation of aluminum rivets and plates traveling in roughly the same direction, but it was a gallant vessel. A lesser boat would have gone to Davy Jones locker, but the *Kid* staggered under the additional load and then lurched forward.

Glenn, completely unflappable, looked almost bored and didn't appear to have noticed the deluge. Wayne deigned to glance at the swirling mess of diving gear and sandwiches behind us and phlegmatically muttered, "We'll pull the bungs out when we get up to speed, and it'll drain out." Then, with a length of dripping kelp rakishly snagged around his neck like Snoopy's scarf, and with his mouth set in a cavalier smirk, he rammed the throttle forward as the next wave in the monstrous set threatened to topple on top of us. That's when the engine stopped.

Using the last of the *Kid*'s meager momentum, Wayne spun the wheel hard to starboard, and we found ourselves in the spot that surfers work so hard to attain; the perfect takeoff position on a large wave. Surfboards, of course, are designed for that role. Aluminum boats are not, although the steep inclination did make it possible for most of the water that had poured in over the bow to pour out again … over the bow. There were glimpses of the sandy bottom welling up in coarse brown stains as we skimmed down the face of the wave towards the estuary we'd just left.

Glenn seemed a trifle annoyed by the inconvenience, but roused himself sufficiently to tug a few times on the outboard motor starting cord. When that had no effect, he shrugged his shoulders and settled back to observe, with mild interest, our hair-raising passage back over the bar and into the choppy water inside the river mouth.

Some weeks later, we were heading out across the bar again, this time successfully despite the deteriorating weather. Wayne, in company with Glenn, has dived the Ship's Graveyard innumerable times and knew by heart the bearings for most of the diveable hulks.

"We'll use the echo sounder to put you right on the conning tower of the best sub dive in Victoria.", he'd said. But now the echo sounder seemed to have expired, and it seemed that we'd have to return, frustrated again.

"No problem," said Wayne. "Get the map, Glenn." Glenn rummaged in the tiny door-less glove box set into the dashboard of the *Kid* and produced a limp, sodden scrap of smudged paper. It looked like a shred of the Dead Sea scrolls.

"This," Wayne intoned imperiously, "is the most complete collection of bearings for the Graveyard. We've collected and improved these over the past 15 years".

Glenn seemed puzzled by the paper and rotated it slowly, first clockwise, then counterclockwise. Then he checked the reverse side, all the while glancing from the paper to the coast that appeared every now and again as we bobbed to the crest of a seething comber.

Wayne kept the *Kid* chugging along and periodically peered over the side—as though expecting the heaving, cement-colored water to calm and clarify sufficiently to provide a clear view of the submarine reposing on the seabed more than 30 meters below. Apparently it did.

"Here it is. Yep. This feels like the right spot. Drop the pick."

Glenn reverently folded and stowed the scroll fragment in the glove box and, like a trick rider walking along the back of a bucking bronco, moved forward in the pitching and tossing boat to release the anchor.

Minutes later we were, all three of us, sitting on the gunwales, ready to roll backward into the water. Glenn on one side. Wayne and me on the other.

Balance is important in a small boat, especially in a rough sea.

"On three," said Wayne and started to count.

Glenn dozed off and toppled backward on "one." The *Kid* tipped alarmingly under the combined weight of Wayne and me. Sheer fright flipped us backward just before Bass Strait flooded in over the gunwale.

Almost impenetrable visibility greeted us, but it was more comfortable beneath the surface than on it. We all sank quickly toward the invisible bottom and the waiting submarine. Well, not quite.

Sea-grass beds play an important role in marine ecology. At first glance, they can seem as devoid of life as an unkempt lawn. Look closer, though, and you'll find that sea-grass beds support myriad life forms; fish, shrimp, crabs, mollusks. This particular expanse of sea-grass no doubt supported its fair share of all those; it looked particularly rich and verdant.

But it didn't support any submarines; at least not that we could see.

It wasn't as if we didn't cover a lot of ground looking. Despite our depth, the surge created by the swells funneling through the constriction of Bass Strait after traveling unimpeded across thousands of kilometers of windswept Southern Ocean swept us back and then forward across the sea-grass at quite alarming speed.

The subs we were looking for are all legendary *J* Class vessels. Seven were built by the British Navy between 1915 and 1918. Imaginatively and inspiringly named *J1, J2, J3, J4, J5, J6,* and *J7,* these were regarded as experimental subs. Capable of cruising at 19 knots on the surface under the power of three 12-cylinder diesel engines, they were faster on the surface than any other submarines in the world. Three 1,300 horsepower electric motors enabled them to reach speeds of up to ten knots submerged. They could dive to 61 meters and stay out on patrol for more than a month. Forty-four men manned them.

Conned by Commander Noel Laurence, *J1* and its crew struck decisively against the German High Seas Fleet when they hit and badly damaged the German battleships *Kronprinz* and *Grosser Kurfurst* with a single salvo of torpedoes.

Less fortunate was *J6*, which was sunk with the loss of 14 men when it went sniffing around a disguised British warship—a *Q* ship—off the Northumberland coast near Blythe in 1918. *Q* ships were live bait for German submarines. Heavily armed but disguised as helpless freighters, these ships wallowed around, hoping to attract attention from predatory enemy subs. When one rose to the bait, the *Q* ship dropped its disguise, ran up the Union Jack, and pounced mercilessly. In this fatal case of mistaken identity, *J6* failed to recognize H M S *Cymric* as a *Q* ship. *Cymric* took *J6* to be a German *U*-boat and opened fire.

The remaining six *J* class subs survived the war and were presented as gifts by the British to the Australian Navy. Australia was very grateful … for a while. High operating costs quickly revealed the real motivation behind the British generosity and overwhelmed the usefulness of these subs. Today, there are four of them out there in the graveyard. Two others, including *J1*, lie inside Port Phillip Bay, closer to Melbourne. Salvors stripped out all the valuable metal and machinery before the hulks were towed out to their final resting places and dynamited.

What remains today are hollow shells, fractured and dislocated, but easily recognizable as submarines. Rearing bows indicate their innovative sea-keeping design. On at least one, a conning tower remains virtually intact, and it is possible to sink gently onto the fragments of rusted and corroded plates once trod by the feet of brave and determined British and Australian submariners. On calm days, when clear water floods the strait, it is possible to safely enter the hulls. Little remains to conjure the sense of drama that would have filled these cramped tubes—barely seven meters wide—when they were crowded with anxious, sweating men and noisy, oily machinery. Some lines of narrow tubing rib the inside of the hulls. A few isolated valves and gears protrude. Most of the bulkheads have collapsed.

Cold-water corals and sponges encrust much of the surface, nurtured by the constant ebb and flow of nutrient-rich water. Tufts of algae sprout everywhere. Fish—mainly bull's-eyes—hang in the shaded shelter of their artificial reef. Steel, won from the earth, is being returned to the earth by the action of the sea. That's on a calm day.

On this swell-swept day, I did find a small rock. It was sufficient to provide brief anchorage in the heavy surge. Wayne zoomed past twice; once forward, eyes intently focused on some distant point out in the murk, bubbles streaming horizontally out behind him like the smoke from an express steam train. Then backward, upside down, elegant as a blindfolded moose on roller-blades, gesturing dramatically upward with his thumb. We'd have to find the subs on another day.

Back at the boat ramp, Wayne had another idea. "Truk. You know, where the U.S sank all those Japanese ships during the Second World War. Those wrecks should be easy to find!"

24

Hass, Armstrong, and A Very Big Tarpon

Low kunuku scrub moaned softly as the trade winds billowed in from the northeast and passed through the thorns that only goats will eat. Klein Bonaire—flat, uninhabited, and already biscuit dry—baked in the midday Caribbean heat. Robyn sat on a shattered shard of limestone, and rocked like a pendulum, eyes squeezed tight shut in pain, both hands clamped around her right foot, which she was holding up across her left knee. The thorn that had stabbed into her instep was three centimeters long, but only a centimeter protruded through the sole of her thin neoprene bootee. Thankfully, when I gripped the protruding stub between finger and thumb, and pulled it carefully backwards, it came out cleanly and she sobbed in relief.

We'd come here to follow Hans Hass' footsteps, and Robyn's painful discomfort reflected his when he had made the same tortuous walk nearly 60 years ago. He had written, "At the same time the sun burned as if to transform us too into cactus. The cactus jabbed back wherever you put your foot … it was not a pleasant walk." "I'll second that," Robyn had said as she wiped her teary face with a towel and hauled herself to her feet to continue the trudge across the little island.

Bonaire, the 290-square-kilometer island just 80 kilometers off the north coast of Venezuela, together with its smaller offspring, Klein Bonaire, is a harsh gem. Lava, welling from a volcanic vent in the seabed, laid the foundation for Bonaire 70 million years ago. As the lava cooled and formed solid rock near the surface of the tropical sea, corals settled and formed the beginnings of fringing reefs. Over the eons, uplifting of the underlying rock created Mt. Brandaris, 240 meters high. Changes in sea level, as a result of global warming and cooling, have terraced this volcanic mount with at least three distinctive rings of long-dead reef, and one that lives today.

So close to Venezuela, deep in the Caribbean, you could be forgiven for expecting Bonaire to be cloaked in lush rainforest. Not so. It is a desert island. Hard. Bristling with cactus and the abandoned, stunted remnants of aloe vera plantations. Goats, thousands of them, eat any greenery that might withstand the blistering heat. It is difficult to tell the difference between feral and domestic goats. Most of them wander at will, but occasionally some can be seen constrained within bare earth compounds, fenced in by tall fences of transplanted cactus. No barbed wire. No need for it when all the shoulder-to-shoulder fence posts are growing their own barbs!

Quite a lot has changed since Hass visited. For example, divers are now welcome there! Bonaire's entire fringing reef system has been declared a marine park. Near the capital, Kralendijk, on the sheltered west coast, there are numerous resorts, many of which cater to divers. We chose one simply because it promised unlimited diving. Nailed to the wall near the compressor house is a weathered sign that explains how this dive resort operates. It's a clear and thoughtful expression of common sense. It should be written into every diving manual, log book, and C card. Every well-intentioned legislator and every dive resort manager should read it. It was titled the "Armstrong Principle."

"Once a person gets certified and has some experience, there becomes a guide-diver relationship rather than a student-teacher relationship. The guide is then felt to have a minimum responsibility for the diver's actions. That guide is acting in an advisory capacity, should warn of known, obvious hazards, inform of local laws and customs but should not be expected to make basic go/no go decisions where the diver has all facts before them. The ultimate decision is left to the diver's own judgment."

In practice, this means that after a comprehensive briefing, experienced divers like us were free to dive where and when we wanted to. Alone, at night, 50 kilometers from the resort if we wanted to.

Liberating experienced divers to do their own thing brings advantages for less-skilled divers, too, because it allows the resort's guides to offer highly personalized attention to those who ask for closer support. It's an excellent system. And it's safe.

Recklessness should not be mistaken for adventure. Ultimately, safety in the water begins and ends with each individual. If we learn what the risks are, understand how to manage them, know our own limitations, and never exceed them, we'll be as safe as it is possible to be. This is as true when we're driving on the road, working, or swimming in water. Armstrong, whoever he was, recognized that.

Diving on Bonaire is superb and some of the easiest diving you can imagine. Any morning, within ten minutes of getting out of bed, you can be hovering at 15 meters over profuse coral in a swarm of colorful fish, many of which insist on swimming too close to the camera to enable them to be photographed.

Bonaire's western coast enjoys the offshore trade winds almost all year round. Flat, calm water varying in color from the palest ultramarine, to deepest violet waits in every cove. Fifty meters was the deepest water we encountered, but the best diving lies well above that. Our average depths were around 12 to 20 meters.

Bonaire has recognized the value of ecotourism and ensures that its marine park is well protected. For many years now, fishing has been excluded within the 65-meter zone. Early in 1996, a freighter was prohibited from entering Kralendijk harbor because its commanding officer would not verify that his vessel's ballast water had been taken from the open sea. This requirement is to prevent the introduction of polluted water or marine species from foreign ports. Threats of legal action from the ship's owners fell on deaf ears, and the freighter was forced to return to the open sea to dump its polluted ballast water before being allowed to take on cargo in Kralendijk.

Divers are prohibited from wearing gloves to discourage them from touching the coral. Every diver is expected to be able to control their buoyancy so that they can always float above the coral, and not crash down on top of it. Spear guns are banned, too, and the fish have responded. There are only few big fish, though. Flip through the pages of *Diving to Adventure*, and you'll see some of the fish Hass encountered. Perhaps in time the muscle-bound jacks and ox-sized grouper will return.

The biggest fish we saw were tarpon; monster relatives of the common and diminutive herring. Some of them were enormous. Hard and brilliantly shiny—like elegantly shaped sheets of stainless steel. Hass' companion, Joerg, managed to spear a tarpon off Bonaire in 1938. The fish must have long memories. Despite several hours of almost obsessive work, I could not get close enough to secure a respectable photograph.

Often, in early morning, four of these super-fish would be hanging in the slight current on the edge of the reef in front of the resort. Only slight movements of their tails, like lazily idling engines in Pit Lane before a Grand Prix, hinted at the power beneath the scales.

I'd pretend that I hadn't seen them, swim up current, and then attempt to drift backward toward them, using the Plexiglas back plate of my underwater housing as a rearview mirror. That didn't work.

Swimming out to sea, moving down current, dropping quickly to 30 meters, then sneaking back across the sand toward the reef (triggering dignified retreat in fields of garden eels along the way), and angling up from underneath and behind them didn't work either.

Tapping a coin against the camera housing? No chance. Fumbling with a flooding flashlight during a night dive, however, did work. Alone. Fifteen meters down, and the white beam of the flashlight was slowly yellowing as the rising water level attacked the batteries and circuitry. Clouds obscured the moon, so it looked like it was going to be a very dark swim back along the reef toward the resort.

As I tilted the flashlight upward, in the futile hope of at least saving the reflector and the globe, a giant metallic head speared into the lightglow no more then 20 centimeters from my face! If I'd been wearing a frightmeter to record my reaction, I'd now be in the *Guinness Book of Records*.

One disdainful flicker of the tarpon's eye signaled, "see, that's how you get close!" and the silver water rocket silently blasted off into the liquid night. One feeble last glimmer seeped from the drowning flashlight, and then all was black.

Spotting an old acquaintance: One of the delights of being underwater is being able to get so close to the wildlife. Years of prohibiting spearfishing from the fringing reefs of Bonaire, in the Dutch Antilles, has resulted in abundant marine life, most of which has no hesitation in approaching and posing for the camera. This handsome grouper occupied a section of reef within a few meters of our beachside bungalow and greeted us at the beginning and end of every dive we made there. 1996.

25

Polynesian Blue

"I love you!" Robyn's farewell, thrown overboard to churn and dissolve in the wind and blue-white wake of the heeling yacht. Tied to her devotion was the yellow nylon painter of the inflatable dinghy that she'd instinctively released as I slid off the teak marlin board into the slightly less-than-pacific Pacific.

Suspended in the void. Gentle shiver, despite the silky massage of warm, transparent water against naked skin. Abandoning a yacht under full sail in open ocean very quickly reveals how easy it is for a human speck to be lost in the immensity of nature.

No reference points below the surface. Just a vacant, indigo hemisphere around and below. Impossible to judge distance or drift. Above surface, occasional glimpses of the already distant yacht, its apex of silver spar and beige canvas stabbing erratically into view amid the jumbled waves. Infrequently, only when the uplift of a passing swell lifts me higher than most and allows more distant views, the jungled humps of Tonga's Vava'u archipelago stud the eastern horizon.

Rubbery rubbing bump from the dinghy, huddling close as though it, too, shuddered in apprehension of solitude in an alien environment. Hanging mournfully from the chrome ring on its bow was the yellow painter, greening as it reached down into the deep as though searching for an anchorage. No chance of that here. Bottom lays some thousands of meters down. I coiled it and tossed it into the dinghy. Bright yellow again. For a moment, the sun-warmed gunwale, dry and familiar, almost lured me out of the water, too.

Just minutes before, the yacht had been spanking southward, scything its starboard rail through the swell with sails and rigging taut as a guitar string under the strain of the southeast Trades.

David Strawn was at the helm, left foot planted in the middle of the wet teak grid that covered the floor of the cockpit; right foot braced against the starboard cockpit seat to keep him upright. Arms spread like thick spokes across the stainless steel wheel. Salt spray splashing against the anonymity of his rainbow mirror sunglasses. And in those mirrors, reflections of Trudy and Robyn, sitting near the port rail, orange spray-jacketed backs to the wind. Bare brown legs extended across the cockpit; toes stretching to find the starboard seat. As the yacht bowed deferentially under the added weight of a passing gust, they found themselves standing almost vertically.

"So, David, I said. Where are the whales?"

"Right there."

Fact stranger than fiction. As he uttered the cue, a monstrous fluke, streaming sheets of spray, reared up behind Trudy and Robyn. Breathtakingly close. Like a massive rear-projected image in a Wembley rock concert.

"Right there!"

Slate black. Notched with creamy white. Issuing a silent siren call. It was gone before Robyn and Trudy could turn their heads, but the call was irresistible. David had heard it too … but today his duty lay at the helm.

"Go on! Go!" he yelled as he spun the wheel hard to port to bring the yacht up into the wind. Jib and mainsail flapped and clattered. Momentarily, the yacht lost headway. Enough time to scuff my feet into fins and squeeze the tight silicone strap of my mask over my head. Then the hull bucked as the bow fell away to leeward, and the sails again offered themselves to the full force of the wind. I scraped my back as I slid off the marlin board, and the yacht peeled away on the starboard tack.

Robyn's cry echoed among the bubbles as the sea closed over my head. When I bobbed to the surface, the yacht was already disappearing intermittently behind steep, watery slopes. Robyn and Trudy were both standing, clinging one-handed to the rigging and pointing with their free arms to a patch of sea somewhere off to my right. David was hard at work, beginning a series of tacks that would keep the yacht heading back upwind to pick me up. His reference point was my friend, the dinghy.

It took some time to appear. A dark and ominous bulk slowly, inexorably bulldozing its way toward me through the swell. No flamboyant flourishes of the tail. Deliberate. Slow. Too far away to be seen underwater. Each low, rolling breach of the surface revealed that characteristic hump and the relatively tiny dorsal fin. I could see the dorsal fin clearly. Head on. Precisely.

I could hear the whale calling but there was another, strange, noise too; *boosh-boosh-boosh-boosh*.

One subdued splash from unseen flukes, and the whale disappeared from the surface. Solitude returned to my liquid hemisphere. But then a patch of blue deep beneath me began to darken. Like an image rising to the surface of photographic paper, a hazy shape formed. Perceptions of depth and distance returned, accompanied by suspense that Hitchcock might have imagined but could have never created. Like standing in a clearing fog and finding your toes overhanging a precipice. The sheer size. And that noise; *boosh-boosh-boosh-boosh*.

Screaming seemed to be a perfectly natural response. Visceral reaction to confrontation with a gigantic and ominous life form. But the scream hid soundless in my throat.

This leviathan was interested in me. It slowed its vertical ascent and hung, tail down, pivoting slowly so that first its left eye and then its right could inspect this white, minute, and fragile flotsam. So close that details of the callosities encrusting its long drooping pectoral fins were clearly visible. It rose in front of me and, like Moses, parted the waters with its black bulk. Beneath the surface, we met in silence save the mystifying *boosh-boosh-boosh-boosh*.

On the surface, the whale exhaled with the sound of an express train storming through a tunnel as air rushed from its lungs with sufficient velocity to atomize the thin skin of water glossing the area around its blowhole. Cold, fine vapor dusted against the brass-blue sky. Another second, and sheets of muscle and membrane in the whale's diaphragm flexed. Pressure decreased inside its chest cavity, and fresh air whistled through the blowhole to fill the cavernous lungs.

And then the second whale. Smaller. Creamy gray. More hesitant. Peering up at me from the depths beneath my feet. Looming then falling away. Spiraling out of sight. Returning. Then dissolving into the blue. Physically, visually, and audibly, I was dwarfed and hypnotized; a dazzled and mesmerized rabbit about to be hit by an emotional Greyhound bus.

As the closest whale sank alongside me, I desperately searched for eye contact. A chance to connect with the soul of a kindred creature. A tiny eye. Close to the curling, impish termination of its mouth. Just one flicker of movement as, perhaps, its gaze switched from me to the floating dinghy, then back again. A confirming signal that life, intelligence, thought, laid buried deep within this impossibly large being. But no insight.

When the whale left, it just sank, tail first. Rotated as though for one last look at me, then slowly tipped over on its side.

One haunting humpback call probed the deep. The second whale materialized, aligned with its more adventurous companion. Then, with massive, synchronized vertical swipes of their flukes, they disappeared.

Alone. Empty. A void within a void. *Boosh-boosh-boosh-boosh*. That noise. As loud as ever. But now subsiding. *Boosh-boosh-boosh-boosh-boosh*. Finally, I realized its source. My heart. Thumping in my chest. Forcing adrenaline-laced blood roaring through my ears …

Cool water slopped under the small of my back; strong sunlight heated my chest and face. I'd retreated to the sanctuary of the dinghy and lay, eyes closed. Exhausted. Recreating as many of the moments that had just passed as possible. Memory is fragile unless it is supported by repeated recall.

It's appealing to think of reaching out across gigantic spans of evolutionary time. To consider, in some telepathic way, that such encounters create communication between humans and these distant kin. Maybe that happens.

If so, I wonder what message the whales might be trying to send us. If they hand down their own history to each new generation of whales, then perhaps what they'd like to say to us might not be as complimentary as we'd like it to be.

Do they swim away from such an encounter as awed as we? Or do they just wonder if they could, with a bit of a struggle, consume that clumsy knot of clotted plankton?

150   Thirteenth Beach

Synchronised swimming: The humpbacks off Tonga. 1993

26

Wounds of Truk Lagoon

It was the kind of evil darkness that made the hair on the back of my neck stand up straight. One small, pale fish flitted convulsively from its resting place on the top step of the ship's weed-bewhiskered companionway and streaked away, downward and to my left.

I'd left Robyn waiting by the gaping doorway, and I was now alone. As I moved forward, utter blackness swooped in to envelope me. In the complete absence of light, the feeble beam of my small flashlight seemed totally inadequate and overwhelmed.

Fear welled up within me. It would have been easy to turn back; a relief. Curiosity wouldn't subside, though, and I busied myself with a routine calming check of my gauges. Thirty-two meters; 11 minutes elapsed; 1,800 bar remaining in my tank.

I'd entered the wreck of the *Kensho Maru,* and the rules had changed. No longer was I a close but still detached observer. A simple, short penetration—down a corridor, left through one room, right into another—had chopped off the umbilicus of dim, depth-blued light that connected me with my mortal world.

Now I was inside the stillness, the living death of this ship, transported through consciousness and time to the point where history and the present collide and fuse in a cold weld.

Part of me amalgamated into that weld. I knew how to leave this place—a quick slash with my flashlight confirmed that the doorway was where I expected it to be—but I shall carry forever the impressions of that drowned and tilted cabin.

The flashlight beam groped through blackness contaminated by silt, swirling like phantoms roused from eternal sleep by my fins.

Like the slowly unfolding plot of a suspense movie—with its attendant rise in fearful anticipation—the chaos and destruction was revealed to me piece by piece; the boundaries of each defined by the small, dirty-yellow patch of light.

Cable; yards of it. A cup. A broken cup. Sake bottles. Two. Three. Some fabric. The corner of a box. A reading lamp. At the end of the flexible stem, a small bowl-shaped reflector, dulled by corrosion. But in the center of that dullness, the glassy brightness of a spherical bulb. I moved my face closer; squinted my eyes slightly.

The spider-web-thin filament was intact, too. Delicate technology that has survived first the fury of the air attacks that punctured and gutted the ship and then, over the decades, the relentless press of the sea. In such an alien and surreal location, it seemed ironic that such a commonplace object as a light bulb could be so intriguing. The irony is strengthened by the pervasive darkness.

I forced myself to stay with the details; my instincts yearned for the complete scene to be revealed in one brilliant revelation. But there was no such brilliance. Only the constant, constrained beam of my flashlight. Fragmented images piled up in my mind like the shattered war debris before me.

Protruding from beneath a sloping pile of silt was the corrugated hose of a gas mask. Near the top of the silt pile and only partly obscured by sediment, the leather sole of a shoe, heel uppermost; a left shoe, scuffed through where the ball of the foot had rested. Just to the right of it, more deeply buried in the muck, the side and heel of another leather shoe.

I stared, transfixed by those shoes, confronting perhaps the ultimate contrast—that between life and death, or maybe just the contrast between imagination and reality. It doesn't matter. There was no need to breach the sanctity of the muck, to prod for bones, to settle this uncertainty. There was death in this cabin; whether real or imagined, the effect is the same.

My flashlight beam moved on, across the sloping silt to the cabin wall, up to the tightly closed deadlight. Had the occupant of this cabin snatched his last glimpse of the outside world through that porthole before jamming the deadlight closed and screwing the locking ring into place?

If he had, that glimpse would have revealed Mt. Teroken, clothed in shaggy green rainforest, rearing upward from the rocky spine of Moen Island. And blue sky, spattered with white clouds and striped with towering pillars of black, oily smoke from blazing shore installations and dozens of armed, but trapped, Japanese merchantmen.

It was February 1944. America had come to Truk Lagoon, 3,000 kilometers northeast of Darwin, to wreak final and complete revenge for Pearl Harbor. The *Kensho* was one of 70 ships consumed in the conflagration.

The fear-slammed deadlight would have shut out the panorama of destruction and most of the furious rattle of machinegun fire. But nothing could have held out the tumultuous explosion beneath the deck as the fatal torpedo blasted a wide rip in the plates of the hull. For a moment, the tumult returned and I could hear trapped and broken men screaming; ruptured pipes hissing; crackling flames.

My flashlight returned to those shoes. Silence, save for the drubbing of my bubbles, returned to the cabin. And it was time to go. Time and depth had conspired to enforce rules which govern those living in the present. Any longer at this depth would force me into lengthy decompression—and I didn't come down with enough air for that.

I twisted to face the doorway. Again, silently agitated silt-phantoms billowed around me but offered no resistance as I slowly pushed through them to reach the outer cabin and finally the corridor. My blue umbilicus was restored, now more luminous and comforting than before. Ahead of me Robyn waited, silhouetted in the doorway at the end of the corridor, her flashlight a warm, gleaming beacon. Beyond her, open water.

Her eyes, owlishly framed in black silicone, soundlessly questioned me. I wondered how I'd begin to explain the impressions of my solitary sojourn. The best I could manage is a quickly scrawled "Tell you later" on her writing slate. At 25 meters, we began our inclined ascent across the face of the superstructure up to where the anchor line hooked onto one of the kingposts.

At ten meters, we joined Wayne, Ellie, and Graham and stopped. Together, we waited ten minutes to help free our bodies of accumulated nitrogen and to begin processing the accumulated sights and experiences of the dive.

Occasionally, tiny glossy black beads of oil drifted up and past, on their way to the surface. It has taken them over half a century to leak from the wreck. Dark spirits; exorcised from a tomb. It was time to surface.

Overhead, a leaden sky released the first drops of warm, tropical rain. Once we'd clambered into the runabout and were skimming across the lagoon to our mother ship, our speed and our sodden rainbow Lycra suits transformed the body-heat air into a chilly breeze. Wayne sat on the opposite gunwale, silent, contemplative. We were all glad to reach our floating home, shin up the ladder, and retreat into a bitingly hot shower.

Late that afternoon, in the few minutes before the sun dropped into the sea, I stood alone on the poop deck. The rain had stopped; the bruised sky had fragmented into a jumble of red-gold tinged clouds. Gentle wavelets lapped and slapped against the sides of our imperceptibly rising and falling hull. Thin, windblown oil slicks, formed from the oil drops escaping from the wrecks, streamed across the surface of the lagoon; slightly bluer than the green water. Slightly more lustrous. The sun sank and tropical night stretched its black cloak from horizon to horizon …

Dazzling sunlight ricocheted from the glass and blindingly white walls of Guam's InterPacific Resort. The entire inner compound, with its pool, palms, and soft green lawns, was suffocatingly hot. Not too hot for the Japanese golfers, though. Twenty or 30 of them. Behind the loose-strung brown nets, they were resolutely swinging and sweating their way through buckets of balls.

Beyond them, the exuberant clamor of countless teenagers and children—mostly Japanese—happily shattered the sapphire pool water into sparkling cascades. Beyond that, the open shade of the Grotto, the kitschy counterfeit cave which serves as a bar. Ice-cold Asahi beaded the glass with condensation and eased my thirst.

An hour later, thirst drove seven elderly Japanese golfers from the practice range into the Grotto. All men. Stout men. Colorfully wrapped in holiday clothes. All with gray-flecked crew cuts. They shuffled and scraped seven chairs into a rough circle around one of the low tables and waited for the American bartender to serve them. Most of them lit cigarettes, and a steel-blue pillar of smoke floated up toward the spotlight recessed into the synthetic rock of the ceiling. Rapid-fire conversation and laughter rippled around their table. One of them glanced toward the bar and caught me staring. He nodded in sudden, surprised politeness. Embarrassed, I returned his courteous nod and turned back toward the bar.

Some days later, we were nodding and smiling at each other again. This time in the crowded lobby of the hotel as we joined the queue at the checkout desk. He was encumbered with his bright yellow golf bag. I was laboring with my diving bag and camera box. His eyes settled on the new, vividly red, white, and black souvenir sticker on top of the camera box. In large calligraphic bamboo characters it spelled out "Truk Lagoon, Micronesia."

A hint of agitation flickered across his face and froze the half smile on his lips. It's as though, distracted, he'd forgotten the smile was there. He looked first at me and then turned to rap one of his companions on the shoulder. I was briefly scrutinized by the companion; a furtive yet obvious glance over his shoulder. A short exchange in Japanese passed between them. Then he returned to me, and in rich tones of broken English, he asked, "You visit Truk?"

"Yes. I dived on the wrecks there."

His ebony eyes studied my face as though he was searching for some unspoken, and perhaps unspeakable, details. Finally, he responded. Just three words. "Ahhh. My brother …"

His voice retreated. His gaze focused on an image more than 50 years away and fell toward the floor. With shoulders now slightly sagged, he nodded without looking at me and turned back into the queue. Images of the oil slicks, streaking across the face of the sea, bobbed to the surface of my memory. The wounds of Truk Lagoon are still weeping.

Indelible memories: After more that 50 years in the sea, this cargo manifest is still legible on the shattered bridge of the *Kensho Maru*. Truk Lagoon is littered with the bombed and torpedoed wrecks of about 70 armed Japanese merchant ships. They were attacked and sunk by avenging U.S. warplanes, operating from aircraft carriers out in the Pacific during the Second World War. Operation Hailstone, as the series of attacks were called, gutted the already battered Japanese fleet, and, in one sense, balanced the ledger for the Japanese attack on the U.S. fleet at Pearl Harbor.

Truk offers more accessible wrecks in a confined space than anywhere else on Earth. Most are deep. All are war graves. Over recent years, substantial effort has been made by Truk and Japanese authorities to recover the remains of as many Japanese sailors as possible. Ceremonial cremations on shore allow surviving family members closure and a chance to finally pay their last respects to long dead loved ones. Even so, the wrecks in Truk Lagoon remain as memorials to the many still unrecovered dead. 1992

27

The Fish that Roared

A discarded white polystyrene cup, floating near the landing, irritated me. Apart from the landing, this was the only sign of human presence; a sign that whomever had drunk from that cup had not appreciated the beauty of the surroundings. I lay on the sun-warmed wooden slats of the landing and reached out to pluck the cup from the water.

Through my own shadowy reflection, I could see past the surface glare and down to the bottom; mud and weed gently sloping away to a dark, rocky ledge about 12 meters down. Sharply cold water dashed over my hand as I retrieved the cup; it went into my dive bag. Freed from the irritation, I took more interest in my surroundings. A quiescent, azure pool. Thick walls of khaki-streaked green rushes. Several dead trees; one of them providing a perch for white herons and a small black-and-white cormorant. Golden summery air, hot and humming with insect life. This was Ewens Ponds.

It was 20 years ago to the day that I last visited this spot. Then it had been simply to spend some time snorkeling between deep scuba dives in the numerous caverns close to here. Compared to the exhilaration of those dives, snorkeling in Ewens Ponds was no more than an anticlimactic diversion to stave off surface-interval boredom. Today, more on a whim than anything else, I'd come to scuba dive.

Befuddled bureaucrats have not closed Ewens Ponds, as they have the other freshwater dives in the area, to competent divers who do not hold cave-diving qualifications. Ewens Ponds can be dived by anybody, and it is often crowded. Today, in the middle of the week, I was alone. I'd chosen to forego the first ponds and the free-flowing channel that connects all three major ponds. Here, I'd been told, there was a large school of bream in the third and deepest pond, and it was those I was keen to see. They're common enough, but they're more usually found in estuarine waters that are often not very clear. At Ewens Ponds was an opportunity to photograph them in transparent fresh water with better than 100-meter visibility.

Cold and quietude closed over my head as I eased myself off the landing and sank as gently as I could. Blue sepulchral stillness imposed its own discipline on me. My breathing became shallow and slow as each drumming burst of bubbles from my regulator seemed to demand an apology for the disturbance it caused. Three meters above the silt and rotten-weed covered bottom, I adjusted my buoyancy and hung suspended in water so clear it could have been air. Away across the mixing bowl-shaped pond, the school of bream meandered in single file over rolling meadows of green weed; they looked just like cattle plodding over a lush paddock toward the milking shed.

Directly beneath me now lay the rocky ledge I'd seen from the surface. A slight exhalation restarted my descent, and my neoprene-buffered knees soon gently bumped down onto jumbled and shattered limestone rocks. Off to the right, the ledge widened out into a ragged-mouthed cave.

The bream had now crossed their submerged meadow, and they were herding together in a nervous huddle under the floating mat of rushes that fringes the pond. I hoped that curiosity would overwhelm their fear and allowed myself to fall face-down across the rocks and out of sight. My horizon was the edge of the meadow, the line where it abruptly fell away into the rocky ledge.

Ten minutes went by. Heat seeped from my body. A cautious peek over the edge of the meadow revealed the bream, still under the rush-mat, pondering their next move. I settled back into a more-or-less comfortable position. Ten more minutes; chilly minutes. Then I saw the eye. A meter away. Staring at me. A solitary eye swaddled in filmy green weed. Motionless. I stared back. Then it moved; a barely perceptible flicker, but enough to show that whatever was attached to the eye was giving me the once-over. It flicked back to its original position. I edged closer, trying to make sense out of the cryptic image in front of me. Too close!

A foot-long fish decided enough was enough. It sprang up out of the weed and roared at me like an angry lion. Well, it was a silent roar—but it had the same effect. It jolted me backward. Totally piqued, the fish dashed off. I watched it go in astonishment. It turned and settled on another patch of weed about seven meters away and, as if to make sure I didn't disturb its repose over there, it roared at me again!

It was a congoli, an interesting Australian native fish capable of living in salt or fresh water. So adaptable is the diminutive congoli that it will even survive sudden transportation from salt to fresh water. Ambush is the congoli's preferred method for securing a meal. Insects, small crustaceans, and worms are typical fare. Ambushing, of course, requires patience. There's probably nothing worse, after careful selection of a hiding place and long periods of waiting made tolerable only by imagining the taste of the next morsel to haplessly wander past, than to have some clumsy intruder blunder in, scare off all the potential meals, and reveal your hiding place. No wonder this fish was irritated with me. I found myself talking to the damn thing. "S'truth! All I'd wanted to do was take a few photographs of bream … I didn't mean to upset anybody!" No effect. It just sat there and scowled at me.

By this time, I was shivering. The bream were still dithering under the rushes, so I quit and surfaced—a humbled intruder being asked to leave a private resort.

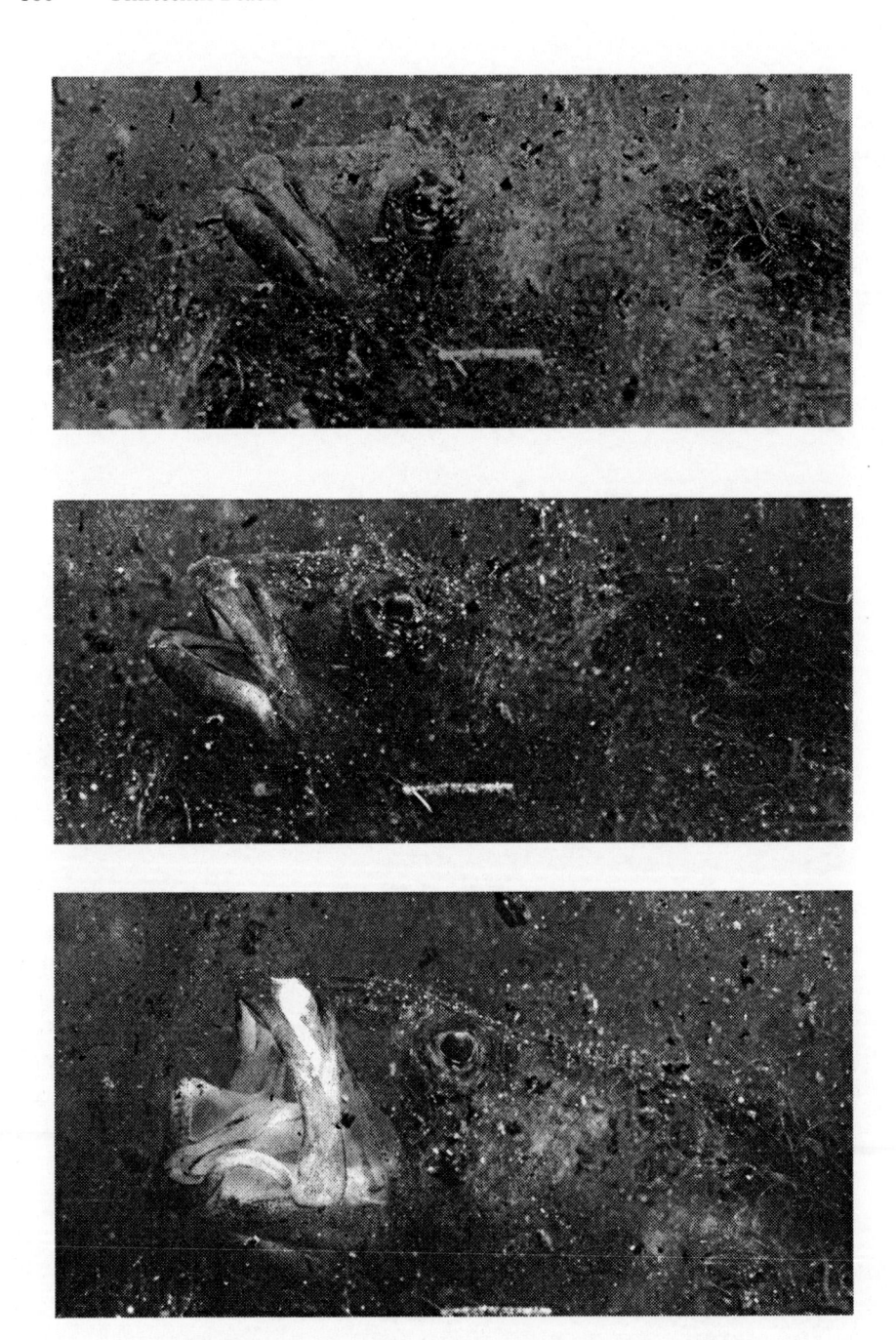

The fish that roared; Ewens Ponds, South Australia, 1989.

28

From Xarifa to the Danube

It never occurred to me in our early years that, while Hass' adventures might be reachable, he might also be. It took the passage of more than 30 years and then the death of Jacques Cousteau to stir the motivation to go out and find this man who had so significantly influenced the course of my life.

Hass was not easy to meet. From the time I was advised that he was still alive, it took six months to arrange the meeting. The easiest solution was to attend a symposium in California where he was a guest speaker, but I didn't want to meet him in a crowd and compete for the chance to speak with him.

Vienna was where he had lived and planned his Caribbean adventure. He had written about that city, and he still spent a lot of time there. It seemed to me that would be the most appropriate location to meet him; if he would agree to a private meeting in the first place. We could only get a commitment that "there is some chance he will be in Vienna" for a week in October 1998. We were requested to call his office during that week to confirm that he was there and had time to see us.

Robyn and I flew to Vienna on the strength of that noncommittal commitment. We strolled the banks of the Danube—gray-brown and never blue—listened to Mozart and Strauss performed in the same Vienna Konzerthaus that premiered much of their music, and sat enchanted by the Vienna Boy's Choir singing in 400-year-old St. Joseph's church—all the while wondering if we'd finally meet Hass.

We called him again on Wednesday morning, and he provided us with an address on Sonnenfredesgasser.

"Come at 11," he said. At ten to, we were standing in a worn, stone-stepped doorway off a narrow doglegged street close to St. Stephens Platz. The street ran like a dreary shaded canyon, a crack in the academic landscape, confined on both sides by the unbroken and stern 18th century facades of the four-story university buildings. Perhaps it was this dreariness that fuelled the search for enlightenment.

At precisely 11, I pushed the buzzer for his apartment. Hass answered immediately; his voice thin and reedy through the tiny speaker.

"Hello?"

"Professor Hass?"

"Yes?"

"Can we come up?"

"Yes."

In his postscript to *Diving to Adventure,* Hass wrote of his own feelings when he was granted an audience by William Beebe, the inventor and designer of the abyssal diving bathysphere: "With pounding heart I entered the laboratory, where I was immediately confronted with the great savant. I shook his hand ... I showed my pictures and had the great joy of seeing that they made a good impression ... and I believe my work could not have had any finer reward."

When Robyn and I stepped out of the elderly, creaking elevator in the University of Vienna and found 80-year-old Professor Hass waiting to greet us, my heart skipped a beat, too. When Hass shook my hand, my eyes briefly brimmed with the sheer pleasure of physical contact with him. It had been 40 years since he had last dived anywhere, but he hadn't lost his passion for the sea, the environment, and the human exploitation of it. Our visit had interrupted his preparation for a lecture he was giving in the university that night; his topic, "the politics of water."

He was highly amused when I showed him the title page of my now battered copy of *Diving to Adventure*; Robyn and I had carried it with us when we went to dive at Bonaire. We used it to retrace Hass' footsteps there and to lead us to some of the same reefs he'd swum. At the end of the trip, I'd asked the manager of Captain Don's Habitat to stamp the title page as he would do a diving logbook.

We chatted through the pages of the book with Hass; a unique experience for me to share history first-hand with the man who made it. Then he signed *Diving to Adventure* for me.

Rustling paper caught his attention as we neared the end of visit. Robyn was unwrapping a framed and signed triptych of my underwater black and white photographs. Like Hass with Beebe "I showed my pictures and had the great joy of seeing that they made a good impression ... and I believe my work could not have had any finer reward."

Ironically, although Hass really showed the way, ultimately it is Cousteau, the industrialist, who capitalized on the flood of human interest released in part by the international fame and acclaim that Hass earned with his courageous, educated inquisitiveness. Analysis is likely to show that it is Cousteau who has had the greater effect on human exploration of the sea. His innovation and invention, beginning with the revolutionary promotion of the automated aqualung, ensured that he was strategically anchored at the mouth of the channel through which military and industrial resources poured for the exploration and exploitation of the sea.

Hass, the naturalist, took a different path. Cousteau took command of the ocean-going research vessel, *Calypso*, crewed it with scientists and technologists, revved up his motors, and powered off to conquer inner space. Hass sailed with Lotte, his wife, and a small team of scientists in graceful *Xarifa*, looking for the meaning of life and trying to sustain that quest with his insightful, slightly quirky films and books. It was industry versus idyll; human development versus enlightenment.

Enlightenment is costly. After two global expeditions aboard *Xarifa*, Hass eventually gave up, docked his beloved vessel for the last time[1], and walked away from his life at sea into a new career exploring the realm of natural philosophy.

But on his first expedition to the Caribbean, the currents of inquisitiveness that would carry him around the globe were only just beginning to gather strength and momentum. In *Diving to Adventure,* he created, with humor and a highly personal style, a mirror of my own yearning.

Hass plainly showed that it was possible to reach this other world where encounters with the extraordinary became everyday occurrences. Meeting him, feeling the warm press of his hand in his study in Vienna, was further proof that he was right.

---

1. Forty years later, in 1998, Hass finally reboarded Xarifa in Monaco as a guest of its current owner, the CEO of a global beverage company.

2000s

29

Southwind over Erie

Ice-water lies like a blanket, spread in the dimness, across the bed of Lake Erie. At a depth of 42 meters, the temperature had fallen to just eight degrees Celsius. In the gloomy stillness, the unswung davits on the inverted hull of the *John J. Boland Jr.* confirmed the suddenness of the catastrophe that overtook this lake freighter and sent it to the bottom 68 years ago.

It was 10 in the morning. Overhead, unseen, the glorious blue sky of the northern summer arched above the lake. Warmed by the June sun, Jim Herbert's *Southwind* tugged impatiently on the mooring line as a northwesterly breeze gouged the surface. Sixteen kilometers off the port beam, low green hills marked the American shore and the *Southwind*'s home port, Barcelona Harbor.

This is a lake. Even though it is the second smallest of the Great Lakes, it is immense and has the feel of the sea. As we'd bullocked into the breeze on the way out, *Southwind* had dipped and rolled in the swell. Spray had erupted from the bow and spattered down over the deck. But it was sweet freshwater spray and left no taste of salt on our lips.

Now my lips were numb with cold. Murky blue-green water had closed over my head when I stepped off the *Southwind* to begin the descent. Visibility had been three or four meters; water temperature a comfortable 22 degrees Celsius.

Swaddled in the comfort of a seven-millimeter-thick wetsuit, I'd dropped slowly down the descent line to ten meters and settled there to check my gear—and deal with the apprehension nagging at the back of my mind. This was my first dive in the Great Lakes. Jim's final instruction as he slapped me on the shoulder and gave me the all clear to go had underlined one of the hazards faced by divers in very cold water.

"If your regulator freezes and goes into free flow, you get it turned off real quick and open up this spare Poseidon reg. You understand?", he'd said waving the spare regulator fitted to the manifold of the twin tank system he'd loaned me for this dive. "You understand", he repeated, locking his steady gaze with mine.

"Understood", I'd replied.

As the air compressed into a scuba tank is released into the first stage of the diver's regulator, it rapidly and dramatically chills. This causes no problem if the temperature of the surrounding water is significantly above the freezing point of zero degrees Celsius. Heat from the water warms the regulator and prevents any moisture in the air from forming ice crystals within it. If the temperature of the water approaches the freezing point, though, there might not be sufficient heat in the surrounding water to prevent ice formation. Exertion, resulting in heavy demand for air, increases the flow and therefore the risk of freezing. So does inhaling and simultaneously venting air from the scuba tank into the diver's buoyancy vest. Usually, if a regulator freezes, it will freeze in the open position and allow air to rush out of the tank continuously.

This is a double-pronged problem for the diver. At depth, a free-flowing regulator will quickly empty a scuba tank. And while the air is rushing out unchecked, it continues to cool and prevents any accumulated ice crystals from melting. A diver confronted with this dilemma must either begin surfacing immediately, snatching breaths from the continuously streaming regulator, or must close off the frozen regulator and switch to an alternate regulator system. Spare regulators, commonly carried to enable two divers to share the air in a single tank in an emergency, are of no use because they are attached to the same frozen first stage of the system. So, in extremely cold water, scuba tanks need to be equipped with two separate regulator systems.

Staring down the descent line toward the yet-invisible wreck of the *Boland*, I mentally rehearsed loosening my harness so that I could wriggle around to reach the tap on the valve of my tank to switch to the back up system if my regulator froze.

At 20 meters, most of the sunlight disappeared, absorbed by the cloudy water of the upper layers. At 25 meters, a sharp thermocline. Seven degrees centigrade. The biting cold immediately caused an ice-cream headache as my sinuses recoiled from the frigidity. Oddly, though, the visibility increased dramatically. Suddenly, the wreck of the *John Boland* lay plainly below me.

Visibility had extended out to about 30 meters. Clear cold water. Everything so still. No current. None of the familiar rhythm and crackling static of the open sea. No blue monochrome here, either. In its place, drab gray-brown. Zebra mussels are responsible for the startling clarity. Billions of these tiny bivalves are literally sieving particulates and pollutants from the Great Lakes. With bodies rich in fats, they're able to store high concentrations of heavy metals and other toxins.

Each mussel in the uncountable horde is capable of filtering up to a liter of water every day.

Unfortunately, though, they are also devastating the ecosystems of the lakes and other U.S. waterways. Introduced in foreign ballast water when the St. Lawrence Seaway created direct access to the lakes from the Atlantic and essentially connected the inland ports of the lakes with those of the Black Sea in Europe, zebra mussels have no natural predators in U.S. waters. They cover every underwater object in Lake Erie. Every square centimeter of the *Boland* seems to have been sprayed with rough, brown-textured coating. But zebra mussels are not the only illegal immigrants in the lakes. Around 130 foreign species have penetrated the lakes and rivers of the northeast U.S. Most of them have proliferated since 1959 when the St. Lawrence Seaway replaced the older system of canals and locks. Sea lampreys, carp, freshwater snails, and many others have torn gaping holes in the original food webs of the lakes and rivers and caused irreversible change to aquatic environments.

So it was a vastly different Lake Erie that overwhelmed and fatally embraced the *Boland* on that October night in 1932. Overloaded with a cargo of coal and under-prepared for the worsening conditions, the *Boland* was commanded by Captain Edward Hawman. He'd followed what was then common practice and, for the short voyage from the U.S port of Erie in Pennsylvania to Hamilton on the Canadian shore, he'd allowed the holds to be filled to overflowing and had not bothered to batten them down with covers over the open holds. The low, rolling American shore initially offered protection from the buffeting of the southwesterly gale. Hawman and his crew headed out into the night with that wind astern.

Sixteen kilometers out, they faced the terrifying reality of a Great Lakes' tempest and tried desperately to retrace their path back to the American shore. Broadside on to the steep, tumbling waves, the *Boland* was helpless. Smothered in raging water, caught with open holds, it quickly succumbed, suddenly capsized, and sank. Somehow, in the storm-tossed blackness, Hawman and 14 members of his crew managed to find and clamber aboard a wildly rearing and plunging lifeboat that had been torn free as the freighter went down. Four less-fortunate men went down with it. Unknown now, grieved then as lost sons, brothers, husbands, or fathers, freed of mortal care, they now rest somewhere in this chilled tomb. In the stillness of the deep, it is difficult to conjure the violence and dread that had preceded their demise. There is peace here.

In this peace and solitude, sadness settled over me as I gently bumped down onto the upturned hull near the rudder. Thoughts of my own father soaked into my consciousness. We'd shared our last conversation just a day before this dive. He'd been on his deathbed in Australia and, as he struggled to surface from the waves of delirium washing over him, he'd reached out to me with uncharacteristic honesty and humor.

In those too brief moments, connected only by the ethereal radiation carrying our voices back and forth between the hemispheres and the seasons, we enjoyed as close and amiable a conversation as I could remember. Contrary to his habitual denial that he was "on top of the world," he'd admitted that he was having "a bit of a rough time of it at the moment." An air of wry humor underpinned that confession; Monty Python's Black Knight claiming the loss of an arm to King Arthur's sword to be just "a flesh wound." He was in deep trouble. He knew it, and he knew that I did, too, but that didn't seem to be causing him distress. Perhaps he'd seen the end of his mortal life coming quickly and realized that the crossing held no demons for him. Perhaps he could see the blazing green eyes and auburn hair of my mother, dead just three weeks before, beckoning him through to the other side.

He inquired persistently about Robyn and her well-being and revealed his too-often muted love for her. He inquired about my plans for the weekend. When I'd explained the plans to dive on the *Boland*, he'd taken detailed interest.

That was unusual. In all the years I'd been diving, I think he had seen me enter or leave the water maybe twice. At first, perhaps in support of my mother's fears, he'd violently opposed my early attempts to dive. When the active opposition ended, defeated by my rebellious adolescent refusal to accept his prohibitions, it was replaced by passive disinterest; at least on the surface, although I know that he'd secretly taken my mulloway trophy tray to work to show his mates.

I told him what I knew about the wreck and the conditions I'd likely encounter. It's difficult to know how much he really understood, but he even inquired about the depth and whether or not the water would be clear. I promised to let him know.

"Enjoy it, lad", are the last comprehensible words that I can remember before my sister gently lifted the phone from his hand and allowed him to sleep. He died a few hours later.

For an hour after receiving the news of his death, Robyn and I considered canceling our trip to Lake Erie to make the trip home for the second funeral in a month as quickly as possible. But then I began to think that this would deny him his last wish and instruction for me, and we delayed our departure for Australia by one day; time enough to drive to Lake Erie from Pittsburgh, dive the *Boland,* and safely fly afterward.

He had shunned the sea as a young man after inexplicably losing his ability to swim, never willing to try a mask and snorkel, even when I'd towed Dorothy, my mother in her late sixties, face down, stiff as a plank but squealing with excitement, across a few shallow coral gardens on Western Australia's northwest shore. So I'm still mystified by his request after my mother's funeral that we hold her ashes until his own death, combine them with his own, and then commit them both to the sea.

Aboard *SS Strathnaver*, plowing with its cargo of hopeful migrants across the Indian Ocean toward Australia in 1959, my parents had often stood at the rail, gazing out across the blue wastes and gasping in European amazement as sheets of foam tossed aside by the ship seemed to magically transform into shoals of scattering flying fish. To my mother, a poet, they'd been "glittering cascades of diamonds" as they leaped in their thousands from the rumbling monster cleaving the surface of their world.

My parents were 45 years old, had two kids and eight dollars in their pocket when we left Wales bound for Australia. Perhaps, in their time at the rail, they could put the anxieties of their life aside and find solace in the simplicity and certainty of the open sea and sky. Perhaps, at the end, with all the decisions and trials of their lives behind them, they'd decided to go together to the place where they'd found solace. Perhaps this dive with me is a reconnaissance trip.

Whatever the reason, the ghost of my father, Thomas Charles Hughes, was at my shoulder as I pushed off from the hull and, together, we began a slow, measured swim down the port side.

Soft silt cushioned the crash of the *Boland* into the lakebed. Eighty meters long, it lies not quite completely upside down with its starboard side buried in the muck. The single stout propeller and the rudder, frozen at midships, stand out clearly. Aft cabins are reasonably intact. At the bow, so is the pilothouse from which Captain Hawman saw his ship's destiny etched in the flying spume.

Cold water becomes a preoccupation on a dive like this. Water conducts heat away from the human body about 28 times more quickly than does air. Soon, midway along the hull of the *Boland*, my hands were numb with cold, my fingers were completely without feeling, and I realize that they are probably going to be useless if I need to react to any equipment failure. I realized then that, if I was to dive here again, I was going to need more efficient gloves.

Even so, it was difficult to leave the surreal surroundings of this wreck. Every detail so clearly visible. So still. Silent. Drab. Cold. Intriguing. I wanted to hold on. But it was time to let go. To begin the ascent, and the journey home to Australia. My father was anxious for the final act in his 67-year, sometimes stormy, romance with my mother to unfold.

Up through the thermocline, where my hands felt as though they'd abruptly been plunged into hot water and the pain of returning blood circulation began. Through the cloudy water that the zebra mussels can't reach. And on up toward the surface, where the *Southwind* waited with Stars and Stripes flapping briskly beneath a glorious blue June sky.

Down deep, dim and cold. The wreck of the *John Boland Jr*. Lake Erie, USA, 2000

30

Xel-há

Mayan seafarers, charting the sun and stars of the Mexican skies and computing their way with their knowledge of mathematics as they pioneered Caribbean trade routes, first settled on the island of Cozumel sometime during the 5th century. The Mayan culture was probably close to its peak then.

Ruined by centuries of war with rival Toltec tribes, a succession of famines, and finally, the swords, guns, and germs of the invading Spanish conquistadors, the Mayans were exterminated by the end of the 16th century. Stargazing observatories, pyramids, temples, roads, and some dwellings, all crumbling on the shores and in the jungles of Cozumel and the Yucatan peninsula, mark their passing.

Pirates swarmed in the brain-baking heat here in the 17th and 18th centuries, marauding from their lawless bases first on the bloated treasure fleets of the Spaniards and later on the merchant shipping of the colonizing Dutch, Portuguese, English, and French.

And it was because of a Frenchman that Robyn and I stood on the beach, just south of San Miguel on Cozumel and stared out at an armada of modern-day invaders surging out to sea. Dive boats. Heading for Palancar Reef. We counted 30 boats in one loose squadron, each with about 20 divers aboard.

That famous Frenchman, Jacques Cousteau, and his aquanauts revealed Palancar Reef and its potential for diving to the world in the early 1960s. Palancar forms a section of the fabled Belizean Barrier Reef, second in length (although admittedly a very distant second) to Australia's Great Barrier Reef. It had been on my list of places to dive ever since I'd seen Cousteau's television shows and read some of those first articles in *Skin Diving* magazine. Cozumel was then only an isolated, underdeveloped source of chicle—the natural chewing gun derived from the sap of the chicozapote tree. As we chewed our bottom lips and watched the hordes of divers heading out to the reef, we began to think that we should have come here earlier.

A line of buoys marked the outer limit of our hotel snorkeling area at the southern limit of development outside San Miguel. Just a few meters farther south lay the entrance to Chankanaab National Park. Our first inquiry at the hotel dive center convinced us that there would be little chance of finding a local boat owner to take us out for some private diving; it would be the dive boats or swim out to the reef from the shore.

Robyn relaxed on the beach with a margarita, already knowing the answer. I duck-dived under the rope connecting the marker buoys and headed out in flat water with just a slight northerly current to test the feasibility of hiring tanks and swimming out to the drop-off. Robyn was right. It is a long way to Palancar from the beach; well over a kilometer across flat bottom with little of interest on the way.

Next morning, we were sweating in the sun on a dive boat with nine other divers ("maximum of six," the sign on the booking kiosk had said). A delightfully polite Mexican dive master held up the iridescent green quacker on the end of an airline attached to his tank's first stage regulator and said, "Remember please, I make noise like duck and you come quick and I show you what I find." He squeezed his quacker, a device we had never seen before, and it did indeed sound like Donald Duck.

"Now" ... *quack, quack* ... "stay close and we all have good time. ¿Any questions?"

Up to this point, I'd been fussing around, adjusting my new buoyancy compensator, a Rig Mark II. This is a fearsome piece of equipment—all black, which cleverly integrates elements of design borrowed from SWAT teams, meteorologists, and turtles. It has so many D-rings dangling from it for attaching pieces of equipment that you could be excused for thinking it was a chain-mail vest. But it's in the combination of Kevlar and hardened nylon body armor that the true character of the Rig can be found. The Rig is clearly a contraction of its full name; the Rigid!

Threatened with amputation by predator or propeller, the diver wearing the Rigid can simply retract all four limbs into this tough assemblage of plates, straps, buckles, and bulletproof fabric and be confident of survival. In the absence of any threat, it is possible to flap arms and legs in almost any direction. It's even possible to move the head a little from side to side.

If the diver discovers a sunken vessel capable of being salvaged, it would be a simple matter of attaching lifting lines to the D-rings and pressing the inflation valve. The Rigid is capable of inhaling half a tank of air in a single gulp, inflating its massive bladder and providing sufficient buoyancy to zoom the diver and booty upward like a radio-sonde attached to a weather balloon. I'd ordered it from a catalog without actually seeing it and must have overlooked the "*designed by Arnold Schwarzenegger" at the bottom of the page. It's a durable and effective accessory, but the Rigid does take some adjustment to get it to sit comfortably.

… quack, quack … "¿Any questions?"

"Er … yes, I do have a question."

"¿Si?"

"Your instruction to 'stay close' to you means 'at least be on the same side of the island as you', right?"

Robyn rebuked me for the unprovoked challenge with a sharp jab in the ribs, but the dive master just laughed jovially, let out a couple of happy *quack quacks*, and said, "Si! Let's go diving!" … *quack, quack*….

This was Santa Rosa Wall. It's not a clearly defined wall, though. A ragged line of deep bommies and gutters, rich with life, extend down to about 40 meters and create a highly complex and interesting section of the Palancar reef system southwest of Cozumel. It's the kind of place that you could dive in for weeks without exhausting the potential for interest and discovery. The dive plan, though, appeared to be a down-current sprint behind the dive master, following Indian-file through swim-throughs, and then, whenever Donald Duck bleated at us, lining up like customers at a monopoly hotdog stand to be served, one at a time, with a viewing of whatever the dive master had determined to be compulsory viewing. At one stage, he appeared to be wrestling with an octopus, although it might have been some other type of dive-master device. It was difficult to be certain through the thicket of human arms and legs surrounding him.

Robyn and I tried to ignore the persistent *quack quacking* and drifted down to about 30 meters toward a large burgundy-black basket sponge. Sheltering in the bowl of this sponge was the tiniest yellow triggerfish. As we peered down over the rim of the sponge, it lay slightly over to one side to keep us in sight, nervously flitted its gossamer-thin pectoral fins, and performed several anxious circuits. And then another presence joined us. Massive down-turned mouth. Beady eyes perched high up on its head, flicking up and down as it puzzled over what was going on. It was a stout black grouper, about a meter long, and it was hanging suspended at Robyn's shoulder, intensely interested in what we were up to.

It attached to us like a stray dog as we worked our way along the reef. Whenever we stopped to peer into a hole or under a ledge, it would gently bustle its way in to stare over our shoulders or under our arms.

I always have trouble reconciling the fact that we eat fish at times like this. I wouldn't call this type of encounter "communication between the species," but it certainly reveals richer detail of life form and character than can be gathered from more distant observation. We became quite attached to our well-mannered and curious sea stray.

Eventually, though, as we angled up through a gutter between bommies toward the sand flats that extend back from the drop-off toward shore, the grouper turned and drifted away into deeper water. We watched it go and ... *quack! quack! ... quack! quack!*

A few more dives like that and I'd seen enough of Palancar, at least from the deck of one of the many dive boats. They provide inexpensive and convenient access to the reef for people who prefer to dive in numbers and who thrill to the journey across a section of reef under the care of an experienced dive master.

Perhaps if those divers had been taught that safety in the water isn't dependent on numbers and that there's often more to be seen by staking out a few square meters of reef and staying put until the tankful of air is consumed than there is by swimming continuously along a predetermined path, there would be more divers willing to spend time alone in the water and more enlightened operators to help them do it.

Nevertheless, there's no doubt that this is a wonderful reef. Chankanaab National Park pulsed with schools of barracuda and jacks. Colorful corals and sponges created picturesque outposts for blue-striped grunts and orange squirrelfish.

Palancar Breaks was less exciting. Muted and subdued outcrops of coral, some blanching from disease and succumbing to a covering growth of algae, offered less habitat than the more dramatic sections of reef. Fish were scarce.

Wind and strong currents prevented any of the boats taking trips out to the Maracaibo Deep on the extreme southern tip of Cozumel from going. We couldn't find any independent boat owners who might take us out, drop us off over an uninhabited section of reef, and simply wait for us to surface. We skipped the last three dives that we'd already paid for and went off exploring the island on our own.

Beyond the mangroves and tidal lagoons of Punta Sur, the road crosses Cozumel and leads to the exposed southeast coast. Harsh, windblown, and undeveloped, this coast doesn't offer the calm water and protected conditions of the west coast. Although judging by the photographs at the Punta Sur ecological park, there would be some exciting, if short-lived, diving to be done with the alligators in the lagoons!

Entering the sea from the rocks on the east coast demands care. Sea urchins add their bristling spines to almost every crack and crevice in the rough-razor coral rocks. Short, sharp dumping waves rear up, collapse, and then drag themselves back across the rocks to join the next incoming swell. Once an entry point has been found, timing becomes everything. Pick the peak of the incoming wave, pitch forward into it, kick strongly to gain some forward momentum, and be in deep enough water to avoid being keelhauled on the rocks as the supporting water suddenly dips and gathers to form the next wave.

It was worth at least a snorkel swim here, though. Swell-swept reefs have the same bleak beauty of weather-lashed heaths and moors. No luxuriant gardens of coral or waving sea fans here. Bare rock. Stubby tufts of isolated coral. Poorer visibility. Probably no more than 15 or 20 meters. Wrasse and small surgeonfish hugging the protection of holes and cracks. Close under the choppy surface, a few needlefish.

Anything that isn't cemented into the bare rock plain, braced within the fissures that crosshatch it, or capable of moving into shelter simply isn't here. It's piled up in the heap of rocks and debris on the shore. Life in the sea is hard and brutal wherever it is, but on the face of seaward-facing reefs like this, the disguise of color and abundance is stripped away. This is truly an evocative environment.

After half an hour swimming in the lumpy water beyond the surf, it took me another 20 minutes to find a way back in to dry land without being shishkebabed on sea urchin spines. And then another five to unsuccessfully chase a young thief whom Robyn spied attempting to pilfer our calypso-colored rental Volkswagen as she left it to meet me on the beach. He disappeared empty-handed into the bush, probably an inhabitant of one of the sea-wrack shanties stranded here beyond the tide of opportunity and employment that washes the west coast. Or perhaps he just found it easier to steal than to work. This was the only unpalatable experience we had with the people of Cozumel. It is indeed a friendly and hospitable place.

Next day, we booked a ferry ticket from San Miguel across to Playa Carmen. Tulum, the only walled Mayan city and perched on the coast of the mainland Yucatan, looked like an interesting place to visit. "Take snorkel gear for Xel-há," the ticket agent had firmly advised. We'd seen Xel-há advertised. It looked like a theme park.

"No, no," protested the agent, "world's largest natural aquarium. Must see."

Tulum spells out the grandeur of the Mayan civilization more eloquently than even the pyramids and ball courts at Chichen Itza in the central Yucatan. Dull white, sagging with age, but essentially intact, Tulum slowly crumbles like a bleached skeleton atop the low cliff overlooking the blue Caribbean.

Juan Dîaz and Juan de Grijalva, forward scouts for the waves of Spanish conquistadors who would follow, became the first Europeans to describe Tulum when, in 1518, they "sighted a city or town so large that Seville would not have appeared bigger or better … a very tall tower was to be seen there …"

Tulum was known as "Zamal" to the Maya. "Morning." It was here that their Yucatan Empire first welcomed the rays of the rising sun. Geometric patterns and intimate knowledge of the movement of sun and stars dictated the layout of the city and the placement of its key buildings. Mayan architects had a strong sense of design, and all the major buildings show pleasing and symmetrical lines. Even today, preserved from the peeling sun in deep alcoves and recesses, traces of the bright colors that adorned the buildings can be seen; blues, orange, reds, black, and white.

Zamal's distinctive tower was a beacon for Mayan merchant seamen. It was the trade generated from their romantic cargoes of honey, tobacco, spices, latex, the long, green tail feathers of the male quetzal bird, jaguar skins, pearls, maize, jade, obsidian, and cotton that underpinned the Maya culture.

Europeans changed all that. By the time pirates such as murderous Welsh buccaneer Henry Morgan and Frenchman Jean Lafitte had established hiding places here in the late 17th and early 18th centuries, Zamal had become Tulum, and Tulum was beginning to fade into a splendid ruin of coral rock.

"What about Xel-há?" Robyn asked.

We looked again at the gaudy brochure that the earnest ticket agent had pressed into our hand. It looked like a cross between Disneyland and Waterworld, but we were so close and we'd brought snorkel gear with us so … what the hell.

Xel-há is a graphic illustration of what the world would be like without spectator sports such as football, tennis, cricket, baseball, and basketball to distract the masses who might otherwise find their way out onto the reefs. At Xel-há, the masses have found the reef.

There were thousands of people. By comparison, the dive boats of Palancar were lonely outposts of isolated humanity. People were crowded around the entrance to the park like the millions of emperor penguins waiting out the winter on Heard Island. And we were there, too! Lined up like the rest of them, putting forward our money to buy a ticket to swim in the world's largest natural aquarium" with the world's largest crowd of swimming people. Robyn looked at the expression on my face as I gaped at this astonishing multitude glossed with suntan lotion and spangled with every known hue of fluorescent beachwear and swimming accessories. She burst out laughing. I made her promise not to tell anyone we'd done this.

Xel-há is a surprise, though, and a credit to the people who created the management plan for this wonderful natural asset. For a start, the entrance fee, about $20, covers everything—well, everything except a swim with the captured dolphins in an adjacent pool complex; that's extra. Bars and restaurants, well-serviced, friendly relaxed establishments, serve as much drink and food as you can consume; all covered by the entrance fee. Want an inner tube or snorkel gear to float down the river to the sea? Showers, towels, security lockers? Just help yourself. It is neither necessary, nor in our experience, possible to even offer the restaurant waiters a tip.

Mexican legend credits Mayan gods with the creation of Xel-há. It was their masterpiece in beauty, and they named it "Xel-há, the place where the waters converge." Those waters begin as a narrow spring, welling up from limestone aquifers beneath the lowland tropical forest. The spring becomes a river and flows out of the forest into what was, in millennia past, a passage between the ramparts of a coral reef. Now the walls of the reef form the cliffs of Xel-há and channel the river down to the sea.

After several piña coladas to fortify ourselves, we joined the chattering torrent of holidaymakers as it wound its way to the spring. Under the natural constriction of the encroaching forest, we were forced into single file as we approached the jump-off point for our journey of discovery. A small wooden deck allows access to the crystal water. After the searing heat of the afternoon, the chilly water took our breath away.

Trees and roots and branches and leaves pressed in on all sides at first but quickly gave way to a wider waterway. Robyn led the way off to the side of the channel and—here was another surprise—we soon found ourselves alone. Most of the people were swimming, floating, or splashing their way down the middle of the river, 20 or 30 meters away.

Wide fractures have dug deeply into the cliff face. In places, massive chunks of rock have slipped away from the face and tilt down into the water. The result is a labyrinth of blue and shaded grottoes in, under, and around the weathering rock. They are crowded with fish. Even more interestingly, in the upper reaches of Xel-há, the fresh water pouring down from the spring floats on top of the denser seawater washing in from the Caribbean. Freshwater fish swim contentedly above their saltwater cousins, separated by nothing but a nearly invisible boundary of dissolved salts. Nearly invisible because the differing densities of the two bodies of water diffract light differently. Where they swirl together, they bend and distort light so that, at times, the fish beneath us appeared as though were swimming through a hall of county fair trick mirrors; sometimes fat and short, sometimes stretched and skinny. Or maybe it was the effects of the piña coladas.

We spent hours here, easing ourselves into the shadows between house-sized blocks of rock, waiting for our eyes to adjust to the gloom, and then getting up close and personal with all kinds of curious fish as they went about their business in the crevices and swim-throughs—hidden from the thousands of people making their own happy way down the river.

As we drifted down into the slightly murky waters near the end of the channel, a loggerhead turtle, nearly a meter long, surfaced alongside us, exhaled a bubble of air, eyed us curiously, snatched a breath, then flipped over into a dive and accelerated away toward the sea with a few strong flipper strokes.

Xel-há is a haven for turtles. This is one of the few places on the Yucatan Peninsula where they can come ashore in safety to lay their eggs in the sand. The eggs don't stay there, though. Xel-há staff quickly dig them up and rebury them in a guarded turtle hatchery. When the eggs hatch, the tiny turtles are held until night falls and then released into the sea, safe from at least the daytime predation of gulls and crabs. Even so, only one in a thousand will survive to play their role in reproduction of the species.

When we turned from watching the turtle, we were confronted by a group of six large silvery jacks. Strong, sleek, hunting in a pack and apparently oblivious to the increasingly dense human traffic, they swam slowly around us several times, big baleful eyes watching closely for any sign that we were disintegrating into something they could eat.

Xel-há shows that wildness is not easily completely lost in the sea. There are other examples, of course. Trunk Bay, on St, John in the U.S Virgin Islands, is one of the most beautiful beaches in the Caribbean and therefore one of the most heavily trafficked by people. Turn up there when a cruise ship is in St. John, and it would be possible to walk many meters out into the water on the bobbing backs of snorkeling tourists, sink-proofed with floaties and inflated lifejackets, all intent on experiencing the Trunk Bay snorkel trail.

Yet, swim out around to the point of rock that juts out from the beach, and there's a wave-tossed point that dissuades inexperienced divers from visiting. Shoals of silver baitfish hang among the bubbles and foam close to the rocks. Barracuda, jacks, and needlefish streak in from the blue to feed on the shoals, which pulse and flash as they dodge in desperate attempts to avoid oblivion in the jaws of the predators. The fact that several hundred people might be just around the corner has no effect on this life and death drama. Farther out in slightly deeper water, sea fans festoon the ledges facing the open water, and reef- and bottom-dwelling fish abound. We dived here alone, untroubled by anyone else.

It's a similar situation at Black Rock Point on Maui in Hawaii. Two arms of black lava jut out into the Pacific here, like the extended claws of a crab. On the point, the waves surge over the rocks, and there are many more fish here than anywhere else along this stretch of coast. The reason is that Black Rock Point is actually in the grounds of a Sheraton Hotel. Spearfishing is prohibited, so the fish have no fear, and most of the hotel guests don't swim far off the beach. Some of the hotel staff did cast sidelong glances, though, as my old friend Mel Johnson and I squelched back through the lobby carrying our gear after spending an hour in the water off the point.

"Just walk through as though we're guests here and they'll never know," was Mel's advice.

No such need at Xel-há; everyone was squelching around carrying their gear. It's an impressive place, though. Both the Maya and our ticket agent were right. When time is short and wilderness is not available, Xel-há—the place where the waters converge—is where we can converge with the natural world to which we all belong. I'd go there again.

Speed machine: A young barracuda cruising along Palancar Reef, Cozumel, Mexico, 2000.

31

Wolf in the Sun

Drifting along with Robyn, submerged in a cold-green Galapagos current with graceful but brutish hammerhead sharks ghosting in and out of the foggy visibility, dismissed the boredom often associated with an idle decompression stop.

The Galapagos Islands lie a thousand kilometers off the Pacific coast of Ecuador. Charles Darwin was here, aboard the research vessel *Beagle,* in 1835. He came looking for knowledge and insight, and the animal life he observed on the Galapagos helped form his understanding of natural selection and the consequential evolution of species.

Pirates, sealers, and whalers came, too. They came to plunder the wildlife for food and profit. Despite their merciless assaults, these stupendous shards of volcanic rock today still offer breathtaking engagement, on land and in the sea, with natural abundance. Remote and fabled, expensive to reach, they had remained an elusive destination—a "one day we'll dive the Galapagos" type destination.

As often happens if a goal is held and nurtured for sufficient time, circumstances seem to fall into place. Now, a world away from the site of my first dive in Australia in 1960, I was floating five meters below the surface of the heaving Pacific, acutely aware of my isolation and thrilling in it.

All night, our dive boat had pitched and rolled northwest across the Pacific accompanied by ghostly white, swallow-tailed gulls feeding handsomely on squid and fish startled into revealing movement by our throbbing, phosphorescent passage. Descendants of the northern sabine gulls, the swallow-tailed gulls have probably turned to hunting at night to avoid the major difficulties confronting life as a gull in the tropics; blistering heat and the merciless airborne piracy of frigate birds.

In the cooler air, hidden from sight, constantly, hauntingly crying out to stay in touch with their invisible mates, they're free to hunt the small fish and squid that rise closer to the surface at night. By the time the black frigate birds rise into the morning sky on their skull and crossbones mission, the swallow-tailed gulls are dozing contentedly on the lava rocks with full stomachs.

At dawn, the 200-meter sheer cliffs of Wolf Island appeared on the horizon and caught the first rays of the rising sun. No other land was visible. An hour later, we could see the faint bulk of Darwin Island lying beyond Wolf, at the extreme northwest boundary of the Galapagos archipelago.

Overhead, thousands of blue-footed boobies, pelicans, and red-throated frigate birds soared and searched for the schools of fish that would become their first meal of the day. Suddenly, like flights of arrows from medieval archers, hosts of boobies and pelicans would fold back their wings and plummet in their hundreds into a patch of sea.

Frantically leaping fish would attract more birds, and the sea would boil and froth as they dived, snapped up fish, and flapped their way into the air again. Every successful boobie had to defend its catch from the marauding frigate birds. Rising boobies were attacked relentlessly, grabbed by the legs or tail by the frigates until, in panic, some of the boobies ejected the fish they'd just caught. The frigates snapped up falling fish before they hit the water, and the boobies were freed to fish for their uninvited guests again.

Closer to the island, fish were under attack from hair seals and sea lions. One large bull sea lion surfaced from the deep blue close to the boat, with a fat flapping snapper clamped in his jaws. Crunched into submission by stubby, dirty-yellow teeth, the hapless fish gasped silently and died. Unable to swallow his meal whole, the sea lion bit deeply and shook the snapper in the same way that his distant relatives, the dog and the bear, shake prey to kill and dismember it.

Bright red flesh appeared as the sea lion thrashed a chunk of the snapper free and the bulky carcass skipped a meter across the surface. Frigates swooped immediately, but the snapper was too heavy for them to carry off. The sea lion ignored their frantic and raucous attack, swam in to reclaim his meal, and flayed off another bite-size piece of fish.

Thousands of dolphins sped past and around the boat. Off in the distance, hunting or playing, perhaps being hunted themselves—it was impossible to tell—dozens of dolphins were leaping well clear of the water, flexing and falling back to the surface with an exuberant splash. An eagle ray launched three times into the air. We were entranced—not surprisingly. These are, after all, Los Encantadas—the enchanted islands of history.

Herman Melville, author of the whaling classic *Moby Dick*, wasn't enchanted by them, though. Coming here as he did aboard a whaling ship, laboring under a shriveling sun to cut down the flesh and blubber of slaughtered whales, and living day and night with the hot smoky stench issuing from the fiery furnaces of the blubber pots, he can be forgiven for describing the islands as "five and twenty heaps of cinder dumped here and there in an outside city lot."

Volcanic cones and lava flows shaped Melville's opinion. Lava—bubbling molten rock gushing from a fissure in the Earth's crust 3,000 meters down on the Pacific seabed—gave rise to these islands and continues to build them. Baked by Equatorial sun and dampened by only light rain, most of the islands do resemble piles of cinders. Lush cloud forest occurs up on the peaks of some islands that penetrate the cloud base at about 300 meters.

On his way home across the blue Pacific, soothed by the balmy trade winds and the thought of the money he would take from his share of the rendered whale oil barreled in the hold, Melville must have realized that "five and twenty heaps of cinders" wasn't going to work as a title for a short story he'd written about the Galapagos. He reconsidered his opinion, and the short story was titled "The Enchanted Isles" after all.

Jaimie, our skipper in the Galapagos, saw the islands in the same light. He was a gentleman in every sense of the word. A quite veteran of the Ecuadorian Navy he was careful at sea and considerate of all his passengers and crew. One morning, he'd interrupted me as I stripped off and prepared to pull on my wetsuit; he'd noticed a sweat-rash under one of my arms and came, un-requested, to offer some balm that would ease the itchiness. He made us welcome in small groups on his bridge while he navigated us between the islands, and most evenings after dinner he could be found in the dining salon, reference books and charts spread open on one of the tables, enriching our experience of the Galapagos with science and anecdote.

They came out from Baltra to get him one morning; a crew from the dive charter company in a high speed inflatable. Jaimie's teenage daughter had been abducted, raped, and murdered in Guayaquil. We all stood on the rear deck, in that peculiar silence that presses down on people in unspeakable shock, as he emerged from the salon, embraced two or three of us who had struck up particularly close relationships, and stepped without a word into the waiting Zodiac. The replacement skipper, equally distressed, quickly introduced himself, then disappeared into the privacy of the bridge to get us underway for the day. The muted atmosphere on board persisted till the end of the voyage.

Galapagos offers insight into the natural abundance of our planet. Staggering amounts of fish congregate here. So does a bewildering diversity of wildlife.

Nowhere else on Earth is it possible to swim with tropical fish, fur seals, whale sharks, and penguins, all on one dive.

Powerhouse for all this life, is the nutrient-rich Humboldt Current, pouring up from the deep south and reaching all the way to the Equator. Feeding time appears to be any time. Dolphins, hammerhead sharks, tuna, sea lions, and, of course, the boobies, pelicans, and gulls are constantly attacking the dense schools of smaller fish that seemed to fill the water around us in every direction.

Only once before, out in the Coral Sea, had I seen sharks chasing live food in daylight. Here at Darwin Island in the extreme northwest of the Galapagos archipelago, it was common to see three- and four-meter-long hammerhead sharks hunt and catch large fish. Only a few scales flashing like scattered sequins and the open-gaped convulsive swallowing of the sharks gave evidence that a life-and-death drama had been played out right in front of us.

With one meal safely swallowed, the sharks would resume their lazy vigil, expending only just enough energy to maintain station against the current. When another tempting fish swam close enough, we'd be treated to another rush of blinding acceleration—and another small cloud of glittering scales.

Galapagos sharks schooled among the rocks. Sleek members of the same family as bull sharks and whalers, they showed neither timidity nor aggression. At the end of one drift dive along a cliff face on Darwin Island, as we angled our way slowly toward the surface, Robyn and I found ourselves accelerating in the current as it whipped around a buttress of rock and veered away from the island.

As we adjusted our buoyancy to hang at five meters, we encountered a large school of Galapagos sharks. Heading in the opposite direction, swimming casually into the strong current as though it didn't exist, they came along head on to us and, with barely a flicker of curiosity, passed around, below, and between us in what seemed to be an endless bustling procession.

Each shark, up to three meters long, seemed intent on only one thing; following the sharks in front of it. Only our streams of bubbles seemed to have any noticeable effect on them. No shark seemed willing to pass overhead. On the surface, I looked down as Robyn clambered aboard the inflatable tender that was infallibly loitering right where we needed it. The school of sharks was still pouring in toward the island. A mesmerizing torrent of large, lithe fish.

Later, close in, near the striking arch that stands off Darwin Island, just one shark mesmerized us. Solitary. Huge. A whale shark. Languidly swimming at 20 meters, mouth agape, sucking in tons of microscopic plankton. The world's largest fish, dependent for food on the sea's smallest creatures.

We swam hard to reach this fish; and even harder to match its speed. After six minutes, the shrill beeping of my computer caused me to check my gauges. Four minutes of air left at the present rate of consumption. I slowed and watched my first whale shark disappear into the void on its ceaseless patrol, propelled by a three-meter-high tail sweeping slowly through a 10-meter arc.

Evolution has generally not favored giants; their sheer size makes them inefficient converters of food into energy. Massive dinosaurs no longer clomp clumsily through our forests and swamps, in part because they could not compete with the evolving mammals that could do more with less. Modern elephants, whales, and whale sharks are exceptions. They're still with us, although, in this constantly changing environment that we know as planet Earth, there's no guarantee that any species, including our own, can adapt quickly enough to cope and compete forever.

While we have them and while we're here to share the Earth with them, giants are uniquely able to offer us a different perspective on ourselves. We can be awed by the sprawling beauty of a landscape and marvel at the towering machines and buildings spawned by our intelligence and industry.

But to swim alongside and to be dwarfed by a free, giant living fish in its own wild environment and to be humbled by the simple majesty of it … that puts human achievement and hubris under a totally different light. The isolation, the very wildness of the Galapagos as a backdrop for such encounters, heightens the experience.

Safety, both on board and in the water, was the highest priority for our entire crew. The pre-dive briefings were thorough. As we left the mother ship and boarded the inflatables for the run to the dive spots, the skipper, deckhands, and inflatable pilots fussed over us, checked our gear, and generally watched over our well-being. While we were in the water, the inflatable pilots ceaselessly patrolled the area, drifting with the current, watching our bubbles, and pouncing forward to retrieve us as soon as we broke surface. The divers were never left in any doubt that they'd be seen within a very short time of breaking the surface, even when some divers were swept farther than expected. On one occasion, Robyn and I chose to allow the current to carry us over the shoulder of a reef and around a blunt headland rather than attempt to surface through thick, billowing foam in rough water at the base of the cliffs.

When we did surface in quieter water beneath the towering cliff and hosts of screaming seabirds, we were out of sight of the mother ship and the small fleet of inflatables. The current was bearing us farther away by the moment. Beneath our feet, groups of the ever-present Galapagos sharks cruised on their way up current.

There was no other sign of human presence anywhere to be seen. We could have been the only people on the planet.

I began scrutinizing the rocks at the base of the cliff ahead of us, looking for some place that we could safely lodge ourselves to wait for the inflatables that we knew would surely come looking for us when all the other divers had surfaced and been accounted for.

Within minutes, though, one of the inflatable pilots had zoomed away from the main dive area so that he could scan the water behind the headland; obviously Robyn and I were not the first divers to take this route. With a reassuring wave of his arm, the pilot showed that he'd seen us and motored the few hundred meters over to us. Such attentiveness is well placed. Galapagos is wilderness diving and we almost lost one of the group as a result of that.

On the surface, with plenty of air in her tank, she almost drowned because, instead of calmly inflating her buoyancy vest, breathing from her tank or through her snorkel, bobbing around safely in the choppy water, and waving to the inflatables, she discarded her facemask and spat out her regulator. Now, to get air, she was dependent on keeping her head above surface. Increasingly anxious and gasping for breath, she inhaled or swallowed water every time a wavelet tumbled over her head.

On the second occasion this happened, as quick as the inflatable pilot was to get to her, he was almost too late. By the time he hauled her over the side of the dinghy, her face was waxen, her eyes were fixed in a wide-open stare, and each shallow, convulsive breath gurgled and rattled dreadfully through her chest. Fortunately, she was resuscitated on the mother ship, where she revealed that she was always apprehensive and often suffered panic attacks in rough water.

Later, her husband etched his own name into the legends of the Galapagos when he managed to allow himself to be plucked out of the sea by a passing wave and deposited three meters up on the side of a small pinnacle of volcanic rock. He was scuba diving at the time, apparently finning along quite happily below the surface when the wave struck. His air tank lodged in a crevice. As the wave drained away, it left him facing out to sea, hanging in his buoyancy vest harness, with arms and legs waving and pedaling like a beetle stranded on its back.

Our Ecuadorian skipper was incredulous. "I never see anything like this. No one ever tried to climb that rock before," he said as he dispatched two crewmen to attempt to land on the rock from one of the inflatables. "At least he can't drown where he is," he chuckled, after intently studying the comical scene through binoculars and convincing himself that his passenger was in no immediate danger. It took the crewmen 20 minutes to free him.

When he returned to the boat, he scrambled up on deck and, with a straight face, seriously announced, "It's just as well I kept my wits about me ... that could have been dangerous," and disappeared below for a shower.

But floating alone with my thoughts and watching Robyn—capable, confident, and calmly eyeing the passing parade of hammerheads—I was struck with the memory of her attempts to swim with her knees tucked up under her chin when she'd seen her first shark in the Maldives. A wave of nostalgia swept through me as I thought of that and all the other places we've dived together. It led to the inescapable conclusion: if this for some reason had to be my last dive, if the adventure were to end here and I had to get out of the water to let someone else in, I would be satisfied.

Darwin Arch, evolving into Darwin's Pillars. And in the green waters beneath it ...

... Steve Sutton swims hard to keep up with the cruising whale shark. Galapagos, 2001

32

From the Irish Shore

One solitary pale gray cod hung suspended in cold apple-green water. It could live for 20 years or more and reach around 90 kilograms in weight, if it escapes the hooks and lines of countless recreational anglers, and the trawl nets of the commercial Atlantic fishing fleets, that, since 1988, have landed more than seven million tons of its kind onto the dinner plates of Europe. That seems to be a forlorn possibility, though.

Cod is arguably the world's most famous fish. It supported and nourished early transatlantic voyagers, including St. Brendan, the adventurous Irish monk in his leather boat, and the Vikings as they probed west and discovered the New World. It formed the economic and nutritional backbone of the American colonies.

Cod fueled the infamous circular slave trade between the North American colonies, Europe, the Caribbean, and West Africa. West African slaves, caught and sold to work in the Caribbean cane fields, produced molasses; molasses was sold to the American distilleries to produce rum; rum was sold in America and Europe for cash; and cash funded highly profitable expeditions to West Africa to extend and replenish the population of Caribbean slaves. Slaves required food, of course, and cod was everywhere to be caught and sold to satisfy their hunger.

Fresh, grilled, dried, fried, salted, and boiled, it has provided the bulk of fish protein for people rimming the Atlantic for more than a thousand years. In that time, it has been hunted from almost unimaginable abundance to the point of commercial and possibly biological extinction.

This one, half-a-meter long and possibly two years old, was the first one I'd seen alive. Knowing that its forebears schooled in their millions made me wonder whether fish experience feelings akin to human loneliness. It's unlikely that a solitary cod would make many new friends outside its own species because they have enviable appetites. They'll eat anything—including smaller cod.

I studied this one long enough to memorize its melancholy features, released my hold on the stubby tuft of algae that was anchoring me, and allowed the surge to wash me over the shelving rock bottom toward the entrance to the sea cave. Visibility was three or four meters. Water temperature was about 16 degrees Celsius. Twenty meters overhead, Atlantic swells heaved up against the black slate cliffs of Oilean an Iasc on the Iveragh Peninsula of Ireland's west coast.

Here, where the Atlantic has drowned the ancient valleys of western Ireland, the relatively warm waters of the Gulf Stream support more prolific marine life than anywhere else in Europe.

In the deep gloom of the sea cave—a wide slot notching well back into the sheer cliff face—the pounding swell rumbled like distant thunder. Occasionally, as our skipper, Martin Moriarty, maneuvered the unanchored *Lochin* away from the cliff face, the cave reverberated with the clattering of the revving diesel engine. Higher up in the slot, well above our heads, two roughly triangular holes penetrated the solid rock and created skylights glowing weakly with dim green light. Urchins, sea stars, crabs, and lobsters crowded together, seeking protection in the jumble of rocks strewn across the cave floor. We could have filled a bag with lobster and crab ... but there was only the one cod.

Somewhere behind me, Steve was making his way across the bottom toward the cave. Steve is a paraplegic. He journeys to his dive sites in a wheelchair. Aided by close friends in whom he places absolute trust, Steve had struggled into his dry suit, buoyancy compensator and air tank, pulled his mask down over his face, and flopped fearlessly off the *Lochin* into the open sea. Two divers went down with him; each one holding a hand and providing the mobility that Steve's legs could not. When he'd exhausted his air supply, he and his companions surfaced in the foaming water close to the cliff. We watched as Steve, floating helplessly but patiently and calmly, waited until he'd been towed into clear water where the *Lochin* could safely move in to pick him up. He's been diving like that for 15 years.

This, our first venture into the Atlantic, had been an interesting experience. We'd been moved by the same waves that tossed spume into the faces of the Vikings as they'd marauded their way down the bleak Irish coast and been introduced to a famous fish and a courageous, inspiring human being and his admirable group of friends. It doesn't get much better than that.

With Robyn safe and warm in the cabin, I zipped up the neck of my spray jacket, walked up to the bow, and stood leaning on the rail as Martin Moriarty spun the wheel, eased the throttles forward, and sent the *Lochin* punching its way back through rising swell and spattering rain toward its harbor on the misty shore of Valentia Island.

33

Iceberg in A Glass

It suddenly dawned on me that what had seemed a romantically exciting idea after a couple of glasses of red wine, one Friday night in our living room at home in the U.S., no longer seemed so romantic.

Gretar had the outboard engine racing. The five-meter-long inflatable Zodiac was skipping and pounding up and down pea-soup green, lumpy swells, scattering puffins and guillemots in frantic flapping panic ahead of it. I was lying, bouncing up and down astride the bucking gunwale, swaddled in a dry suit.

We were close to Surtsey at the southwest extremity of Iceland's Vestmannaeyjar, zooming to get ahead of what we thought were two orcas—killer whales. Iceland, and particularly the cluster of spectacular volcanic islands off the south coast that make up Vestmannaeyjar, is one of the best places in the world to see orcas. They feed predominantly on schools of herring and capelin and, so far, no one has tried to regulate access to them; if you want to do it, you can jump right in with them.

We'd had brief glimpses of black fins breaching the surface amid the jumble of wave tops, and Gretar had accelerated toward a point that he hoped would put us in their path. but well ahead of them so that the Zodiac wouldn't scare them away.

Once I'd kitted up—difficult enough in the constriction of a crushed neoprene dry suit in an erratically frolicking Zodiac—but before it was time to go over the side, I had some opportunity to reflect on Gretar's plan. "So, let me get this straight," I muttered to myself as my gaze vacantly settled on the laminated red rubber of the inflated gunwale centimeters in front of my face. "We're in the far reaches of the central North Atlantic, I'm going to get out of the boat, alone, into the path of what we think are two killer whales, neither of which is Free Willy, and then Gretar is going to 'take the boat away so it doesn't scare *them!*.' This is a good idea?"

Iceland had been on the list of places to dive for some time, but it wasn't the kind of diving destination that appealed to Robyn. Too cold; too rugged. So, while she headed home to spend time with her mother in Australia, I'd trawled the Internet looking for an Icelandic dive guide. Gretar Gretarson was the only one who responded to my e-mail, perhaps because I'd begun it with, "Please don't respond to this request unless you're willing to let me dive alone." We'd agreed to meet in July for what Gretar describes on his website as "an excellent tour for people who are open-minded and like exploring caves, snorkeling in different parts of Iceland, and more. On this tour, you will do many crazy things, leaving you totally exhausted at the end of each day." Gretar didn't realize this, but the craziness and exhaustion actually started in the Dormont pool in Pittsburgh several weeks before I left for Iceland. That's where I took my first dive in a dry suit.

There are several different types of dry suits. Knowing that Icelandic water would be cold, I bought the thickest and warmest I could find—a four-millimeter-thick crushed neoprene "Antarctica" suit made in Sweden. It's a one-piece suit with built in bootees. Entry is made through a wide zippered slash across the shoulders, and then the top third of the suit pulls down over the head. To provide warmth under this blizzard-proof outer shell, I bought a grade-four thermal insulation undergarment. Imagine a billowing and quilted burgundy-colored sleeping bag without a hood, but fitted with arms and legs, and thick enough for camping out on the summit of Everest without a tent, and you'll get some idea of what this looks like.

In addition to the undergarments, dry suits are designed to be inflated with gas—usually air—to provide further insulation and to prevent the sealed suit from collapsing into creases that pinch skin and muscle painfully as the outside water pressure increases during descent. Air conducts heat away from the human body at only about $1/28^{th}$ the rate of water, so in cold water dry suits are far more efficient protection against the cold. That's against the cold. Unfortunately, at the open-air Dormont pool, it wasn't cold. By late morning, the temperature had risen to close to 40 degrees Celsius and, as is usual in green, densely treed Pittsburgh in high summer, the atmosphere was blued and sodden with tropical humidity.

There's another characteristic of dry suits that makes them unsuitable for casual wear on a hot, humid day. They're called dry suits, of course, because they're designed to keep water out. This is accomplished through the use of those cleverly designed waterproof zippers, and what dry suit manufacturers call "seals." Doctors call them tourniquets. Impossibly tight tubes of silicon rubber, the seals squeeze around the diver's neck and wrists and prevent any liquid—water or blood—from passing in any direction. Dragging the neck-seal into place over your head also drags downward any facial feature that isn't composed of solid bone. So there I was, tottering about, arms forced out straight by the unyielding thick suit, lower eyelids pulled down like a bloodhound's, bottom lip trapped under my chin between the neck seal and my Adam's apple, terrifying all the kids and most of their parents, trying to ask the pool attendant to close the rear zipper.

It was a struggle, but I eventually managed to get suited up, heave my tank onto my back, and go into the water up to my waist. This was a surprise, because I'd stepped off the edge into three meters of water in the deep end of the pool. Crushed neoprene dry suits, unlike their tri-laminate counterparts, are extremely buoyant. Add a whiff of air to inflate them, and they can support tremendous weight before they will sink. Twenty-two kilograms of lead were required to stop me from bobbing about like a big empty bottle and let me gradually submerge to the bottom of the pool—and that was in fresh water. Seawater is much more buoyant.

After an hour, I'd become semi-used to the peculiar feeling of suit squeeze around my legs, adjusting buoyancy and easing the squeeze by letting air into and out of the suit through the release valve on my shoulder. After a couple periods of bobbing upside down with my lower legs and feet waving above the surface like Santa Claus stuck head-first down a chimney, I also became reasonably proficient in righting myself and avoiding the trap of letting my feet rise higher than my head. Naturally, the air trapped inside a dry suit always seeks the highest point within the suit. Inverting in a dive causes the air to rush into the sealed legs and bootees of the suit, and the diver is then suspended, upside down, beneath the ballooning legs of the suit. Even more humiliating, if the fins aren't tightly strapped on, the bulging bootees ping them off like corks out of champagne bottles. There are no release valves in the feet of dry suits, so it takes a concerted and decisive maneuver to escape this undignified position.

When I emerged from the pool and staggered into the changing rooms, I thought that the suit must have leaked. My insulated undergarment wasn't just damp—it was saturated. But the suit hadn't leaked. This was sweat. "Must be great for weight loss," the pool attendant enthused.

Gretar, on the other hand, raised one eyebrow and let out a low whistle when I told him how much lead weight I needed to gain. He had to go ratting old weights from some of his mates who were repairing damaged fishing nets. They were to be stuffed into the voluminous pockets vulcanized onto the thighs of the dry suit. With these, and as many regular weights as possible jammed onto my weight belt, and the integrated weight pockets of the Rigid bulging with more, we were ready to go diving.

We began in the Vestmannaeyjar, sitting out a pounding 70-knot gale that blustered in from the northeast and humped up enormous seas. "You have to remember," Gretar had said apologetically, "even though we have 24-hour daylight now, this is Iceland ... not Sunland."

Gretar grew up on the dark precipitous cliffs of the Vestmannaeyjar, and we spent part of the next day nestled in one of his favorite cliff-top haunts near the weather station at Stórhöfði on the south end of Heimaey, the largest island in the group. After climbing down into a shallow crevice just back from the edge of the cliff, we were able to enter the open mouth of a narrow lava tube.

Formed by the cooling and solidification of surface lava, while molten lava continued to flow underneath, this tube would once have been the conduit for a torrent of red-hot liquid rock. Now, in the blackness behind us, the tube wound its way back like a bloodless vein into the cold body of the cliff. Just in front of our feet, it opened to the purpling sky and a dizzying sheer drop to the sea. It was an ideal spot to gauge conditions, and to watch for patrolling whales, all the while being entertained by the comings and goings of countless fulmars, puffins, kittiwakes, and guillemots.

From this aerie, perched like gulls ourselves high above the sea, it was plain to see that we wouldn't be going out to sea for at least another 24 hours. Even though the wind had abated, it had left in its wake a bruised and sullen swell that coursed chaotically through the maze of the Vestmannaeyjar, rearing unpredictably and menacingly whenever it bumped into itself or rolled across submerged reefs.

Slate-gray stains streaked and clouded the sea as far as we could see; evidence that the gale had pumped silt-laden glacial river water well out to sea from the south coast of the mainland. We knew then that we would have to reach as far as we could dare to the southwest to find orcas in diveable visibility.

A day later, from the same observation post, Gretar spied two orcas heading south, parallel to the coast. It was enough to assure him that pods of orcas were following their predicted and usual path, and we hurried back to the harbor to dress in dry suits and launch the Zodiac.

Seamen aboard sailing ships due to leave the safety of Heimaey's tight and snug harbor for the uncertainty of the sea frequently took their ship's boats into a vast sea cave just within the harbor entrance. Here, they could siphon fresh water into casks from a canvas tarpaulin suspended under the roof of the cave. Cold, filtered rainwater dribbles incessantly from the rock above.

Floating in the temporal peace of a cave filled with the incense of salt and seaweed, echoing with the cadence of wind and surf and gulls—in the very place that a sea-faring god could be imagined to live—the seamen would offer their prayers for a safe return from the furies of the North Atlantic. I offered one, too.

Gretar gunned the motor once we'd cleared the entrance to the harbor, and the Zodiac hauled up to planing speed. Starkly illuminated by the strong sunlight breaking through the overcast, the string of uninhabited islands and rocks that make up the Vestmannaeyjar jabbed up out of the sea ahead of us. By the time we'd cleared Stórhöfði and were leaving the lighthouse behind us, we could see the mauve silhouette of Surtsey brooding on the southwest horizon.

Gretar had planned our route carefully. Surtsey was a destination he'd had in mind for some time, and he'd thoroughly thought through the course he would take. Direct enough to minimize the fuel we had to carry but in as deep water as possible to avoid hidden reefs that can send steep swells suddenly spearing into the air.

His father had been lost at sea on a trawler that went down with all hands somewhere between Seattle, Washington and Juneau, Alaska. Whatever catastrophe overtook the trawler struck suddenly. There was only time for one indistinct mayday signal. All that was ever found was a single lifebuoy. With this unresolved loss of his father guiding his ambitions, Gretar has developed the skills and capabilities to support his own resolute sense of purpose and adventure. I had absolute confidence in his seamanship, and we might have needed every ounce of it. Surtsey experiences gale force winds for more than two thirds of the year. Twenty-five meter swells have been recorded here. Even now, at the height of the northern summer, we'd seen one fierce gale whirl in to violently disrupt a short succession of calm, clear blue skies. As Gretar had said, "This is Iceland, not Sunland." But what an experience!

Seething foam heaved up and then collapsed back into the sea around the base of every island we passed. We came close enough to some to clearly see the features of the birds nesting on impossibly tenuous ledges on the cliffs. Birds milled everywhere above us and everywhere across the surface of the sea close to us. Only in Galapagos have I seen more. At one stage, I leaned over and let my bare hand trail in the water. It was cold! Closer to Surtsey, we could see just how bare and forbidding that island is. It only arrived here in 1963.

Surtur was the Norse god of fire and, according to thousand-year-old legend, was capable of generating "steam and the life-feeding flame, until fire leaps high about Heaven itself." Trawler men fishing near this spot, way out to sea on that day in 1963, had reason to believe the legend. A volcanic vent suddenly opened up on the seabed 130 meters below the surface.

Titanic, explosive eruptions followed as molten rock was injected directly into cold seawater. Columns of smoke, steam, and ash rose more than 9,000 meters into the sky. Eruptions continued for four years.

Surtsey today is calm, and the softer deposits of ash and scoria are rapidly eroding away from the harder core of the central vents and a triangular apron of flat lava that juts out to the north, just above sea level. It now covers about three square kilometers. Two smaller islands born shortly after the creation of Surtsey have already succumbed to the relentless battering of the waves and have disappeared again beneath the surface.

We didn't attempt to land on Surtsey. The flat lava apron offers some meager protection from the swell, but the island is a scientific reserve; an ideal laboratory to monitor the natural accumulation of life on new bare rock in the midst of the ocean. Casual visitors could artificially introduce seeds or bugs and reduce the value of the scientific monitoring. Even from our position low in the water, we could see the colonization of birds and, beneath the birds, occasional tufts of tough green grasses, probably seeded by the wind and now fertilized by the birds.

Birds continued to mill around us as we motored away from Surtsey. Then Gretar cried "There!" He'd seen see the fins of two whales.

"Orca?" I shot back, with my heart already starting to thump. Gretar shrugged. "Didn't see them very well."

We didn't see them again. When we got to the point Gretar judged was on their path, he closed the throttle. The Zodiac wallowed to a rapid, lurching halt.

There's nothing wrong with feeling scared, and I *was*. It's what you do while you are scared that counts. What I *really* wanted to do was go home, but this was what I'd come for, so I took a deep breath, let it out, and rolled out of the Zodiac into the water. Gretar idled away over the swells and stood scanning the sea, watching for orcas to his left and me to his right. Beneath me the cold green water became impenetrably dark. I could not see as far down as my feet.

The possibilities stemming from an encounter with orcas here didn't strike me as being particularly attractive. Agile and athletic performers at Sea World in San Diego perform extraordinary aerial somersaulting dives into the water after being boosted skyward on the nose of an orca that rockets upward out of the blue beneath their feet. I was confident that the clumsy, inelegant dry suit, weights, and fins wouldn't allow me to do that. Sea lions in Patagonia unwillingly perform similar maneuvers after being wrenched from the shore by orca that beach themselves to grab a meal then hurl their punctured prey up into the air for a spot of sport before consuming it. I definitely didn't want to play that game. But in the green-black water, it was certain that, if I were to see orca underwater here, it would only be when they appeared centimeters away from my face.

I lifted my head and looked toward Gretar. He raised both hands, palms up, to signal that he didn't know where the whales were. I beckoned him back to pick me up.

We patrolled along the arc between Surtsey and the more northerly islands and as far out to the east as a small three-pointed rock constantly besieged by the heaving sea. We drifted down close to a capelin fishing boat. But we could find neither whales nor clearer water. It was time to head back to Heimaey.

Looking for orca: Gretar heads us out from the lee of Surtsey, Iceland, 2002.

Three more days of fruitless searching followed. Fishermen that Gretar quizzed on the docks reported seeing a few orcas farther out to sea. We did have minke whales hurry past just as we were approaching Heimaey harbor entrance, but that was all. Next morning, we were back on the ferry heading for the mainland and fresh water. Our first destination was Thingvellir.

Given all the volcanic activity in Iceland and the apparently limitless volume of geothermally heated water surging out of the ground all over the place, you would think that there would be a reasonable chance of encountering warm subterranean water almost anywhere, especially at Thingvellir.

It's at Thingvellir, just north of Reykjavik, that you can see proof that Iceland is enlarging itself. The island lies across the juncture of the North American and European crustal plates—and they are drifting apart, taking western Iceland toward the United States and eastern Iceland toward Europe. Admittedly, it's a slow process; the plates are traveling at the rate of about two centimeters a year. Deep beneath the surface, molten rock wells up from under the crust to fill the gap created by the separating plates. Thingvellir sits atop this zone of crustal movement, and the ground here is cracking open as the movement of the plates far below stretches it.

This is ground saturated with fresh water. Pure when it fell as snow in the highlands and now filtered by its long journey to Thingvellir through porous basalt, this is extraordinarily clear water. But it escapes any contact with the molten rock that could heat it. It is cold. How cold?

"Between two and four degrees centigrade," said Gretar. This is where the dry suit would earn its keep.

Thingvellir is the site of the earliest Icelandic parliament. About a thousand years ago, Viking clan leaders would gather here to debate and settle the big issues of the day; they also executed miscreants here. Men were hanged, women were drowned in the clear cold water. The hanging and drowning have ended, but Iceland's parliamentary system has continued unbroken ever since. It is now the longest continuously operating democratically elected parliament in the world. Iceland also probably has more politicians per head of population than any other country on Earth; 63 federal representatives for a population of just 280,000. So, Thingvellir is a historically as well as geologically interesting place to dive.

We parked off the road in a shallow grassy depression; a saucer of softer green among the harsh basalt outcroppings. Black flies—*mee* in Icelandic—made the time we spent kitting up miserable. Individually insignificant, they attacked us in thousands. Small, slow, and persistent but prevented from finding bare skin anywhere else on our bodies, they invaded our eyes, nostrils, and mouths. Too sluggish to be brushed off with a waving hand, occasionally inflicting sharp bites, they took us to the brink of irrational anger within minutes. Only submergence in the water on the other side of the road brought relief.

More than 50-meter visibility greeted us. Gretar had chosen a narrow deep crevice for this dive. We slid into the water from a rocky ledge into a relatively shallow pool, seemingly contained between basalt walls ten or so meters high. To the left, though, the fissure disappeared into blackness under the road. It was into this void that Gretar led me.

It was narrow all the way down, constricted by almost interlocking blocks of basalt jutting out of the walls of the crevice. Intense cold numbed my face and hands. Ahead, the bare rock parted to reveal pitch black, split only by the beam of our flashlights as we probed the depths below us. Gretar pushed deeper than I did. At about 25 meters, I arrested my descent, found enough room to turn to face the direction we had come, and stared up at the small disk of intense blue light that signaled the open surface. As I watched, a solitary arctic char swam, silhouetted against the disk.

Apart from scuff marks on the rocks—caused by falling chunks of basalt jerked loose by the daily earth tremors that vibrate through Thingvellir—there was little to see at this depth. We were soon working our way carefully up between the rocks back toward that beckoning blue disk.

At the opposite end of the pool we'd entered, the water fell away into the bowels of the earth again but, about ten meters down, a horizontal passageway opened up. Gloomy as a tomb at first, it soon became suffused with gray-blue light. It became clear that this was a swim-through into the shallower water downstream. We shouldered past a small group of char and emerged in another shallow pool. There were more fish in this pool, and we spent several minutes here until dwindling air supply forced us to make the return journey through the swim-through and out into the hordes of waiting *mee*.

Next day we were heading along the south coast towards Skogafoss. *Foss* is the Icelandic term for waterfall. In fact "Fossland" would probably be a more accurate name for this harsh, compellingly beautiful island. Compared with the optimistically named Greenland, which is covered in ice, Iceland is predominantly green and relatively free of ice. There are *thousands* of waterfalls there, though.

Skogafoss, just off the main highway that casts a thin black line through the often black lava landscapes of the south coast, is one of the most impressive. This is where the Skoga River takes the 60-meter vertical leap from the highland plateau down onto the coastal plain. At first glance, it doesn't immediately recommend itself as a dive site. It's a dwarfing cascade, thundering down off a cliff into a rockbound gully and splashing out clouds of saturating spray. Below the falls, the river races on toward the sea down a shallow bed that curves away from the plateau through a grassy meadow and then across the lava plain. In the bright sun of the short Icelandic summer, with a vivid rainbow striping the clouds of spray and yellow, purple, and red wildflowers dotting the soft green grass, the area around Skogafoss is strikingly picturesque.

It's still there! Viking legend has it that there's a chest of treasure hidden under the Skogafoss waterfall. If anyone finds it, they will have earned it. Iceland, 2002

Picture: Gretar Gretarsson

Gretar, though, offers this waterfall to his clients as a unique diving experience. Thinking that it would have been useful to have spent a couple of months training with Navy SEALS in preparation for this trip, I became the second client to start the tricky crossing of the pebbly bed of the shallow Skoga River. On foot, below the falls, in the dry suit, lugging close to my own body weight in suit, scuba gear, and lead.

It was necessary to cross the river to gain access to the shelter of a stubby rocky point close to the falls. Once there, speech became futile because of the roar of the torrential falling water, but it was possible to finish fitting fins and mask without getting swept downstream. Then, already buried in dense spray, we could slip out from behind the rocks, pitch forward into the stream, and begin the battle against the current to reach the pool at the base of the falls.

It was a curious sensation. Bubbles cloud the water, but it is clear water. Whenever a brief space appeared between the swirling bubbles, it revealed momentary glimpses of the riverbed and the arctic char that swim here. Gretar and I quickly lost contact with each other.

Clawing hand-over-hand on the bottom was the only way to make progress toward the falls against the racing water. Air poured out of my regulator as though it was stuck in free flow as the exertion pumped through my body. Then, quite suddenly, the current eased.

Ceaseless churning by the plummeting water has scoured out a deeper hollow at the base of the falls. Down here, in this plunge-pool on the riverbed, the rotating water circles back under the falls. At first, the easing of the downstream current in this eddy teased me into relaxing my grip on the riverbed rocks and attempting to observe more details of my surroundings in the peeps allowed by the roiling bubbles.

Arctic char were loitering in the relative calm on the downstream rim of the pool. Sleek, spotted, deep brown-gray on their backs fading to the palest pink on their bellies, these members of the salmon family maintained their position with hardly any visible effort. Without the streamlining or the natural balancing abilities of the char, I couldn't just hang around in the eddy with them. Gentle tugging by the circling current swung me around until my feet pointed upstream, and then the current started to drag me backward into the pummeling falls.

While the poised char watched, I had to resort to furious kicking with my fins and clawing at the pebbles on the riverbed with my hands to avoid the punishment that would surely result from a trip directly under the tons of falling water. Vibration—intense vibration—drummed through the water. Sixty-meter waterfalls are not exceptional by world standards. Angel Falls, the world's highest, tumbles nearly a thousand meters into its plunge-pool in the Venezuelan jungle. But, if you have ever been thumped by even a small breaking wave, you can imagine the energy released by a river pouring over a 60-meter drop—and the incentive it offered to regain the relative calm of the plunge-pool eddy.

After a few round-trip circles like that, I worked my way to the shallow water at the right-hand edge of the falls, drew my knees up under me at the base of some large rocks, and kneeled there, head above the surface, looking directly up into the edge of the falling water. Drenching spray, with drops the size and colour of clear glass marbles, and continuous roar filled the space around and above me. Only in glimpses was it possible to see more than a meter or so in any direction. Periodically, swirling air currents flipped the edge of the curtain of water aside and revealed sizeable slabs of the flanks of the falls. When this happened, it allowed a brief splash of rainbow to glow like a hologram in the finer mist drifting away and down the gully. Here, in the river just a couple of meters from the edge of the main impact zone of the cascade, was an awesome experience of Skogafoss. Inside my suit, I was warm and dry. Braced securely by the rocks at my side and reassured by the sense of self-containment that comes with viewing the world through the window of a face mask, with every breath amplified by the hissing regulator, I just soaked in the sights and sound. Time passed quickly.

Gretar was right. 'Did you feel the power? Isn't that fantastic?" he asked as I washed up inelegantly alongside him on the pebbles and struggled to regain my feet after kicking off from my safe niche beneath the falls and allowing the Skoga to speed me downstream.

It was fantastic. We began the walk back to the four-wheel drive, stepping around happy holiday makers spreading their picnic blankets out on the grass and capturing their own summery memories in the peace and beauty of Skogafoss.

Out of their sight, we'd been allowed into a cold forge to privately witness Nature smithing a notch in the Earth, wielding a hammer of water to shape stone on the anvil of time.

"And now for something completely different," Gretar muttered as he spun the wheel and took us back onto the highway, heading further east.

In the twilight of an overcast evening, it is like driving through a black and white photograph. Black road, dashed with a central white line running like a ribbon through black lava landscapes. Off to the south lies the sea. Brown, whipped into whitecaps by the almost ceaseless wind, it is grinding endlessly at the uncertain shoreline of boulders and pebbles gouged from the bedrock by the creeping, irresistible forces of glaciers. Away off to the north lie the highlands and the glaciers themselves. Vatnajökull is the largest, the most massive in Europe. With ice up to a thousand meters thick, extending over 8,000 square kilometers, it dominates the southwest quadrant of Iceland. But Vatnajökull and the smaller glaciers it feeds it are shrinking, retreating slowly as the Earth enters another cycle of warming.

As glaciers advance, they bulldoze ahead of themselves a wall of earth and rock; it's called terminal moraine. About 200 kilometers east of Reykjavik, the road east runs between a mound of terminal moraine and the coast. Breiðamerkurjökull, one of the smaller glaciers fringing Vatnajökull, had pushed this mound of earth and rock almost to the sea when the current warming cycle began and the ice began to thaw slightly. Without fanfare, in the middle of nowhere, Gretar slowed the vehicle and veered off the bitumen onto a rough track that ran a short way before ending at the foot of the moraine mound.

"What's here?" I asked.

"Come see," Gretar responded casually and led the way up the 15 meters to the top of the moraine mound. "Stunning view" is a cheap cliché, much loved by jaded Sunday newspaper travel writers. It's loathsome and trite and unimaginative, and I would never use it. Except to describe a stunning view. By definition, to be stunned, you have to experience a sudden shock of some kind. Jokusarlon glacial lagoon delivers such a shock. There aren't many places in the world where you can drive off the side of a perfectly smooth bitumen road, park the car, walk a few meters, and gaze across a field of icebergs, but you can at Jokusarlon.

Breiðamerkurjökull's moraine mound has created a towering dam wall, holding back the water liberated as the glacier melts. Several kilometers to the north, across this natural reservoir, the ice sheet continues its glacial creep into the lagoon. Immeasurable forces push the leading edge of the ice deep into the water, but eventually the buoyancy of the ice overcomes the downward pressure. With a thunder-clap roar, great blocks of ice snap off and heave to the surface as icebergs. Wind and current cause them to drift south until they run aground against the steep slope of the moraine mound. They lie there, sculpted by wind and water into fantastic shapes, gleaming in translucent shades of blue and gray, striped with black. Coming as it does suddenly, amidst a drab black landscape, with no warning, it is a stunning view. This was the location for the climactic car chase on ice for the James Bond film *Die Another Day*.

"Are you up for a dive here?" Gretar asked when the effect of the stunning view had eased.

Underwater, the ice creates extensive grottoes. Only 20 percent of an iceberg floats above the surface. Eighty percent is hidden from view. At Jokusarlon, what appears to be separated 'bergs above surface are in fact jammed and interlocked together along the shore of the lagoon. This only became obvious to me when I sank through the pastel green cloudy water midway between the peaks of adjoining 'bergs. I was intending to explore the steeply shelving bottom of the lagoon and perhaps get a glimpse of the interface of ice and rock.

At about ten meters, a pale bottom faded indistinctly into view about a meter beneath me. It was spotted with dark, circular patches—each a few centimeters in diameter—that I originally imagined were sea urchins. Jokusarlon lagoon is open to the sea where the moraine mound has been breached some kilometers further east of our dive spot, so it would not have been surprising to encounter some marine species here. When my knees bumped gently down, though, I found myself settled on a solid expanse of ice. Dense, hard like concrete, slick as glass, it extended beyond the range of limited visibility in every direction. Fine silt had accumulated in scalloped-out hollows and formed the dark spots I'd mistaken for sea urchins.

Slowly, sliding my hands across the ice, skimming my gloved fingers past sprays of fossil air trapped in small bubbles deep in the glassy mass, I moved off to my left. Within a few meters, the ice shelved almost vertically into what I took to be the wall of the 'berg. But, when I rose and attempted to follow this wall up toward the surface, my head bumped into more unyielding ice. I put my hand up to discover a curved dome of ice above me. This was clearly an overhanging ledge, but it was impossible to see how far it extended.

With my pulse jumping up a few beats I wondered if I'd blundered into a small cavern in the 'berg and thought for a moment about the best way to make an exit without the risk of getting lost and perhaps swimming deeper into uncertainty within the ice. In the end, I allowed myself to sink back down the face of the ice, moved some distance back in the direction I thought I'd come, and rose slowly and tentatively with my hand extended protectively in front of my upturned face.

Brighter light soon came reassuringly into view. I was clear of the overhang, but there was an interesting lesson here. I'd gone in without sufficient knowledge and not properly equipped. Diving at Jokusarlon can be compared to some aspects of cave diving, but without the pervasive darkness. As the warmer water of the lagoon penetrates the cracks and crevasses of the fractured bergs, it melts and enlarges them.

In limited visibility, it is easy enough for a diver to unknowingly enter one of the larger voids and, without a line attached to a float on the surface to show the way, it could be difficult to find the exit. Sobered by the thought, I went back to

Iceberg in A Glass 207

the wall of an adjoining 'berg, submerged again, and discovered numbers of minute shrimp, only a couple of millimeters long, scampering over the surface of the ice. I spent the rest of the dive a few meters below the surface, watching them and unsuccessfully trying to determine what they ate.

Later, when we'd surfaced and packed our gear in the vehicle, Gretar led me to the top of the moraine mound again, produced a bottle of good quality Scotch from his rucksack, and invited me to sit on a rock.

"Wait here," he said as he jogged down the slope toward the water with a glass in each hand. When he returned, each glass held chunks of ice.

"Skäl," he said. "Cheers," I replied. We clinked glasses and celebrated the endless day, overlooking the lagoon with seven-year-old whiskey chilled by thousand-year-old ice.

Water temperature of 4 to 7 degrees C awaits divers in Jokusarlon glacial lagoon. In many ways, diving here is akin to cave-diving; but the walls and roof are composed of solid ice, not rock. 2002

Picture: Gretar Gretarsson

34

Cloudbreak on the Abrolhos

Jeronimus Cornelisz had sailed the very water passing under our hull with murder on his mind. In June 1628, he'd lain in his bunk aboard the *Batavia*, staring up into the darkened rafters of his cabin, living out his fantasies of adventure and treasure. Only the creaking and the soft slapping splashes of a ship under sail in the calm aftermath of a southern winter gale disturbed the brooding silence. Somewhere off to the east lay the forbidding west coast of New Holland—today's Australia. Ahead, to the north, lay the *Batavia*'s destination; Java. It was a destination that Cornelisz did not want to reach. Perhaps tomorrow, maybe the next day—it had to be soon—he intended to erupt from his ordered life of commerce into bloody mutiny and from there, into a life of unrestrained piracy.

The stage had been set for Cornelisz' plot 130 years earlier when, in 1498, the Portuguese navigator Vasco Da Gama reached Goa in India by sailing around the southern tip of Africa and across the Indian Ocean. In doing this, Da Gama had thrown open the seaway to the Spice Islands of the East Indies. This was literally a pathway to gold because, in the days before refrigeration, Europeans were forced to eat dried, salted, or semi-rotten meats. Faced with that prospect, they eagerly sought spices to mask the miserable flavors and odors of their food and willingly paid high prices for the limited quantities that were traded overland from the Far East through Europe. Da Gama's route meant that cargoes of nutmeg, cloves, cinnamon, and pepper, along with other goods such as tea, coffee, silk, and Chinese porcelain, could now be shipped cheaply and directly into the teeming markets of the European capitals.

East Indies companies quickly organized in Spain, Portugal, England, and Holland to tap into this source of fabulous wealth. The Dutch established their base, Batavia, near the port of Jacatra on Java, in what is now Indonesia. Britain seized tracts of the Malay Peninsula and Sumatra, Portugal swept into the Moluccas, and Spain swiftly colonized the Philippines. Theirs was not a peaceful form of trade; brutal, murderous competition ensued as the European Christians forced their way into the generally peacefully co-existing Hindu and Moslem islands, crushed any islander resistance, and then fought ruthlessly for supremacy among themselves. Of all the companies, it was the Dutch that dominated. Holland became a superpower on the bloodied profits of the respected and feared merchant warriors who swore allegiance to the VOC, the Verenigde Oostindische Compagnie—the United East Indies Company.

Dutch fervor heightened with the return in 1627 of Peter Carpentier's fleet of seven ships. They were laden to the gunwales with spices, but even more tantalizing was the promise of riches waiting to be gathered from the unclaimed fertile islands on the margins of a vast gulf—today's Gulf of Carpentaria. By "unclaimed," of course, he meant that no other European power had yet tramped ashore to suppress the local inhabitants and exploit their land and labor.

Directors of the VOC acted immediately and set the Dutch shipyards to work building a new flagship. *Batavia* was designed as a plump, spacious ship, about 50 meters long, capable of carrying about 600 tons of cargo.

On its first and last voyage, the *Batavia* led two other ships, the *Dordrecht* and the *Assendelft*, in a small flotilla under the command of Francisco Pelsaert, a high-ranking VOC official. *Batavia* was laden with trade goods—cloth, lead, wine, cheese, and blocks of sandstone masonry prefabricated to form an impressive arch at the Governor's residence in Java. Most valuable of all were the 12 chests of silver coins and jewelry. Coins to buy spices; jewelry to win the favor of rulers and dignitaries in the East Indies. But there was something else, too. Fatally, like the space shuttle *Discovery* launching with the undetected faulty O-ring, the majestic *Batavia* sailed from Texel in Holland on October 27, 1628 carrying the psychopathic Jeronimus Cornelisz.

As they stood out into the North Sea, the skippers of the small flotilla planned on a voyage that would take them south to the Cape of Good Hope on the southern tip of Africa, then east-southeast into the reliable winds of the southern Indian Ocean, and then, with little more idea of their longitude than a wet finger held up in the wind could give them, they would heave around to the north and beat their way up into the tropics. One problem. Australia lay like a brick wall in front of them as they ran their easting down from Africa. If they turned north too late, catastrophe would be their reward.

For *Batavia*, the first discomforts of discontent were gurgling in its belly by the time the ship made Cape Town. Pelsaert was a peppery commander, and he quarreled furiously with the skipper of the *Batavia*, Ariaen Jacobsz. Cornelisz cultivated the seeds of dissent that are sown when leaders fight. It is impossible to judge why, because Cornelisz was on a career path with the VOC that would have probably resulted in him becoming wealthy in his own right, but he'd settled on a plan to seize the *Batavia* and turn to a life of piracy. In the hard-suffering crew, there were many who would join him, including Ariaen Jacobsz. As the featureless horizon of the Indian Ocean encircled the ships, it hid them from the outside world and fed the wild-eyed dreams of Cornelisz.

Storms winnowed *Batavia* from the accompanying ships off the Australian coast, and it found itself alone plugging northward into a warmer climate. Jacobsz nudged the *Batavia* slightly farther to the east, believing that he was minimizing the chance of reestablishing contact with the *Dordrecht* and the *Assendelft* and creating the best chance of success for the mutiny. In fact, he had placed *Batavia* on a direct course for the breakers and reefs of the northern Abrolhos.

These islands had been named by another Dutch captain, Frederick de Houtman, on his way to Java in 1619. Probing tentatively north, just out of sight of the Australian mainland, he'd been startled by the sight of low lying islands fringed with reefs rearing abruptly to the surface out of deep water. "Abrolhos!" he had warned, using the Portuguese term for "keep your eyes open!"

On the night of June 4, 1629, the mainland coast was only 70 kilometers away to the east. *Batavia*'s masts and yards, cruciform symbols of the European domination it carried, dipped and swayed gracefully against the fixed stars blazing out of the utter blackness overhead. Moonrise cast a bright silvery sheen across the water.

Jacobsz saw the breakers, but sailors on watch convinced him that he was only seeing the light of the moon dancing on the wave tops. Jacobsz shrugged. Unaware of the debate going on the deck above him, Cornelisz dreamed and plotted. And *Batavia* plowed on toward its destruction on Morning Reef.

At four in the morning, 375 years later, the 20-meter mast of Wayne Osborn's *Cloudbreak* traced its own series of elegant arcs through the same constellations that had shone down on *Batavia*.

We'd battled a gale through the last night and day to get to this point, too. It spun out of a series of northwesterly low-pressure systems that had rotated black storm clouds across the southern half of Western Australia for days, pinning us in the rain-lashed marina at Fremantle with winds in excess of 50 knots. *Cloudbreak*, fully provisioned and ready for sea, had strained at its moorings; we'd chafed at the inactivity. For the four of us, it was a welcome reunion; Wayne is based in Perth, Glenn flew in from Melbourne, Gerard traveled from China, and I came from the U.S. Ahead lay a 550-nautical-mile round trip, most of it in the blue water of the open sea, and we were all keen to go.

Eventually, the meteorological forecast offered a respite from the endless procession of fronts. The wind eased a little, and Wayne decided to cast off. We had some difficulty at first getting the bow of the yacht to come round into the wind, and this led to a dramatic series of maneuvers in reverse that took us in and out of most of the dead-ends in the marina. There were some tense moments in these as quickly approaching seawalls and moored boats had Wayne as busy as a one-armed violinist, working at wheel and throttle. But this at least gave us several opportunities to farewell, then greet, and then wave farewell again to Wayne's wife, Pam, who by this stage was convinced that she'd made the right decision to stay home.

In the open sea, 40 knots of wind had gusted in from the northwest, hammering the yacht with six-meter swells and three-meter seas as we'd clawed our way north from Fremantle.

A long night: Forty knots of wind pound *Cloudbreak* and the weather report offers little respite. Wayne Osborn at the chart table, computing course and position, 25 kilometers off the Western Australian coast in the small hours of the morning.

I'd missed most of the action during the first night on *Cloudbreak*, furious at my impotence, too ill with seasickness and vertigo to be anything much more useful than a green, bilious cushion lying on a seat on the leeward side of the cockpit. Glenn and Gerard lurched around in the tumultuous darkness, drenched in flying spray, dealing with their own waves of nausea, jibing halyards, splicing tacks, folding sheets, vanging booms, and doing all the other endless and mysterious tasks that Wayne determined to be necessary to keep the yacht moving forward against the wind. I've probably got some of those terms confused but, given the circumstances, I think I've done well to remember any of them at all.

Abrolhos! Keep your eyes open! In calmer conditions, Gerard Kennedy scans the sea at first light as *Cloudbreak* creeps toward the entrance of Goss Passage, Abrolhos Islands, 2003.

Like *Batavia*, *Cloudbreak* had been separated from its consorts, *Tramp II* and *Calypso V*, by the weather. Once, briefly in the middle of the night, we'd caught distant glimpses of their running lights, one off to port, the other to starboard, as they pounded north, 20 kilometers or so offshore. But that was all we saw of each other. Unlike *Batavia*, we did have radio contact. As I lay there in misery, hearing snatches of radio calls crackling up from the chart room speaker, I wondered if they were actually traveling on the same planet as us. A typical conversation went something like:

"*Tramp II, Tramp II*, this is *Calypso V*. Over."

"Roger *Calypso V*, this is *Tramp II*. Go ahead Dennis. Over."

"Roger, Graham. Just checking in. Everything OK? Over."

"Roger, Dennis. Yes. Splendid. Running on 327. 40 over the deck. That new clew ruffle-splitter is working perfectly. Jolly good idea to fit that for this trip. Over."

"Roger, Graham. Pleased to hear that. We're on 319. Thought we'd sneak a bit more sea room before we open the pinot and start the movie. Probably break into the cucumber sandwiches shortly. Over."

"Roger that Dennis. Good show."

"Good show, old chap. *Calypso V* standing by."

Such is the phlegmatic and genteel world of the experienced and competent yachtsman. Meanwhile, in our cockpit on *Cloudbreak*, "MOVE! Move your fucking legs! Quick! *hhhooorrooooorrrch!!!!!!*" Gerard made a gallant attempt to clamber over me in a desperate lunge for the lee rail and added a bold, burnt-orange stripe of ravioli and meatballs in tomato sauce to the Jackson Pollock-style accumulation of pre-owned food adhering to the gunwale and stern quarter.

I was eventually able to rise after about 18 hours when the weather abated somewhat, and Wayne gave me the helm for a while to help get my mind off the rebellion going on in my head and stomach.

Our course, keyed into *Cloudbreak*'s on-board computer and monitored with the help of satellites hiding among the stars, was calculated to lead us safely into Goss Passage, the narrow, serpentine gap between Morning and Evening Reefs—but we had our eyes wide open too; computers have been known to crash!

When *Batavia* hit the reef, the grinding shudder of the collision caused widespread panic. Three hundred and sixteen people crowded the tilted deck to learn their fate. They were shipwrecked 3,200 kilometers from the nearest civilization. Pelsaert ordered all the heavy cannon to be thrown overboard in an effort to refloat the ship. No effect; *Batavia* was permanently impaled. Pelsaert then concluded that there was no chance of saving the ship and ordered the masts to be cut down to lessen the pounding of the hull against the reef. This, he hoped, would at least slow its disintegration and perhaps give the people on board some chance of survival. Some hours later, gray light, advancing from the east ahead of the sunrise, eased back the darkness and revealed a grim and inhospitable scene.

"That's Traitor's Island," Wayne said as he helmed *Cloudbreak* sharply to starboard to enter Goss Passage. We were in calm water now. The storms of the night lay behind us and, just as the shipwrecked souls on *Batavia* had experienced, we were getting our first look at the Abrolhos as the damp darkness dissolved around us.

Traitor's Island is a tiny flat islet of sand and rock lying behind the rampart of Morning Reef. "That's where they first landed from the wreck. But 40 drowned trying to get there. And that's Beacon Island." Wayne checked off the landmarks from the chart. Off to starboard lay a larger island, today fringed with a colorful, cubist-like community of lobster fishermen's huts. "Just imagine the slaughter ..." Wayne said, almost to himself.

We'd seen forensic evidence of that slaughter in the Fremantle Maritime Museum, where most of what remains of the *Batavia* and its cargo has been assembled in one of the most compelling exhibitions of marine archaeology available anywhere. The exhumed skeleton of a young man lies on display in a glass case there. On his skull is the distinctive incision left by the edge of a scything cutlass blade. Most chilling, though, is the testimony of the silent scream issuing from the gaping jaws; they were shattered by the cutlass stroke that slashed open his throat. Madness had descended on the Abrolhos when Pelsaert and a number of sailors, including skipper Ariaen Jacobsz, had gamely set off in a small boat to summon help from Java, leaving the deranged Cornelisz in charge of the survivors.

Cornelisz was certainly a never-say-die opportunist. No matter that the ship he had intended to seize lay strewn across a reef half a world away from Holland. He determined that he could just as successfully launch his pirate venture in the vessel that came to rescue him. But first there was work to do. He had to be rid of the people who would be unlikely to join his pirate crew.

Dour and loyal soldier Webbye Hayes and his men were too strong to be attacked, so they were dispatched to a neighboring island—today's West Wallabi island—in what Cornelisz hoped would be a futile and fatal search for food and water. Hayes and his men instead prospered when they found pools of rainwater, lizards, and tammar wallabies. These were the living relics of the time, 7,000 years ago, that this group of the Abrolhos formed part of the mainland. As the edge of the continent frayed to the east, it left behind these chunks of harder rock—and stranded on them, the ancestors of the animals Hayes and his men hunted for their own survival.

Meanwhile, Cornelisz launched into systematic, uninhibited serial murder. In three months, Cornelisz and those crewmen and passengers who joined him, drowned, shot, stabbed, bludgeoned, and hacked to death 125 innocents; men, women, and children. Emboldened by the bloodletting, they mounted two assaults on Hayes and his group. This resulted in Hayes ordering the erection of the first known European structure in Australia, a simple fort of loose limestone rocks. Both assaults failed and, in the second, Cornelisz was captured. At last, the end of the massacre was in sight.

Pelsaert reached Java, was given command of the *Saardam*, and eventually retraced his course to the *Batavia* wreck site. He was welcomed back by the first rowing race held in Australia. Mutineers, desperate to secure the ship and avoid judgment, struck out from Beacon Island. Hayes and his men, equally desperate to warn Pelsaert, bent their backs from West Wallabi. Unfortunately for Cornelisz and his followers, Hayes won.

Pelsaert's vengeful rage sprayed more blood over the Abrolhos. Cornelisz died, after having both hands amputated with a shipwright's chisel and mallet, on a gallows set up on Long Island, just across Goss Passage from the scene of his crimes. Some of his followers went the same grotesque way. Two others were marooned on the mainland near the mouth of what is today known as the Murchison River; Australia's first European settlers. How long they survived is not known. The remainder lived long enough to wish they'd been left on the mainland with them. They were keelhauled and flogged back to Java and were then burned alive, broken on the wheel, or mutilated with red-hot tongs and then hanged.

There's no happy ending to this story. Webbye Hayes was killed in battle shortly after returning to Europe. Pelsaert, despite his heroic voyage from the Abrolhos to Java in a small boat and his recovery of 11 of the 12 chests of silver from the wreck site, was harshly criticized for losing the ship and then abandoning the survivors to the horrors of Cornelisz. Reviled and disillusioned, he died in 1630.

On the surface, apart from the fishermen's huts, little has changed on these "islands of angry ghosts" as author Hugh Edwards labeled them. When Wayne steered *Cloudbreak* through the reefs into a safe anchorage on the northern tip of East Wallabi Island, we found ourselves in an uninhabited bay, enclosed by low limestone headlands and backed by a white sand beach that rose gently into a low scrub-covered dune. Five mooring buoys and the triangular passage markers are the only signs of human presence. The islands' disturbing history feels quite close.

Underwater, though, when we went out to dive the reefs aboard Wayne Williams eight-meter *Littlesport,* it was quite different. We anchored first in the lee of a platform reef just off Long Island, within sight of the place where the handless corpses of Cornelisz and his fellow mutineers would have swung until they had decomposed.

It was disappointing. In clear water, we could see dense thickets of stag horn coral extending down the sheltered gutters of the reef. Deeper, in less protected water, the stag horn gave way to extensive expanses of plate corals. But there were very few fish. One solitary jack bustled in close then zoomed off into the blue. A small Western Australian jewfish ducked for cover under a ledge. Juvenile coral trout hovered apprehensively. Small demoiselles and basslets flitted nervously deep within the protection of the stag horn. A largish baldchin groper flashed away in blind panic. We'd really expected more.

Coral reefs here lie at a biological crossroads; they are the southernmost living reefs in the Indian Ocean, but the warm Leeuwin Current sluices through them, drawing tropical fish from the north to mix with the cool-temperate fish from the south. The same reefs form a foundation for a large portion of the Western Australian rock lobster fishery. We did see lots of lobsters.

In the early 1990s, the Western Australian government moved to protect the conservation, economic, cultural, and historical values of the Abrolhos and created a comprehensive management plan for the islands. Among its wide-ranging features is a series of Reef Observation Areas, where fish stocks can be given a chance to recover from the fishing pressure that has depleted them. We dived there, too, and found little difference. In time, hopefully, the management plan will yield results and return to the Abrolhos the level of abundance that must have coursed for centuries around the wreck of the *Batavia*.

We passed the wreck site, pounded by heavy surf, one last time as we eased out of Goss Passage between Morning and Evening reefs and set a southerly course for home in bright sunshine and a lively breeze. *Cloudbreak* surged forward into a glorious day at sea. In mid-afternoon, a whale idled past. Shortly after, we skimmed past a large basking shark, doing just that—basking on the surface. Albatross wheeled effortlessly around us. Gerard perched for hours on the bowsprit, nothing before him except blue sky and bluer seas.

Later that day, Graham, skipper of *Tramp 11* traveling some distance inshore of *Cloudbreak,* was forced to start his engine and rev it in neutral to shoo away a humpback whale that was sidling alongside and showing no signs of wanting to leave before nightfall. When darkness did close in on us, and we began to enter the northern fringes of the low pressure ridges still scouring the southwest of the state, the wind and swell picked up again. We went through another rough night, but at least with the promise of a spanking breeze to carry us quickly home.

Twenty-four hours later, as we snugged *Cloudbreak* down for our second night at sea, we'd lost the wind. In its place came hesitant, gusty breezes; first from the east, then from the south, then back to the east. Instability wobbled through the atmosphere. Lightning flickered in the west. Confusing weather reports came in from different coastal weather stations: a possibility of a storm front north of Jurien Bay from one; a possibility of localized thunderstorms somewhere south of Jurien Bay from another. We called the weather service in an attempt to clarify this, but without success. The meteorologists were plumbing the charged atmosphere for clues, but the incoming data revealed no patterns on which they could confidently base a forecast.

Wayne took in most of the sail—and the wind died to a zephyr. We hauled up more sail to catch what we could, and a violent squall burst out of the northwest, shoved *Cloudbreak* over onto the port rail, and set us frantically dropping the mainsail and furling the jib. Then the wind rushed away out into the night just as quickly as it had pounced upon us.

We motored from there with the jib furled and the mainsail double reefed with the boom lashed down, tugging and banging against the lashings like a chained bear whenever an unpredictable gust of wind nipped in from some direction to torment it. Cold, damp air settled over us as we hunched down in the sheltered space behind the dodger. Like a brilliant pulsing star, the white light of the Rottnest Island lighthouse appeared on the western horizon, 21 nautical miles off the starboard bow; confirmation that we were on course. Muted by low revs, the diesel continued to push us south, its exhaust grumbling and gasping into the water as the following seas jostled up under the stern. *Cloudbreak*'s easy rolling glide became a harder clash with the water as the swells of the open ocean, tripped and deflected by Rottnest Island and its outlying reefs, changed into restless, uncertain seas.

As we drew closer to the coast, eerie orange light, cast up by the unseen suburbs, glowed over the eastern horizon. Glenn sat silently in the rearmost corner of the cockpit, eyes fixed on some point away to the south.

"What do you see, mate?" Wayne asked.

Glenn let out a deep sigh and answered quietly, as though speaking to himself, and without taking his eyes of the point ahead, "Just a chance to sleep lying down, without having to wear a lifejacket, wet-weather gear, a safety harness, deck knife, flashlight, and a personal rescue beacon hanging round my neck … and to know that I'm only going to see my meals once."

Nearly four hours later, we entered Gage Roads and began the tricky task of navigating through the winking, blinking confusion of thousands of lights on shore, on channel markers, and on ships entering and leaving Fremantle harbor. Ahead, through that artificial constellation, lay the marina. Disentangling those lights and plotting a safe course through them kept us busy through the early hours of the morning.

One more squall swirled through the marina and set the masts and rigging of the moored yachts jangling and wailing in the wind as we finally eased in between the breakwaters. Toward the west, the crescent moon yellowed and sank past an upwardly curling wisp of ragged cloud. The wisp bisected the crescent and, for a moment, created the resemblance of eyes blazing through a black mask, staring at us across the dark water. One last baleful glare from the angry ghosts we'd left

250 sea miles behind us? Or, perhaps, from the spirit of that young murdered Dutchman who lies immodestly uncovered in a glass coffin, just 300 meters from where *Cloudbreak* strains against its moorings, as though anxious to be off on the next voyage.

35

Last Ascent

Choppy water, scuffed up by the stiff offshore early morning breeze, made snorkeling on the surface difficult. The whales were somewhere ahead of me—I could distinctly hear them clicking—but they were wallowing on the lumpy surface, up-sun, and even when I could snatch a quick glance in their general direction from the top of a tumbling wavelet, they were hidden in the dazzling brassy glare.

There were two of them. We'd seen them from the inflatable Zodiac minutes after the excited cry from the *vigia* had come over the radio. "Ohhhhhh! Cachalot! Cachalot!" Through powerful binoculars, from within his aerie on the flanks of dormant Pico—the volcano that gives this island in the Azores its name—he'd seen the angled spouts of vapor that clearly distinguish sperm whales from other whales. With precision honed sharp by years as a whaling lookout, and speaking in the native Portuguese, he quickly relayed distance and bearing to Michael, our guide and skipper.

"Cachalot … sperm whales", Michael confirmed. The outboard bit deep as he spun the wheel, pushed the throttle lever forward, and sent the orange Zodiac zipping and bouncing in a froth of white on blue towards the seaward horizon.

"There!" Robyn, her windblown hair haloed by the low sun, was first to see them. Once again, the whale was given away by the puff of vapor that issues low, forward and to the side from its left nostril. We were about six kilometres out to sea and they were several hundred metres dead ahead. Michael pushed the Zodiac off to the right in a wide curve, to take it far behind, and away from the track of the whales. When he'd put us well to seaward of them he killed the revs and the Zodiac whispered along on a course that gently converged with that of the whales.

It was June, 2005, and this is what Robyn and I, and Wayne and Pam Osborn had come for. We'd applied for and been granted permission by the Azorean authorities to enter the water to observe and record behavior of these enigmatic mammals, the largest of the toothed whales. The Azores, spectacular volcanic peaks, erupting from the same mid-Atlantic Ridge that creates Iceland, Ascension Island and Tristan da Cunha, lie on the same latitude as New York and Lisbon. Surrounded by deep oceanic water, they are one of the best locations on Earth to observe sperm whales close to shore. Frank Wirth, ebullient German born filmmaker, expert in natural history, and owner of Pico Dive in Madelena had provided us with the Zodiac and his two best whale-spotting guides, Michael Costa and Artur Hörner.

Now, in close quarters, we all watched intently the two whales on the surface. Two gray-black backs, sloshing and awash like a low reef at mid-tide. Downwind as we were, we could clearly hear their periodic exhalations "*Phwaaaah! Pohh!*"

"They've been up for a while so they're probably going to dive anytime now," Michael declared. Sperm whales, super predators that they are, make their living catching their prey, principally squid, far away from prying human eyes in the blackness of the abyss at depth of up to perhaps 3000 metres. Pre-eminent researcher, Hal Whitehead calculates that the world's estimated 300,000 sperm whales gulp down about 75 million metric tons of squid and other cephalopods annually! That's about as much as the weight of edible fish that the entire human population drags out of the sea every year. How they're able to actually do that—in the dark, faced with prey that are far more agile and speedy swimmers than they-is not yet fully understood, but they spend far more time at depth, chasing food, than they do on the surface.

Typically, they'll be underwater working hard for around 45 minutes at a time. Consequently, the ten or 12 minutes that they spend on the surface between dives is critically important for them. In that time they replenish their lungs with air, and their blood—up to three metric tons of it in larger whales—with oxygen. It was a period of recuperation that we did not want to interrupt.

But, after watching them for a few minutes more Michael changed his mind. "They're not going to dive for a while. They're socializing. You can go in. Be careful. Be quiet"

I'd been ready to slip over the side from the time we'd inched carefully to within swimming range—about 100 metres. My thin wetsuit brupped against the inflated rubbery pontoon of the Zodiac as I eased myself into water. Chilly rivulets of water wriggled their way past my collar, down between my shoulder blades and sent an involuntary shiver through me. Wayne ran his eye over my camera housing to confirm that it was properly sealed, and then lowered it into the water. With a little wave towards Robyn, I pushed away from the Zodiac to begin the long slog towards the whales.

In conditions like this, against the wind and the water and the drag of a large underwater camera housing, with ankles weighted to eliminate the risk of fins splashing on the surface, it really *was* a slog. In water somewhere around 1000 metres deep, there is no hope of judging progress by watching the seabed pass below. Every time we swam here we felt as though we were invisibly anchored in the center of an inverted transparent blue liquid hemisphere, pounding away with our fins, with lactic acid burning in our aching legs, seemingly all to no avail—until the looming mass of a sperm whale materialized out of the blue haze.

These were all solitary swims. Only one diver is allowed in the water at a time. It's akin to being on safari in Africa and taking it in turns to get out of the jeep, take the camera, and sprint across the savannah to photograph giant elephants, hoping that none of the big cats that you can't see, but you just *feel* are watching you, don't pounce before the jeep circles back to collect you. For the one in the water, the adrenaline pumps, but the task at hand crowds out the phantoms of fear.

When I stood in the boat though, watching Robyn heading for her first eyeball to eyeball encounter with a whale, way off on her own in open ocean, it starkly illuminated her vulnerability, and cast a shadow of apprehension for her safety across me.

When she'd made first contact though, when she'd watched the whale approach her, glide past and dive beneath her, then lifted her head and punched the air with elation, my heart had soared. Such is the price and reward of looking for adventure with the one you love! But this morning, it was my turn to go in on the whales.

I kicked hard and downwards a couple of times to raise my head as high out of the water as I could, in an effort to get a bearing on the two whales, but without success. Instead, I glanced back to be guided by the outstretched and pointing arms of those in the Zodiac. I had no idea whether I was getting closer or not, although the sharp periodic "Click! … Click! Click! … Click" told me that they were still there and heightened the suspense and excited anticipation that was rising in me.

In different combinations and frequencies those clicks serve as communication between whales and as a critical tool for echo-locating, and, some researchers speculate, for perhaps even confusing or immobilising, the squid on which they depend. No other animal can rival the sound energy that a sperm whale is capable of producing. This is yet another only-partially understood aspect of sperm whale biology. If you can imagine an elephant with its trunk split, with the left nostril dedicated to breathing, and the right nostril trumpeting into a megaphone, then you have a reasonable analogy for the sperm whale's sound system The megaphone is the spermaceti organ, the ponderous oil-filled cask from which the whale derives both its boxy head and its name; early whalers mistook the oil in this organ for semen.

Finally, as a wavelet slopped me upwards, and the water fell away from my facemask, I caught sight of one of those emblematic heads, slightly raised above the surface about 40 metres away. From my position, it was lined up almost precisely with the cloud-wreathed conical peak of Pico, rearing 2351 metres up off in the distance, so I finally had an easily visible mark to lead me forwards. I dug in with renewed effort.

Moment's later, much sooner than I'd expected, I had a whale in sight. Just a purpling smudge in the blue at first. Ahead and slightly below me—about five metres beneath the surface. It was sinking. Not diving, just sinking slowly, slowly on its side, watching me approach. It's eye, and the almost comically little paddle-shaped pectoral fin, it's white mouth, and a large gray-white patch on its side were all clearly visible. It was probably eight or nine metres long. These are wonderful, impressive, mysterious, massive creatures and I was mesmerized by it. Such a giant. Yet so timidly retreating into the depths. Seemingly curious enough to want to watch me as it went, but apparently not curious enough to stay. I swam until I was directly overhead of it, and lay staring vertically down at it until it disappeared.

Then I raised my head to look ahead again and jumped with surprise. There were not *two* whales here. There were five! Just meters ahead: a socializing group, dominated by an 11 metre long female and ranging through a variety of sizes down to a young calf. The female lay just below the surface, horizontally, her side towards me, watching me. Arrayed around and below her, the smaller whales hung suspended in a variety of postures—upside down on their backs, head down, tail down—as though strewn carelessly by capricious liquid wind. One, inverted with its tail flukes casually flopped down like a relaxed hand on a limp wrist, had begun sinking slowly into deeper water.

The calf sank a little too. In fact that's how it first came into sight, dropping head down to peer at me from under the belly of the large female. Sperm whales, like elephants, often care for their young communally so it was impossible to know whether this was a calf with its mother, or one under the temporary care of another female while the mother foraged in the blackness far below.

Whatever the relationship, finding myself in such intimate proximity to the calf triggered some fear in me. Before this expedition I'd found nothing in the literature to suggest that sperm whales would react aggressively towards humans in the water. But few animals will passively accept a perceived threat to their young. Heart pounding, I stared intently at the large female. Tossing up and down on the choppy surface made it impossible for me to be completely still, but there was no reaction from the whale. She just floated there, her wrinkled bulk dominating my field of view.

One of the smaller whales—if any whale can be described as small by the humans they dwarf—rolled over onto its back and swam slightly closer—and added another ten beats a minute to my heart rate. This gave me the clearest view I'd yet had of the remarkable white mouth of the sperm whales. Closed, as this one was, the whiteness appeared like luminous lipstick delineating the long, spindly jaw. What advantage is conferred on the whale by this coloration is uncertain: squid attractor or signaling device to other whales? No one knows. It is certainly one of the most immediately visible features as a sperm whale approaches underwater.

From the Zodiac we'd seen many whales heaving their flukes up into the air as they began a vertical dive—the upraised "hand of God" cascading water and feared, with good reason, by open-boat whalers around the world. Today though, in this encounter, each of the whales I'd seen descending had been simply sinking rather than purposefully powering downwards with massive swipes of their flukes.

And so it was with the remaining whales in this group. Continuously clicking, in loose formation, they simply started to fall slowly from the surface. I filled my lungs and swam down in parallel with the large female and the calf. This immediately roused the curiosity of the calf and it leveled out of its own headfirst descent and turned toward me. In turn, this attracted the attention of one of the smaller whales. Like a watchful older sister reigning in a wandering toddler, it quickly but gently nudged the calf back into close formation with the matriarch.

For me, this was a period of elation tinged with frustration and sadness. Elation at the shoulder-rubbing closeness I'd been afforded by these immense animals. Frustration and sadness with my inability to follow them further. So far distant is their everyday world from our own, so difficult is it for humans to study their hidden lives in detail, that they may as well have been heading for the dark side of the moon.

I was forced to arrest my descent, frame one last photograph, and then watch as the three of them, as though with arms linked, continued their downward journey until they dissolved into the blue-black beneath me.

When I raised my face towards the surface to begin my ascent, I got another shock. I'd dived far deeper holding my breath than I believed myself capable at my age. Focused intently on the whales, I'd subconsciously shut out the desire to breathe, and I was now faced with a long haul to reach the surface.

There was an uplifting force within me though. Part of it was certainly the encounter with the whales; the knowledge that I'd achieved what we'd come here to do—get close, and knock out some creative shots of animals that few people ever get to see alive. But there was something else too; impossible to define at the time. I rose through the cool blue water, warmed from within, and free from any anxiety to resume breathing.

When I hit the surface, 30 metres or so from the Zodiac, Artur Hörner, himself a former member of the German free-diving team was in the process of entering the water to come looking for me.

"You were down for ages! We were getting worried" The tone in Robyn's voice and the expression in her eyes reflected uncharacteristic anxiety.

A month later, lying in bed in Manhattan, awake in the early hours of the morning, I had reason to wonder if that mysterious uplifting force had been a spiritual messenger, sent to tell me that that wonderful ascent had been my last. During the previous day, my doctor had called me with the results of some tests confirming that I had contracted prostate cancer.

This was sobering news, but, as I've been able to do so many times in our life together, I was able to draw strength and inspiration from Robyn. Eight months earlier, she'd carried herself with extraordinary courage and composure after her skin specialist detected a life-threatening malignant melanoma on her back. To our great relief, the surgery had been successful, and Robyn had emerged from that period of sinister pain and menacing uncertainty with an even more positive view of the future than she had displayed over the years. Now it was to be my turn.

It was a rough and potholed trail through surgery and recuperation, and more than once, as I traveled along it, I cast gloomy backward glances at the receding memories of the whales off the Azores. But, just as it had when it drew me down the unpaved limestone road from my parent's house to the shore at Christie's Beach in the 1960s, the sea pulled on me as the moon pulls on the tides. Gradually, stroke by stroke, I brushed out the bleak and disturbing memories of the past months, and replaced them with vivid imagery that recaptured the sensual caress of the deep blue.

Buoyed by this, and by Robyn's limitless support, I regained the determination and the fitness to convert imagination into reality.

I was going back into the water, and there was no doubt about where I would do so: I'd finally figured out just what that spiritual messenger had been trying to tell me. There is no way of knowing with any certainty that we are about to enter the water for the last time, nor when we have made our last ascent. Thankfully, there are far too many unpredictable cross-currents in life to allow for that. Happiness lies in living every dive, every experience and encounter with those we love, as though it *could* be the last, and treating it with the same sense of awe and wonder as the first.

May 2006

Three thousand kilometres off the coast of New York, 25 kilometres off the coast of Pico Island in the Azores, Michael Costa slowed the Zodiac.

I slipped over the side and reached up for the camera that Robyn held ready for me.

She paused before she released her grip of it—just long enough to fix me with that bewitching gaze that confirms the ascendancy of our own spiritual connection. Then she laughed, let me take the camera, and blew me a kiss.

Exhilarated, and trembling with boyish anticipation of what lay ahead, I struck out across the violet-gray surface of the open Atlantic to put myself into the path of a pair of oncoming sperm whales.

###

Sperm whales descending into the abyss off the Azores. 2005

Scientific Names of Species Mentioned in the Text

Angelfish.   *Family: .Pomacanthidae*
Arctic char   *Salvelinus alpinus*
Baldchin groper   *Choerodon rubescens*
Banded sweep   *Scorpis georgianus*
Banner fish.   *Heniochus sp*
Barracuda   *Sphyraena barracuda*
Basking shark   *Cetorhinus maximus*
Basslets   *Anthias sp.*
Bigeye trevally   *Caranx sexfasciatus*
Black grouper   *Mycteroperca bonaci*
Blacktip whaler   *Carcharhinus limbatus*
Blue-green chromis   *Chromis viridis*
Blue groper   *Achoerodus gouldii*
Blue morwong   *Nemadactylus douglassi*
Boarfish   *Pentaceropsis recurvirostris*
Bream.   *Acanthopagrus australis*
Bronze whaler.   *Carcharhinus brachyurus*
Butterfly fish.   *Chaetodon sp*
Bull's eyes.   *Pempheris sp*
Cleaner wrasse   *Labroides dimidatus*
Clown triggerfish   *Balistoides conspicillum*
Cod   *Gadus morhua*

Congoli	*Pseudaphritis bursinus.*
Cryptic cardinalfish	*Apogon coccineus*
Dog tooth tuna	*Gymnosarda unicolor*
Drummer	*Kyphosus sp*
Dusky morwong	*Dactylophora nigricans*
Eagle ray	*Myliobatis australis*
Flathead	*Platycephalus fuscus*
Flying fish	*Cyspselurus furcatus*
Fusiliers	*Caesio lunaris*
Galapgos shark	*Carcharhynchus galapagoensis*
Hepatus tang	*Paracanthurus hepatus.*
Humpheaded wrasse	*Cheilinus undulatsu*
Leatherjackets	Family *Monacanthidae*
Lionfish	*Pterois volitans*
Luderick	*Girella tricuspidata*
Magpie perch	*Cheilodactylus nigripes*
Mullet	*Mugil cephalus*
Mulloway	*Argyrosomus holopeditus*
Needlefish	Family *Belonidae*
Old wife.	*Enoplosus armatus*
Pantherfish.	*Cromileptes altivelis*
Potato cod	*Epinephelus tukula*
Queen triggerfish	*Balistes vetula*
Rainbow runner	*Elegatis bipinnulata*
Red bass.	*Lutjanus bohar*
Red morwong	*Cheilodactylus fuscus*
Samson fish	*Seriola hippos*
Scaly fin.	*Actinochromis victoriae*

Scientific Names of Species Mentioned in the Text

Sea sweep	*Scorpis aequipinnis*
Silvertip whaler	*Carcharhinus albimarginatus*
Snapper (southern Australia).	*Chrysophrys auratus*
Snapper (northern Australia)	*Lutjanus sp*
Snapper (Galapagos)	*Lutjanus sp*
Snook	*Sphyraena novaehollandiae*
Southern blue-fin tuna	*Thunnus maccoyii.*
Spanish mackerel	*Scomberomorus sp.*
Sperm whale.	*Physeter macrocephalus*
Stonefish.	*Synanceja horrida*
Sweetlip	*Family: Haemulidae*
Tarpon	*Megalops atlanticus*
Tiger grouper.	*Mycteroperca tigris*
Trevally.	*Pseudocaranx sp*
Western Australian jewfish.	*Glaucosoma hebraicum*
Whale shark	*Rhiniodon typus*
White shark	*Carcharodon carcharius*
Whiting.	*Sillaginodes punctata*
Wobbegong	*Orectolobus sp.*
Yellowtail kingfish	*Seriola lalandi*
Zebrafish	*Girella zebra*

Selected Bibliography

Allen, Gerald R. Swainston, Roger. **The Marine Fishes of North-western Australia**. Western Australian Museum, 1988

Badger, G.M. (ed), **Captain Cook, Navigator and Scientist**, Australian National University Press, 1969.

Benham, Clarrie. **Diver's Luck**. Angus and Roberston, 1949

Carefoot, Thomas. **Seashore Ecology**. University of Queensland Press, 1977

Cousteau, J.Y. **Silent World.** Hamish Hamilton, 1953

Edwards, Hugh. **Islands of Angry Ghosts**. Hodder and Stoughton, 1966.

Fisher, James. **Rockall**. Geoffrey Bles Limited, 1956

Flinders, Mathew. **Voyage to Terra Australis**. G&W Nicol, 1814

Gordon, Bernard L. **Man and the Sea**. 1980

Hamiliton—Patterson, James. **The Great Deep**. Random House, 1992

Hass, Hans. **Diving to Adventure**. Jarrolds, 1952

Hass, Hans. **Men and Sharks**. Jarrolds, 1949

Hass, Hans. **Under the Red Sea.** Jarrolds, 1952

Hutchins, Barry. Swainston, Roger **Sea Fishes of Southern Australia**. Swainston Publishing, 1986

Idriess, Ion L. **Forty Fathoms Deep**. Angus and Robertson, 1937

Jackson, Michael H. **Galapagos; a natural history**. University of Calgary Press, 1993

Kelly, Saul. **Lost Oasis**. Westview, 2001

Kurlansky, Mark. **Cod.** Vintage, 1999

Laffin, John. **Damn the Dardanelles**. Doubleday, 1980

Laseron, Charles F. **Ancient Australia**. Angus and Roberston, 1954.

Lineaweaver, Thomas H; Backus, Richard H. **The Natural History of Sharks**. Andre Deutsch Ltd, 1970

Loss of the *Admella*; Minutes of evidence and proceedings of Commission. Adelaide, 1859

Marchant, Leslie. **France Australe**. Artlook, 1982

Moorehead, Alan. **Gallipoli.** Hamish Hamilton, 1956

Morne, Hakon. **Caribbean Symphony.** Elek Books, 1955

Mudie, Ian. **Wreck of the Admella.** Rigby, 1966

Myers, Robert F. **Micronsesian Reef Fishes**. Coral Graphics, 1989

Napier, S. Elliott. **On the Barrier Reef.** Angus and Roberston, 1929

Pugh, Marshall. **Frogman: Commander Crabbe's Story**. Scribner, 1956

Severin, Tim. **The Spice Islands Voyage**. Little, Brown and Company, 1977

Sigurjonsson, Sigurgeir. **Lost in Iceland**. Forlagid, 2002

Sobel, Dava. **Longitude**. Fourth Estate Limited, 1996

Stewart, William H. **Ghost Fleet of the Truk Lagoon**. 1985

Villiers, Alan. **Grain Race**. Charles Scribner's Sons, 1933

Villiers, Alan. **The Last of the Wind Ships**. Harvill Press, 2000

Wachter, Georgann & Michael, **Erie Wrecks East**. Corporate Impact, 2000

Whitehead, Hal. **Sperm Whales: social evolution in the ocean**. University of Chicago Press; 2003

Young, Louise B. **The Blue Planet**. Little, Brown and Company, 1983

Notes on Thirteenth Beach

Thirteenth Beach and the dunes beyond it fringe the southern edge of the peninsula that shelters the western arm of Port Philip Bay from the boisterousness of Bass Strait. They were created from the sands swept up from the exposed seabed by the persistently strong winds of an ice age about 125,000 years ago. At that time, the dry seabed created a land bridge linking mainland Australia with Tasmania. As a flat sandy plain studded with granite peaks that offered habitat for game animals, it enabled early waves of migrating Australian Aboriginal peoples to penetrate as far south as any human beings had ever ventured at that time. Wathaurong tribes-people were the first to occupy the area around Thirteenth Beach, at least 25,000 years ago.

When the spinning Earth wobbled slightly closer to the sun or perhaps when the nuclear furnace of the sun temporarily flamed into greater incandescence, the global glaciers sweated. Sea levels rose and flooded across the land bridge. This trapped and isolated the Tasmanian Aboriginals and protected the marsupial predators trapped with them from the more efficient competition of the placental wild dog—the dingo—which had been introduced to the Australian mainland by later Aboriginal migrants.

Shallow and tempestuous, the gap between Tasmania and the Australian mainland became a funnel for swells driven around the globe by the incsant Roaring Forties. Captain James Cook suspected its presence in 1770, but it was intrepid English explorer and navigator Mathew Flinders who named this body of water "Bass Strait" in honor of his close companion and fellow adventurer, George Bass. They proved its existence by circumnavigating Tasmania in the ten-meter-long sloop *Norfolk*. That was in 1798.

Escaped convict, William Buckley found his way here in 1803. Buckley became infamous as the Wild White Man and lived with the local Aboriginals for 32 years. Europeans arrived in numbers from about 1835, eager to colonize the rich lands between the coast and the Otway Ranges. The hunter-gatherer Aboriginal people were overrun as they lost their traditional lands to farms and their health to the virulent new diseases, such as influenza, that the Europeans brought with them.

Today, although it is close to Melbourne and the towns of the Surf Coast, Thirteenth Beach remains mostly undeveloped. Marram grass has been introduced in an effort to stabilize the sand dunes. Introduced rabbits and foxes run in destructive abundance, but this is a place where it is still easy to reach out and touch the sea. Limpid and blue in summer, ruffled with brisk breezes in spring and fall, thundering with Hawaiian-sized, gray-green surf in winter, Thirteenth Beach sees it all. Our home for some years in Australia overlooked Port Phillip Bay, near here.

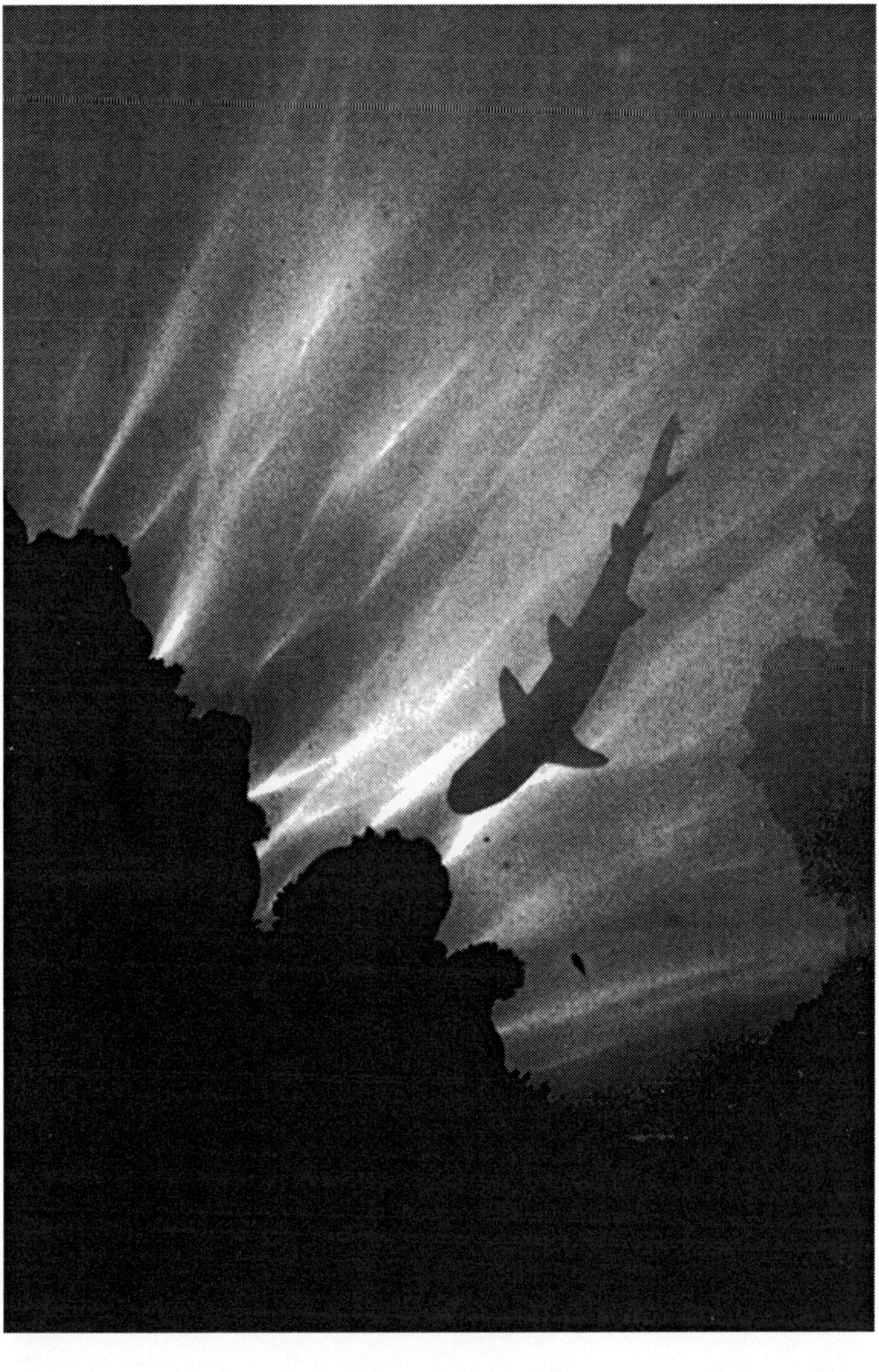

About the Author

Picture: Robyn Hughes

Wade Hughes is a Fellow of the Royal Geographical Society and a Member of the Explorers Club. He began diving as a 12-year-old in southern Australia and began his writing career when he was 17 as a weekly summertime skin diving columnist for Adelaide's major daily newspaper, *The Advertiser*. Since then, he has dived extensively within Australia and in salt and fresh water locations in such widespread destinations as Egypt, Malaysia, Thailand, the Maldives, Florida, California, Hawaii, the Great Lakes, Great Barrier Reef, Ireland, Truk, Palau, Tonga, Fiji, Iceland, Greece, Turkey, Mexico, Gibraltar, Jamaica, the Dutch Antilles, Virgin Islands, Bahamas, Azores, and Ecuador. His underwater photographic art has been exhibited in a number of galleries, including a one-man exhibition commissioned by the Great Barrier Reef Marine Park Authority. He has authored nine books. Wade has been married to his equally adventurous first wife, Robyn, for 29 years. They live in New York and Australia.

Order your copy of *Thirteenth Beach* at www.thirteenthbeach.com

978-0-595-31098-2
0-595-31098-2